FASHION SEWING
FOR EVERYONE

Also by *Adele P. Margolis*

HOW TO DESIGN YOUR OWN DRESS PATTERNS

PATTERN WISE

THE COMPLETE BOOK OF TAILORING

THE DRESSMAKING BOOK

HOW TO MAKE CLOTHES THAT FIT AND FLATTER

DESIGN YOUR OWN DRESS PATTERNS

FASHION SEWING FOR EVERYONE

Adele P. Margolis

Illustrated by JUDY SKOOGFORS

Doubleday & Company, Inc., Garden City, New York

1974

Dressmaking

ISBN: 0-385-08543-5
Library of Congress Catalog Card Number 73–15356
Copyright © 1974 by Adele P. Margolis

To my granddaughter
ANDREA
who, though only seven, can already
sew a fine seam

FOREWORD

Wouldn't it be great if one could just glue, tape, weld, or wish together one's clothes instead of stitching them? Someday in the future, fashion and technology may make this both desirable and possible. Until then, we'll have to settle for the more traditional (and admittedly, more laborious) hand and machine sewing. Don't despair! Even stitched clothing need not take forever to make, nor need it look—shall we say, uninspired? It's all in knowing how.

It matters not whether you are young, old, or in between; whether you sew once a month or every day of your life; whether you sew for fun or earn your living at it. To produce something truly beautiful, the same rules apply to all.

This is a book for everyone who loves to sew. Not just plain sewing, mind you, but *fashion sewing*. There's a difference! It's the difference between chore and excitement, between have-to and want-to, between the routine and the creative.

Yes, it takes time—but really not too much time. And, yes, it takes effort—but it's really not that hard. You'll forget them both when, on appearing in your newest creation, your astonished public awards you the supreme accolade, "You didn't make that, did you? It's positively gorgeous!" Then just bask in the glow of their admiration. And plan your next project.

Philadelphia, Pennsylvania   Adele P. Margolis

CONTENTS

PART I

SIMPLE STYLES THAT STAGGER

FAST FASHION
The Whip-it-up-and-wear-it Department

Every sewer likes to spell her more ambitious projects with the kind of dress she can whip-up-and-wear. After all, it's a relief to have something that doesn't take forever (it only seems that way) to make. Besides, one really does need to have something to wear while the more important ventures are in production.

Want a sure-fire way of making an entrance of a mere arrival? Appear in a simple dress made of fascinating fabric in an arresting design, color, or texture. It's fast fashion!

Clever Rather Than Costly: The Fashion Impact of Fabrics

It's cleverness in the use of fabrics that makes fashion news, not cost. An original way of using a classic material, a classic style of an unexpected material, a bold use of a brand-new material. With few seams, few darts, few details, fabric itself can carry a fashion impact.

Fig. 1

Take the simple design in Fig. 1. Just a front and a back, a scooped neckline and no sleeves. It could be a beginner's exercise in sewing. In a nondescript material, this style could be just plain dull. But . . .

How wildly wonderful it would be in a fur fabric (Fig. 2a), how exciting in a bold print (Fig. 2b), how unusual in suede (Fig. 2c), how elegant in velvet (Fig. 2d), how dazzling with glitter trimming (Fig. 2e). One could hardly slip unnoticed into a room wearing any of these. Each would proclaim your presence as if it were a fanfare.

The formula for instant attention? A simple style in a staggering material. It's guaranteed to get results every time.

Fig. 2

The Sensuous Sewer

If you are one who can look at a bolt of cloth with a cool eye and a hard heart, or if you can casually and unseeingly walk past a counter of materials, you don't have the instincts of a sewer. But if every rag and remnant can set you a-dreaming, welcome to the clan. Fabric is the siren song for sewers. It lures us all—novice as well as seasoned sewer, sixteen as well as sixty.

There are sensible ways to choose fabrics—if you are sensible—or faint-hearted. For instance, the following fabrics are easy-to-handle: solid colors, medium weights, plain weaves, firmly woven, all-over surface designs, two-way design units, cottons, linens, and some woolens.

Somehow, despite their known difficulties, the hard-to-handle fabrics always seem the most appealing: stripes, plaids, checks, blocks; silks, woolens, and man-made fibers like nylon, Dacron, polyester, etc. (unless they are blended with natural fibers); raised surfaces—looped, napped, fuzzy, furry; very stretchy, very loosely woven, very sheer, very heavy, *very* anything.

The first category (easy-to-handle fabrics) will present fewer problems for early ventures. However, if you have sufficient eagerness, determination, and patience (it takes lots of this!) to carry you over the rough spots, then do choose a fabric from the second category (hard-to-handle fabrics) and learn to master it.

In either case, choose a fabric you love. If you don't enjoy the color and feel of the fabric while you are working on it, chances are you won't wear it. A sewer just has to be sensuous.

How to Separate the Girls from the Women: Choice of Fabric

What separates the girls from the women is often the choice of fabric. More mature sewers tend to stick to the classic and traditional fabrics. That's because, in the main, they are reaching for elegance and longevity in their clothes. Young sewers know a dress is not forever. This makes them more adventurous, unconventional, and ingenious in their use of fabric. Of the young, one expects the unexpected in the use of material.

Of course there are big moments in the life of any girl when she, too, may want the elegance (a wedding gown, for instance). When this is so she turns to the more classic fabrics.

Fig. 3

From a fashion standpoint, it's a good thing to have both classic and off-beat fabrics to choose from.

Pick a Pattern

There's much you can do with a length of cloth. You can wind it around you like a mummy (Fig. 3a). You can wrap it around you like a sari (Fig. 3b). You can drape it like a toga (Fig. 3c). You can cut a hole in it for a poncho (Fig 3d). You can carve out sleeves and have a caftan (Fig. 3e). Or add an obi and have a kimono (Fig. 3f).

All of these are simple, stylish, satisfactory, very easy to make. And, you don't need a pattern. Just a flat length of cloth.

The only trouble with all of them is that they were designed for other times and other places. While they may be fun to dress up in, they are not particularly well-suited to our complex way of life.

When it comes to more intricate styling or clothes designed to conform to the figure, *a pattern is essential.* You may buy one, you may make one yourself, or you may just have the pattern shape in your mind's eye.

Easiest, of course, is buying a pattern. There are many from which to choose all the way from easy-to-make to designer originals. There is something to be said for reaching a bit beyond your experience but you'll have less frustration and struggle if you grade yourself as a sewer and choose the degree of pattern difficulty you can comfortably handle. As your skill increases, upgrade your pattern choice.

You may be one who never quite finds what she has in mind. You've dreamed up something the pattern companies haven't—yet. Pictures of what's "in" are flooding the fashion pages but it may be months before any of the new styles are in the pattern books. Perhaps you had better learn to make your own patterns.* It's easier than you would suspect.

Playing Darts: Shape by Dart Control

It's no magic and no mystery! It's those clever little darts and seams that convert a flat length of cloth into an eye-catching, figure-enhancing, breathtaking gem of a garment. How do they do it? By

* *Design Your Own Dress Patterns* by Adele P. Margolis, Doubleday & Company, Inc., gives easy step-by-step directions.

Fig. 4

shaping a flat length of cloth to fit the curves of the body. This system of shaping is called *dart control*.

This is how dart control works. Say your hips measure 34 inches and your waist measures 23½ inches. The garment must fit at both waist and hips despite their difference in measurement. You need some way of handling that 10½-inch differential. One way is to shape the garment by darts (Fig. 4a). Other types of control are seams (Fig. 4b), pleats (Fig. 4c), smocking (Fig. 4d), gathering (Fig. 4e), and so on. Any device is acceptable just so it provides enough cloth where the figure is larger and "takes it in" where the figure is smaller.

Wherever on the body there is a difference between two adjoining measurements (bust and waist, hips and waist, lower shoulder blades and waist, upper shoulder blades and shoulders) or wherever movement creates a bulge (as at the elbow) you will find some form of shaping is necessary.

Dart control always represents a relationship. It is the difference between a larger measurement and a smaller adjoining one. The greater the difference, the greater the need for control. The smaller the difference, the less the need for control. Obviously a figure that has 35½-inch hips and a 23½-inch waist (12-inch difference) needs more shaping than one with 34-inch hips and a 24½-inch waist (9½-inch difference). It is not whether a figure is short or tall, heavy or slim, which determines the amount of shaping it needs. It is the relationship between two adjoining measurements.

DART CONTROL FOR COLUMNAR FIGURES

However heavy, slim, short, tall, columnar figures *need less shaping* because there is less difference between adjoining measurements (Fig. 5a).

DART CONTROL FOR HOUR-GLASS FIGURES

However, heavy, slim, short, tall, hour-glass figures *need more shaping* because there is more difference between adjoining measurements (Fig. 5b).

Dart control is the basic structure of all fitted clothing whatever the design. Its rules apply to children's, boys', and men's clothing as well as to girls' and women's.

Fig. 5

Fig. 6

Not What They "Seam": Shape by Style Lines

Some designers are very clever at incorporating structure into design so that you may find it difficult to discern just where the shaping does occur (Fig. 6).

Here is how you can tell. Place the pattern sections side by side with the grain lines parallel to each other.

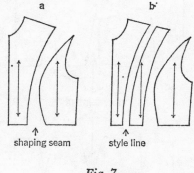

shaping seam   style line

Fig. 7

Do you see the darts that form on the seam line? This is the control (Fig. 7a). When the sections of the garment are joined, the control is hidden in the seam.

Not all seam lines are control lines. Some are style lines just there for decorative effect (Fig. 7b). You can always tell which seam is a shaping seam by making the above test.

In design, one can play great games at hiding the control in style lines that divide an area into interesting spaces.

In Fine Shape: Dart Control Where Needed

Whether in darts or in seams, *the dart control is placed just where it is needed* (Fig. 8).

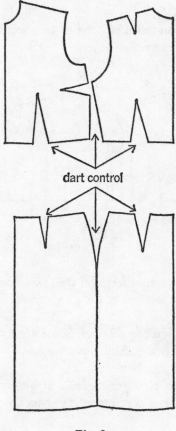

dart control

Fig. 8

In the bodice, since the bust area needs the most shaping, the largest amount of control is placed in front. In the skirt, since the buttocks area needs more shaping, the largest amount of control is placed in the back. The logic of this is apparent. Note that shaping is also found on the side seams.

The dart control of front and back can be subdivided.

Fig. 9

One large dart produces one large bulge. One small dart produces one small bulge. To avoid or minimize a large bulge, the dart control can be divided. The division may be on different seam lines (Fig. 9a) or on the same seam line (Fig. 9b).

Pinwheel Patterns

The fascinating thing about dart control is that while the amount of control remains constant, it may be shifted or divided so that it appears anywhere on bodice, skirt, or sleeve. There is only one rule: the darts (and shaping seams) must originate at an outside seam and end up at or pass over the crest of a figure curve. It's as if the high point of the curve were the pivot of a pinwheel from which the control can be swung in any direction (Fig. 10).

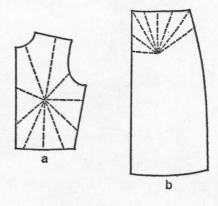

a

b

Fig. 10

Design by Darts

A different position for a dart means a new design for a garment (Fig. 11).

The shaping is in no way altered by the position of the control. It doesn't make any difference whether the darts come from the center, sides, top or bottom. Exactly the same shaping results.

Meant for Each Other: Fabric and Pattern Co-ordination

The pattern has a design. The fabric has a design. When the two are put together, they must look as if they were meant for each other.

On a paper pattern you can put darts and seams wherever you want them. Not so on fabric.

The fabric already has a design of its own built right into it by the way in which it is woven, knitted, or printed. A dart or seam stitched

Fig. 11

into the cloth will interrupt the flow of *its* design. What the sewer has to do is to anticipate what will happen to the fabric design when the darts and seams of the pattern design are stitched into it. If the effect is pleasing, one can safely go ahead. If the effect is unpleasing, something must be changed—either pattern or fabric.

Note what happens to a simple vertical waistline dart in various materials.

In Fig. 12a, the vertical dart is perfectly acceptable, for in no way does it disturb the plain-weave, solid-color fabric.

In Fig. 12b, the waistline dart cuts right into the flower. What a pity! You bought the material because of that beautiful flower. Why destroy it?

Horizontal stripes are easily matched and balanced on the vertical dart (Fig. 12c).

Vertically-striped material produces a chevron shape (Fig. 12d). This may or may not be objectionable depending on the width, color, and location of the stripes.

A vertical dart in a diagonal material is hopeless. It produces an unsightly distortion of the fabric design (Fig. 12e). Diagonals, either woven or printed, are difficult to incorporate into design.

Having trouble visualizing the effect of dart control on fabric? Try one of the following:

1. In buying fabric, fold the material into a dart or seam similar to that of your pattern. Note what happens to the fabric design.

2. Trace the prominent lines or motifs of the fabric on the pattern. Pin the darts or seams closed. Note what happens to the fabric design.

More garments are spoiled by lack of co-ordination between pattern and fabric than by anything else in sewing. When the fabric and pattern work together, the result is a success. When fabric and pattern fight each other, the result is a flop.

Fig. 12

THE OPENING SCENE
Zippers and How to Install Them

Easy as the construction of a shift dress is, there are a few techniques involved that must be mastered. Not only for this simplest of all projects but because they are necessary for your more complex ones. Besides, a constant struggle with the "how-to's" will rob you of the fun of sewing.

One of the greatest inventions of all time must surely be the zipper. Can you imagine what it must have been like in days gone by to get into a dress via dozens and dozens of snaps or hooks and eyes? As if the getting-into and getting-out-of clothes by this means wasn't bad enough, imagine the chore of having to sew them all on.

What kind of zipper and how to insert it depends on the design of the garment and the fabric of which it is made. Zipper installations run the gamut—from completely exposed (Fig. 13a) to completely hidden (Fig. 13d), with the standard settings, both regulation (Fig. 13b) and slot-seam (Fig. 13c) in between.

Fig. 13

The Standard Zipper Closings: Best by Hand

Let me tell you the easiest, fastest, most foolproof way to sew a standard zipper closing. Do it by hand! Hand stitching holds well and looks prettier than machine stitching.

Pin the zipper to position. Use a tiny half-backstitch to secure it. Presto! While your sewing buddy is still searching for her zipper foot in that jumble of sewing tools, your zipper is happily in place.

Despite its delicate appearance, the half-backstitch is a strong stitch (Fig. 14).

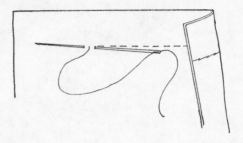

Fig. 14

Fasten the thread on the underside of the material at the right end. Bring the needle to the right side one small stitch ($\frac{1}{16}$ inch to $\frac{1}{8}$ inch long) toward the left. Working back to the right, insert the needle half the distance (or less, if you wish) of the first stitch, slide it along the underside and once more bring the needle out one stitch ahead. Repeat for the length of the seam.

Regulation or Slot-seam Installation: Which?

If the design is "dressy," and the fabric delicate, looped, or the kind that may catch in the teeth of the zipper when it is closed, use the *regulation closing* (Fig. 13b). In the regulation closing, the zipper is hidden by a lapped fold. The lap may be to the right or to the left, depending on which is easier for you to use and which is more consistent with the design. If you're right-handed, choose a lap to the right. If you're left-handed, choose a lap to the left. Only one line of stitching is visible in this type of zipper insertion.

If the design is geometric or the fabric is heavy or pile, use the *slot-seam setting* for your zipper (Fig. 13c). This is also a suitable method for faced or slashed openings, wrist openings, openings concealed in box or inverted pleats.

In the slot-seam closing the zipper is concealed by two folds of material centered over it. There are two visible lines of stitching, one on each side of the closing.

Prepare the Placket

Placket is another name for an opening in a garment used for convenience in putting it on. When a zipper is the placket closing, the placket must be prepared to receive it.

1. With right sides together, stitch the garment below the placket.
2. Press the seam allowances open.

For a slot-seam closing, continue to press the opening along both seam lines. *Pressing now* makes it easier to set and stitch the zipper. It also eliminates the need for pressing when the insertion is completed— often a more difficult procedure.

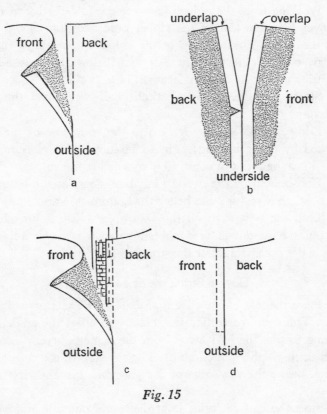

Fig. 15

For a regulation closing a little more preparation is necessary.

1. Turn and press the upper seam allowance. This becomes the overlap. Mark the under (back) seam line with guide basting (Fig. 15a).

> Guide basting is an almost continuous line of uneven basting. Using a double thread of contrasting color so the basting will be clearly visible, make a series of long stitches on the right side of the material and short stitches on the underside.

2. Now clip the under seam allowance at the end of the placket to the seam line (Fig. 15b).

3. Fold the under seam allowance to form a ⅛-inch extension (Fig. 15c). This becomes the underlap. Press.

How to Stitch the Regulation Zipper

1. Working from the right side, place the folded edge of the extension over the right side of the zipper tape allowing enough room to work the slider. The top-stop of the zipper is placed ⅞ inch below the raw edge of the garment (¼ inch below the cross seam line) —a little more if the fabric is heavy. Pin to position.

2. Starting at the top, hand stitch (half-backstitch) the extension (underlap) to the zipper.

3. Bring the fold of the overlap to the seam line of the underlap (marked by guide basting). Pin to position. This placement of the overlap has the merit of completely concealing the zipper.

4. Half-backstitch the overlap in place. Start at the bottom of the zipper. Stitch across the end below the bottom-stop and continue to the top. Keep the welt even all the way up. As you approach the top-stop, pull the tab down. This makes it easier to preserve a narrow welt in the slider area. Complete the stitching (Fig. 15d).

How to Stitch the Slot-seam Zipper

1. Place the fold of one edge *slightly beyond the center* of the closed zipper. This small correction is necessary to offset the tendency of the stitching to pull the fold away from the center, thereby exposing the zipper teeth (highly undesirable). The top-stop of the zipper is placed ⅞ inch below the raw edge of the garment. Pin the zipper to position.

2. Start the half-backstitches at the top of one side and work down the length of the zipper.

3. Pin the second side of the zipper in the same way as the first—that is, the folded edge slightly beyond the center of the zipper.

4. Stitch across the bottom below the bottom-stop and continue up the second side. Make the welts even on both sides.

Just because you have the latest sewing machine, don't make the mistake of thinking that every operation must be done on it. Some are best accomplished by hand sewing. No worries about pulling the material off-grain, matching cross seams and stripes, stretching the fabric, ragged stitching. One zipper successfully put in by hand and you'll understand why it is *the* method used in expensive and custom clothes.

How to Set and Stitch the Exposed Zipper

The bared teeth of a zipper need not be fearsome. They may be decorative. Consider a heavy industrial-type zipper (Fig. 16a) or a contrasting color (Fig. 16b).

a

b

Fig. 16

FOR A ZIPPER SET IN A SLASH

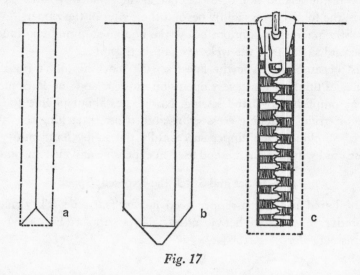

Fig. 17

1. Mark the center line of the opening on the garment.

2. Measure the width of the zipper teeth. Add a tiny bit to the measurement for slide-fastener clearance.

3. From the center line of the closure, measure over half the amount determined in step 2 on each side for the entire length of the zipper. Mark with basting thread.

4. Continue the marking across the end of the opening (Fig. 17a).

5. Reinforce the corners with small machine stitching (Fig. 17a).

6. Slash the center line of the opening. Slash diagonally to each corner (Fig. 17a).

7. Working from the right side, turn under the seam allowance along the line of guide basting. Press (Fig. 17b).

8. Pin the folded edge of the closing to the zipper tape.

9. Topstitch close to the fold (Fig. 17c).

FOR A ZIPPER SET IN A SEAM

Zippers may be set into seams with only slight variations of the above method.

When the zipper is set above or below a stitched seam, omit step 1.

When setting a separating zipper, omit steps 4, 5, and 6.

The Great Deception: The Seam That Is Really a Zippered Closing

It's not only the exposed zipper that is decorative. In its own sneaky way the invisible zipper is too. With this type of installation, the only break in the continuity of the fabric design is that of a normal seam. No one need ever know there's a zipper nestling beneath that smooth seam line.

There are two types of invisible zippers. One is a featherweight nylon coil for lightweight fabrics. The other is a metal-tooth chain for heavier-weight fabrics. They are both installed in the same way.

A special zipper foot must be used for each type. It has two small grooves to hold the right and left sides of the zipper in place and to guide the stitching in a straight line. The smaller-grooved foot is for the nylon coil; the larger-grooved foot is for the metal zipper.

Before setting, flatten the nylon coil, which has a tendency to curl up. Press it flat with your finger or with an iron. Only the tape should be visible when the zipper is set.

In all other installations the seam in which a zipper is set is stitched first, leaving an opening for the zipper. One does just the opposite with the invisible zipper. *The zipper is installed first;* then the seam below it is stitched.

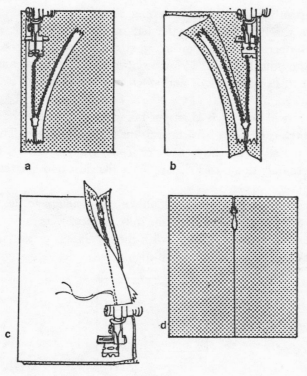

Fig. 18

1. Place the *opened* zipper face down on the right side of the fabric. The coil or teeth are placed on the seam line while the zipper tape is in the seam allowance. The top-stop of the zipper is placed ½ inch below the cross seam line.

2. Slide the zipper foot into position so the coil or metal fits into the appropriate groove and the needle can be lowered into the center of the hole. Insert the needle. Lower the presser foot. Stitch from the top of the tape until the foot touches the slider at the bottom (Fig. 18a). Lock with backstitching.

3. Pin the second side of the zipper to the second side of the opening on the right side of the fabric. The tape is set the same distance from the top as in step 1.

4. Set the groove of the zipper foot over the coil or metal. Bring the needle down into the tape through the hole. Lower the presser foot. Stitch the second side as in step 2 (Fig. 18b).

So far, so good. It's easy. It's fast. However, the next part is a little more difficult.

5. Close the zipper. Place the right sides of the fabric together below the zipper with seam lines matching. Pin.

6. Slide the zipper foot to the left of the zipper so it clears it, making it operate like an ordinary zipper foot. Insert the needle through the outside notch, ½ inch above the zipper end and 1⁄16 to the left of it. Lower the foot and stitch to the end of the seam (Fig. 18c).

7. There will be 1 inch of zipper tail extending below the installed zipper. Stitch each side of the tape to the seam allowance. This stitching must not show on the right side. *No stitching* shows on the right side. Successfully done, this closing looks like just another seam (Fig. 18d).

Theoretically, steps 5 and 6 should be easy enough to do. Actually it is hard to be precise because of the bulk. Some sewers find it easier to stitch the seam *below* the zipper with the regulation presser foot, then come back and backstitch that half-inch length (step 6).

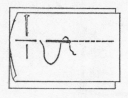

Fig. 19

The backstitch is done in the same way as the half-backstitch with this exception: when working back to the right, the needle is inserted at the point where the preceding stitch ended (Fig. 19). The cloth is encircled with stitches. Before the advent of the sewing machine, this stitch was the one that was used for joining two layers of cloth.

A good rule to follow for all your sewing: when a procedure is too difficult for you to do by machine, do it by hand. Hand stitching came first and it still makes up a large part of fashion sewing.

Matching Cross Seams, Plaids, Stripes, or Motifs at Zipper Openings

When a zipper is installed by hand stitching, one has perfect control in matching cross seams, plaids, stripes, checks, and motifs. It takes a little more doing when the stitching is done by machine.

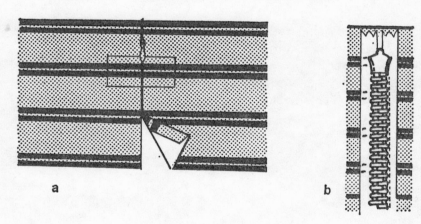

a   b

Fig. 20

1. Machine stitch the first side of the zipper as usual.
2. Fold under the seam allowance of the second side. Using masking tape, tape the fabric to position on the right side matching exactly all cross seams, plaids, stripes, motifs (Fig. 20a).
3. Machine stitch.
   (a) *Standard zipper:* topstitch; remove the masking tape.
   (b) *Invisible zipper:* turn to the wrong side. Pencil mark the zipper tape at each seam line or unit (Fig. 20b). Remove

the masking tape from the right side. Open the zipper. Match the markings on the zipper tape with the seams, lines, or motifs of the fabric. Stitch as usual.

There is no all-purpose zipper or zipper installation. Choose whichever type seems best for the design and the fabric of the garment you are making.

LET'S FACE IT!

Finish by Facing

You could ignore the whole finishing bit and let Nature take its course. In which case your beautiful dress would be outlined in a raw, ragged (eventually a fringed) edge. Not many designs call for such casual treatment.

You could bind the raw edges with bias or braid, with leather or lace, with ribbon or rickrack, with fur or feathers. All of these are fine finishes—in their fashion.

Let's face it! Nine times out of ten, *the finish is by facing.* When the edge to be faced is a straight one, the facing is generally an extension of the garment turned back at a foldline (hemline) to form a hem (Fig. 21a). When the edge to be faced is a shaped one, the facing is a separate piece of fabric cut in the same shape, size, and grain (Fig. 21b).

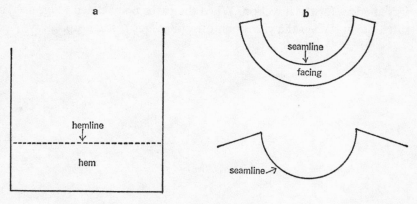

Fig. 21

Face What and What Facing?

When the dress fabric is opaque, smooth, and light-to-medium weight, use self-fabric for the facing.

When the dress fabric is transparent, cut a facing of flesh-color net, tulle, marquisette, horsehair braid, or any other transparent material.

When a dress fabric is heavy-weight, rough, shaggy, pile, or any other raised surface, use a lightweight, smooth lining material for the facing.

Hold That Line: Staystitching

Before attaching a shaped facing, the edge to be faced must be preserved by staystitching.

Staystitching is a line of machine stitching close to the seam line. It fixes the length, the shape, and the grain of the edge to be faced. When a curved edge like a neckline or an armhole needs to be clipped for better fit, make the staystitching right on the seam line.

Use any thread and 8 stitches to the inch. These are small enough to stay the edge and large enough for easy removal should that be necessary. Otherwise, the staystitching may remain permanently in the seam allowance where, hopefully, no one will ever see it.

To preserve the grain, *staystitching must be directional.*

Stitch with the grain. The rule is: stitch from a high point to a low one, from a wide point to a narrow one (Fig. 22a). The latter takes precedence over the former.

The yarns of the material actually point the way. Examine the frayed edges for the direction. When the yarns point down (Fig. 22b), stitch down. When the yarns point up (Fig. 22c), stitch up.

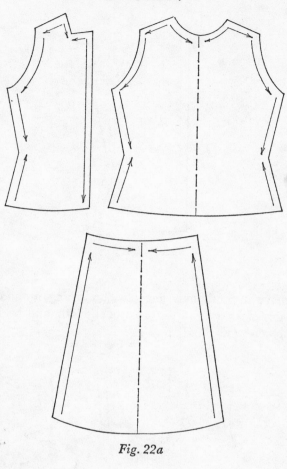

Fig. 22a

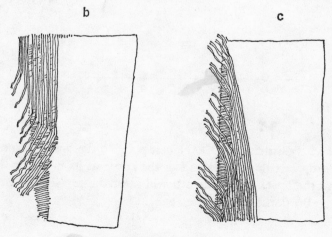

Figs. 22b and 22c

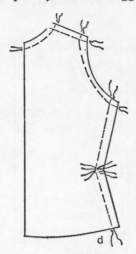

Fig. 22d

Never make a continuous line of staystitching around a corner. Break the thread at the end of a row of stitching and begin again in the new direction (Fig. 22d).

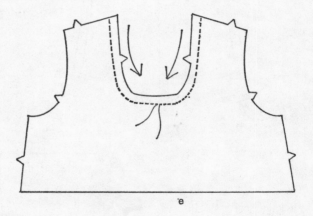

Fig. 22e

On a curve, stitch from the highest point to the lowest point. Break the thread, start the second half of the curve at its highest point and stitch to the lowest one, where it will meet the previous line of staystitching. Break the thread (Fig. 22e).

Just to make sure that your stitching has in no way departed from the original size and shape of the pattern, compare your staystitched edge with the original edge. Pull up the thread on any stretched edge. Clip the stitching in a few places to release a pulled-up edge. Staystitching must preserve the line of an edge, not distort it.

Staystitch all curved or angled edges that need facing. And while you're at it, staystitch all other curved or angled edges of the garment immediately after cutting and marking. The only edges that dare be excluded from staystitching are those that will eventually be eased into others (the sleeve caps, for instance) or that will not join any others (like the outer edges of facings). Even at that, if the fabric tends to ravel, it is wise to staystitch those edges too.

Staystitching may seem a tedious task and you may be tempted to skip it. Don't! In the much handling during construction it is so easy to stretch and pull the fabric out of shape. You certainly wouldn't want that.

Facts About Facings

One of the telltale signs of amateur sewing is a facing that keeps popping into view. In fashion sewing, every step in the cutting and application of facing to garment must contribute its bit to preventing this.

SIZE OF FACING MAKES A DIFFERENCE

A facing must be cut slightly smaller than the edge to be faced. This shortened length does several very important things.

1. It fits the inside of the garment. *An inside curve is always shorter than an outside curve.*

2. It makes the neckline or armhole (or whatever else is faced) lie better against the body.

3. It makes it possible to *roll the seam that joins facing to garment to the underside—out of sight.*

The simplest way to shorten a facing is to take a larger seam allowance at the shoulders in a neck facing or at the underarm in an armhole facing (Fig. 23a).

When a garment has an unusual style line, naturally, its facing must have a similar one. To shorten such a facing in any one place would throw off the precise matching of the shaped seam lines. Instead, make tiny tucks in the facing pattern in several places so the over-all shape is preserved (Fig. 23b).

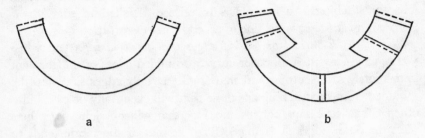

a   b

Fig. 23

How to Apply a Separate Neck or Armhole Facing to the Garment

1. Join the front and back neckline facings at the shoulders. Join the front and back armhole facings at the underarms (and shoulders, too, if necessary).

The facing seams should match the garment seams. This is particularly important to remember if, in fitting, you made any changes in the position of the seams.

2. Press the seam allowances open.

3. Trim the facing seam allowances so they are narrower than the garment seam allowances. This is called *grading*.

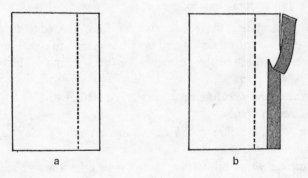

a   b

Fig. 24

In fine sewing we never permit one edge to end directly over the other (Fig. 24a). This produces a bumpy ridge. Instead we stagger or layer or *grade* widths of seam allowances so that the bulk is diminished *gradually*—hence the word, *grading*. This beveling eliminates unsightly lumps (Fig. 24b).

The final width of each seam allowance is determined by the thickness of the fabric. Sheer fabrics can be trimmed to a narrower width than heavy fabrics.

Eliminate Bulk and Release Strain

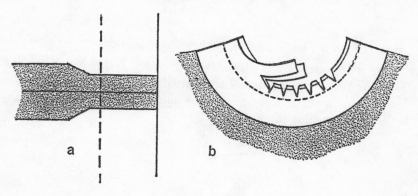

Fig. 25

1. Free the cross-seam areas of bulk by trimming away some of the seam allowances (Fig. 25a).
2. With right sides together, matching centers and seams, pin the facing to the garment stretching as necessary to make edges meet. Stitch the two with the facing side up. Be sure to keep the seam an even distance in from the raw edge.
3. Clip the curved seam allowances to the seam line (Fig. 25b).

A straight facing is no problem. Stitch, grade the seam allowances, and just turn back. A curved or shaped facing is another matter. It cannot be "just turned back." The cut edge is considerably shorter than the length against which it will rest when the seam allowance and facing are turned to the inside. The seam allowance must be clipped to provide the span that will equalize the lengths. Without this, neither seam allowance nor facing can lie flat.

To Finish the Facing

1. Press the seam allowances open a small section at a time. It is easier to do this on some curved surface like a tailor's ham (page 293).

A crisper finished edge results when the seam allowances are pressed open first before the facing is turned to the inside.

2. Grade the seam allowances. Make the seam allowance to be worn to the outside the wider one.

3. Turn the facing to the inside, rolling the joining seam to the inside too. Press.

4. Finish the outer edge of the facing in any of the ways suggested for edge finishes (page 65).

To Be Sure: Topstitch or Understitch

One more operation is necessary to keep the facing "in its place." This one positively guarantees that it will never slip into view. The facing is anchored with *topstitching or understitching*. Either one may be hand or machine stitched.

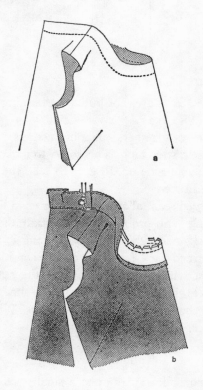

Fig. 26

TOPSTITCHING (Fig. 26a)

Since topstitching becomes a decorative feature, choose whatever kind of stitching, whatever stitch size, however many rows of stitching, and whatever thread will be most effective. The thread may be matching, contrasting, thick, thin, embroidery floss, buttonhole twist, or mercerized cotton.

Mercerized cotton thread for topstitching can be effective if used double for both bobbin and upper threading. On a single-needle sewing machine use the double thread from two bobbins set one over the other on the spool holder. On a two-needle sewing machine, use the double thread from two spools set on the two spindles. Thread as usual as if the double were a single thread.

Measure an equal distance in from but not too close to the finished edge. Mark with guide basting. If you are an accurate sewer use the machine gauge on the throat plate.

Topstitching can make any seam line more interesting and more important. It emphasizes the architecture of your garment.

UNDERSTITCHING (Fig. 26b)

While topstitching is there for all the world to see, understitching quietly goes about its business unseen.

1. Lift the facing from the outer fabric.
2. Place the seam allowances now caught between the facing and the outer fabric against the facing.
3. From the right side of the facing, stitch the facing to the seam allowances close to the seam line.
4. Trim away some of the seam allowances close to the stitching line. You don't need the bulk they add. There is little chance the facing will rip away through the two rows of stitching.

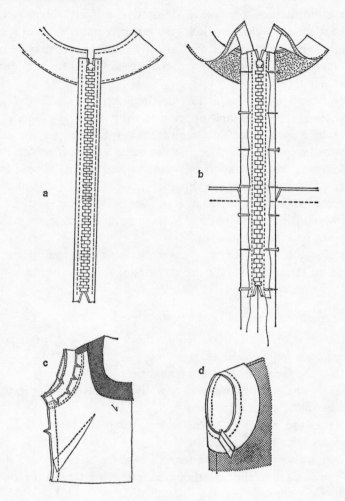

Fig. 27

Some folks think it easier to apply the neckline facing first and then put the zipper in (Fig. 27a). Others say it is easier to fit the garment if the zipper is inserted before the facing is attached (Fig. 27b), indeed, before even the shoulders are stitched.

Some hold it easier to stitch the armhole facing to the armhole before stitching the side seam, then stitching the facing and underarm seam in one operation (Fig. 27c). Others believe it makes a neater and more precise armhole application to stitch the side seams first and then apply the completed facing (Fig. 27d).

One of the first things you must learn in sewing is not to make things hard for yourself. Choose whichever method appears easier to you for a particular garment.

The All-in-One Neck-and-Armhole Facing

It's easy enough to attach neck and armhole facings when they are cut separately or where only one or the other is necessary. For instance: a sleeveless blouse that has a collar needs only the armhole facing; a collarless dress that has sleeves needs only a neckline facing. However, in a sleeveless, collarless dress, both neckline and armhole facings are necessary.

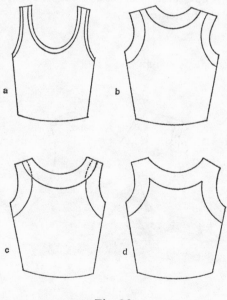

Fig. 28

In a dropped-neckline, narrow-shouldered sleeveless style separate facings for the neckline and armhole would, of necessity, have to be very narrow—little more than bindings (Fig. 28a).

In a more normal-shouldered sleeveless, collarless style separate armhole and neckline facings of regulation width may leave a narrow space on the shoulder where there is no facing-layer of cloth (Fig. 28b). In some fabrics this unsupported channel has a tendency to collapse between the two thickened, faced areas that adjoin it.

On the other hand were the facings to be cut too wide for the shoulder measurement, they would overlap (Fig. 28c).

When facings are cut so they just meet on the shoulder, they may just as well be in one piece. As a matter of fact, most sleeveless, collarless styles are cut so the neck-and-armhole facings are all in one piece (Fig. 28d).

Tricky and Terrific: How to Stitch the All-in-One Facing to the Garment

How to stitch the all-in-one facing to the garment is no mystery, but how to turn that one-piece facing to the underside requires a bit of sleight of hand. The secret? *Leave one seam open.* It may be the shoulder seam or the underarm seam.

WITH THE SHOULDER SEAMS OPEN

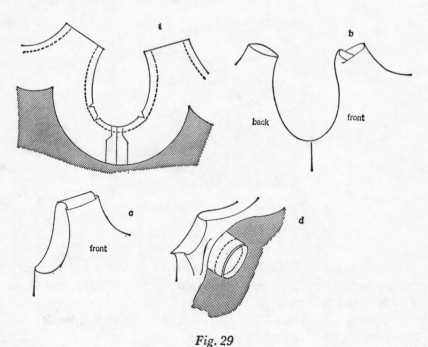

Fig. 29

1. Stitch the side seams of the garment but *leave the shoulder seams open*. Stitch the side seams of the facing but *leave the shoulder seams open*.

2. Press all seam allowances open. Trim and grade them. Free the cross-seam areas of bulk.

3. Place the right side of the facing against the right side of the garment. Match centers, seams, and outside edges stretching as necessary. Pin to position.

4. With the facing side up, stitch around the neck and around the armholes but *do not stitch the shoulders* (Fig. 29a).

5. Trim, clip, and grade all seam allowances.

6. Turn the facing to the underside through the openings at the shoulders.

Now for the tricky part.

7. Turn in the raw edges of the front shoulder about a seam allowance (Fig. 29b).

8. Slip the back shoulder into the turned-in opening (Fig. 29c). Make certain the right sides of the outer fabric are together and the right sides of the facing are together. The neckline and armhole seams must match.

9. Reach up under the facing, grasp the open shoulders and pull them down far enough between the facing and the garment so you can work with them.

10. With right sides together and raw edges and seams matching, stitch the shoulder opening in one continuous circle-of-a-seam (Fig. 29d).

11. Trim the seam allowances and finger-press them open with the nail of thumb or forefinger.

12. Carefully pull the shoulder back to its correct position.

13. Press all outside edges, remembering to roll the neckline and armhole joining seams to the underside.

WITH THE SIDE SEAMS OPEN

This kind of construction can be used when the length and bulk of the garment are not too great and when there is a center front or center back opening.

1. Stitch the garment at the shoulders but *not at the side seams.* Stitch the facing at the shoulders but *not at the side seams.*

2. Press all seam allowances open. Trim and grade.

3. With right sides together, stitch the facing to the opening and neck edges. Stitch the facing to the armhole edges (Fig. 30a).

4. Grade the seam allowances and clip all curves.

5. Turn the facing to the underside, bringing the opening edges through the shoulders (Fig. 30b).

6. Open out the facing so it extends the side seams.

7. With right sides together, seams matching, make one continuous line of stitching to form the underarm seam from the edge of the facing to the hem of the garment (Fig. 30c).

8. Press the seam allowances open. Trim and clip where necessary.

9. Turn the armhole facing to its correct position (Fig. 30d).

10. Press all the outside edges, being careful to roll the neckline and armhole joining seams to the underside.

Master these two techniques and flabbergast all your friends with your magic. They'll never guess how it's done.

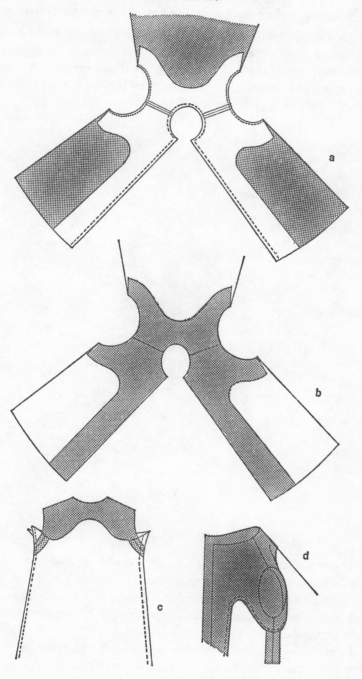

Fig. 30

Facing to the Fore: Decorative Use of a Structural Necessity

In sewing, you will often find places where one can make a decorative use of a structural necessity. Take the facing, for instance. Why hide it perpetually on the underside when it can become an attractive feature on the outside? Perhaps an unusual shape (Fig. 31a), or a contrasting color (Fig. 31b), or a different texture (Fig. 31c).

Fig. 31

Face the Facing

About the easiest and most effective way to cope with a decorative top-facing is to face the facing first and then attach it. There are two bonuses to this method. The facing edge is finished before being fastened to the garment. (It's so much less bulky this way.) The facing's facing functions as an interfacing.

In attaching the facing to the outside of the garment, some of the operations are (understandably) the reverse of those used for applying

it to the underside. Take the matter of size, for example. Since the facing must fit the outside measurement of the garment, make it slightly
larger than the area it is to face. Adjustments are the opposite of
those in Fig. 23: add at the shoulders or slash-and-spread the facing
pattern to enlarge it (Fig. 32a).

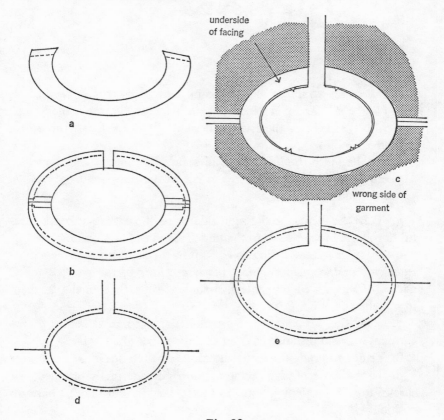

Fig. 32

1. Cut out the facing.
2. Cut a facing for the facing of a lightweight material in a matching color. Make the facing's facing just a tiny bit smaller than the
facing itself.
3. With right sides together, join the facing to its facing on all outside edges (Fig. 32b).
4. Press the seam allowances open. Trim and grade them. Clip or
notch where necessary.

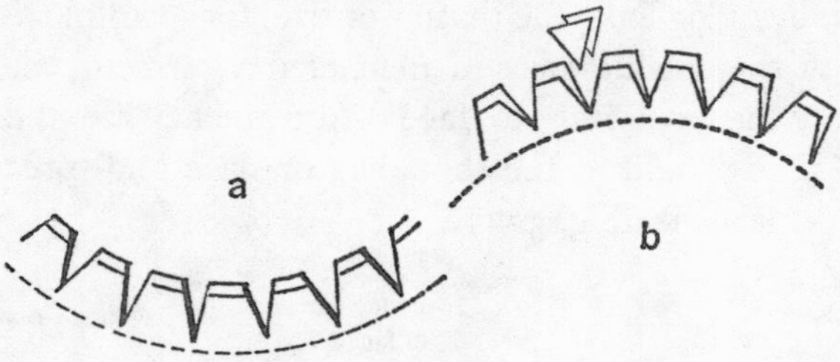

Fig. 33

To release straining clip all seam allowances that curve in (Fig. 33a). A clip is a short snip in the seam allowance made with the point of the scissors at right angles to the stitching line.

To eliminate rippling notch all seam allowances that curve out (Fig. 33b). A notch is a small wedge that is cut out of the seam allowance.

5. Turn the facings to the right side. Press the edges flat being careful to roll the joining seam to the underside. Baste to position.

6. In order for the facing to end up in the right position, *place the right side of the facing against the wrong side of the garment* (Fig. 32c). Match raw edges, centers, shoulder seams. Stretch the garment to match the facing. Pin to position.

7. With the *garment side up,* stitch the decorative facing to the garment an even distance in from the raw edges (Fig. 32d).

8. Trim and grade the seam allowances. Notch or clip as necessary.

9. Turn the decorative facing to the right side of the garment. Be careful to roll the joining seam to the underside. Pin and/or baste to position.

10. Topstitch (Fig. 32e) or slipstitch the outer edges of the decorative facing to the garment.

SLIPSTITCH

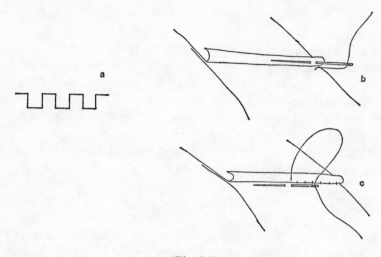

Fig. 34

A slipstitch is an invisible hand stitch done from the right side. It is one of the most all-around useful stitches in sewing so you must learn to do it well.

The stitches are worked from right to left. They slip alternately between the facing and the garment to which it is attached. The motion forms a Greek key design (Fig. 34a).

1. Fasten the thread on the underside and bring the needle up to the surface just under the finished edge of the facing.

2. In order to conceal the stitches, turn back the finished edge of the facing about $\frac{1}{16}$ inch to $\frac{1}{8}$ inch.

3. Slip the needle into the turned-back fold of the facing, bringing it out about $\frac{1}{8}$ inch from the point of entry (Fig. 34b).

4. Make a similar slipstitch in the garment, starting directly under the ending of the first stitch (Fig. 34c).

5. Start the next slipstitch on the facing directly above the ending of the slipstitch on the garment.

Repeat the stitches across the length of the facing. Fasten the thread on the underside.

The turn-back of the facing produces enough slack in the stitches to float the facing on the surface of the garment. The slipstitch produces a line of permanent stitching on the wrong side which is completely invisible from the right side.

Decorative facings can be applied to sleeves, hems, slits, and other openings in the same way.

Slipstitching is also *the* method used for attaching patch pockets, welts, flaps, and decorative appliqués.

Fitting Finish

Whether you choose to boldly expose the facing or modestly conceal it, don't forget the primary function of a facing: it is a fitting finish for a garment.

ROMANTIC RUFFLES

Want to look romantic? Add a frill that frames the face, that froths at the wrist, that flounces at the hem (Fig. 35).

Fig. 35

Don't Be Ruffled by a Ruffle

A ruffle is easy enough to make. You don't need a pattern for it. It can be any width (the heavier the fabric, the wider the ruffle needs to be). It can be any fullness. (A full ruffle is three times the length of the edge it is to join. For less fullness, use less length; for more fullness add more length.) A ruffle can be straight grain or bias. It can be single, double, or layer upon layer.

Whatever else a ruffle is, it's feminine!

How to Make a Gathered Ruffle

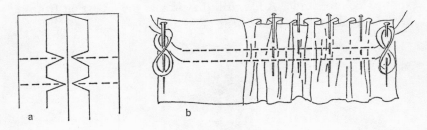

a   b

Fig. 36

1. Staystitch the edge to which the ruffle is to be joined. Section it off into halves, quarters, eighths. Mark with pins, notches, or basting thread.
2. Section off the ruffle in the same way.
3. Gather the ruffle by hand or by machine.

BY HAND

Use a double thread of cotton or silk or a single thread of buttonhole twist. Use running stitches.

Running stitches are tiny, even basting stitches woven through the material with an up-and-down motion of the wrist (as if the hand were a moving part of a machine) while the fabric is held still. When the needle is full of stitches, the thread is drawn through and the operation repeated.

BY MACHINE

Wind the bobbin with heavier-than-usual thread or with buttonhole twist. It is the bobbin thread that gets drawn up. Heavier thread makes it easier to do so.

BY EITHER METHOD

Eliminate the bulk at all cross seams by notching the seam allowances almost to the seam line (Fig. 36a). Make two rows of stitching —the first in the seam allowance close to the seam line, the second ¼ inch away toward the raw edge. Two rows of stitching make for an even distribution of gathers.

4. Pin the ruffle to each end. Place the pins at right angles to the edge.

5. Draw up the ruffle until it equals the edge to which it is to be attached.

6. Fasten the threads at each end by winding around the pin in a figure eight (Fig. 36b).

7. Match the markings.

8. With the point of a pin or needle, distribute the fullness evenly between the markings. Pin frequently enough to hold the distribution in place. Place the pins at right angles to the stitching line (Fig. 36b).

9. With the fullness on top, stitch the ruffle to the garment on the seam line, removing the pins as you sew. In addition to saving the time it takes to baste, this method has another advantage: it is possible to improve or correct the distribution of the gathers as you sew along. If you have any doubts that you can manage this, then first baste with short stitches *beside* the stitching line. Were you to baste right on the stitching line, you would not be able to remove the basting thread once the permanent stitching is done.

Simple Styles That Stagger

Pleated Ruffles Are Pleasant

Pleated ruffles are pleasant too (Fig. 37). More controlled than the bouncy gathered ruffle, they add a soft edging to otherwise simple or severe lines.

Fig. 37

Meet the Pleat

A pleat is a fold of fabric. It may be used singly, in clusters, in a series. Pleats may be even or uneven, pressed or unpressed, stitched or unstitched, shallow or full.

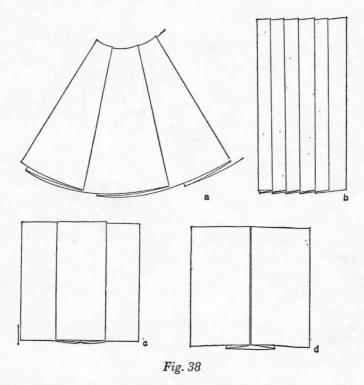

Fig. 38

The most frequently used pleats are side pleats, knife pleats, box pleats, and inverted pleats.

A *side pleat* is fabric folded to one side (Fig. 38a). The fold may be in either direction.

Knife pleats are a series of crisply pressed, even side pleats of any size folded so they all go in one direction (Fig. 38b).

In a *box pleat* the folds turn in opposite directions on the right side and meet at the center on the wrong side (Fig. 38c).

An *inverted pleat* is just the opposite of a box pleat. The folds of two equal side pleats meet at the center on the right side (Fig. 38d). Inverted pleats used in a series are transformed into box pleats.

Ruffles are either knife pleated or box pleated.

To Make the Pleated Ruffle

1. Prepare the length of material in the same way as for gathering.
2. Place pleat markings.

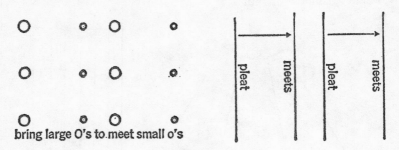

bring large O's to meet small o's

Fig. 39

Pairs of markings are necessary for each pleat—one line of marking for the fold of the pleat, the other for the line to which the fold is brought. On ready-made patterns, the markings are either large O's and small o's or solid lines with directional arrows. Both are supported by printed directions: "Pleat . . . Meets" or "Bring large O's to meet small o's" (Fig. 39).

When no pattern is used, make your own markings. Use a ruler or a gauge to measure.

Generally, each pleat takes three times its width: the pleat (the part that appears on the surface), the underfold (the part that is turned under), the underlay (return) (Fig. 40a).

For fuller pleats, make the underfold and underlay much deeper than the pleat itself (Fig. 40b). For less fullness, make the underfold and underlay much shallower than the pleat itself (Fig. 40c).

3. Lay in the pleats. Baste or press them to position.
4. To hold the pleats in place across the edge to be attached to the garment, hand or machine baste.

three times width of pleat   narrow pleat, deep turn-under and return

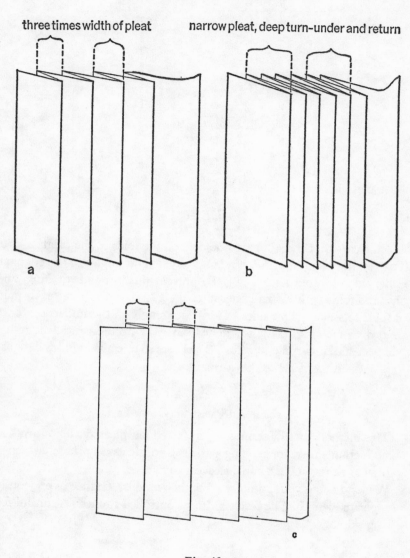

Fig. 40

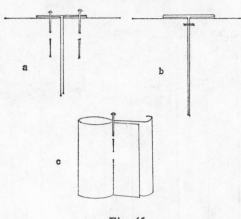

Fig. 41

Take care that the stitching doesn't pull the folds of the pleats apart. To prevent this in machine stitching, pin at right angles to the edge on either side of a fold (Fig. 41a). To prevent this in hand stitching, anchor the folds with a small backstitch (Fig. 41b). Or bring each pair of folds together (right sides inside) and stitch on the underside for a short distance (Fig. 41c). If stitched part way up the width, the result will be a standing ruffle, the kind Pucci uses so effectively in his designs.

5. Attach the ruffle to the garment.

Gathers and Pleats for Other Parts

The methods used for making gathered or pleated ruffles are the same methods used for making gathers and pleats anywhere else on a garment: skirts, collars, cuffs, sleeves, anywhere.

Want to show your mastery of both methods? Gather a previously box-pleated length. The result? Much controlled fullness. Beautiful for a long skirt.

THE HOW OF HEMS

Whether one lets down, puts up or evens out, whether it's a first-time job or a retread, whether it's long, short or in-between, the procedure for setting and stitching a hem is much the same.

Top-to-Toe Continuity Dictates the Length of a Skirt

Skirt lengths are not merely a matter of how-far-from-the-floor or how-much-above-the-knee. It's the total look that determines the length.

A mini skirt or hot pants worn over colored or textured panty hose looks less mini than if worn with sheer flesh-colored hose or none at all. Dark or matching shoes and stockings emerging below a longish skirt make the skirt appear even longer than it actually is.

Whether a skirt is slim or full makes a difference in determining its length. Because a narrow skirt rides up when in motion, you may want to make it a trifle longer than you normally would. Because a full skirt stands away from the body, it is not affected by movement. Therefore you can afford to make it a trifle shorter.

Some fabrics (notably thin silk knits) and some cuts (particularly bias) also have a tendency to ride up when one moves. Skirts of these fabrics may be made a trifle longer to compensate.

How to Decide What the Length Shall Be

1. Consider what's fashionable.

You'll save yourself a lot of inching up and letting down if you have the courage to adopt an incoming fashion rather than wait to be the last holdout. Within the framework of current design, there are always fashionable alternatives that can be flattering.

2. Bedeck yourself in the finery you plan to wear.

From the skin out—the bra, *the* girdle, *the* slip. If you turn up a hem without them on, you may discover your skirt a different length when you do put them on. A garment that is forced to stretch in width to accommodate uncontrolled curves robs the length to do so. Remember that curves take length as well as width to fit them.

From top to toe—the garment, *the* stockings, *the* shoes. In addition to top-to-toe color continuity (which may help determine the length) there is also the very real matter of heel height. Heel height not only affects the number of inches from the floor a hem is to be, it also affects one's posture which, in turn, involves the evenness of the skirt length.

3. Try on the garment.

4. Turn up a tentative length.

You could do it by eye, by gosh and by golly, but you'll find that the services of a willing friend or relative makes for a much more accurate setting.

5. Decide whether the length is becoming to you.

Sit, stand, swirl to test the length at rest and in motion. It is only after having considered all these factors that one can determine whether the length is too short, too long, or just right.

The Hang of It

You certainly don't want your beautiful new dress spoiled by a dippy hem. To avoid this, let the garment "hang out" until the fabric has a chance to settle. Overnight will do for most fabrics. Bias cut and circular skirts take longer—sometimes as much as a week.

It is a good idea to hang up your garment whenever you have finished working on it. By doing so the fabric will have settled by the time you are ready for the hem.

With the Help of a Friend: Setting the Hem

When it comes to setting a hem, a girl needs the help of a friend. It's more than just soul stuff. It's downright practical.

All self-help gimmicks have their drawbacks. Take that handy little skirt marker that squirts out chalk in response to your squeeze of a bulb. By this method, the chalk marker stands in place while you turn slowly as you do the marking. It's that turning that is the hazard. A shift in your position makes for inaccuracy in marking. Then, too, even if the chalk powder doesn't come out in a blob, the chalk may mar some fabrics and may not show on others.

When a friend sets the hem for you, *you stand still while helper and skirt marker move around you.* As for skirt markers, the best one to use is an adjustable-rule, on-a-stand marker that dispenses pins. This is a standard tool and can be bought at most dressmaker supply counters.

1. Set the skirt marker for the number of inches from the floor you've decided the hem is to be.

2. *You*

Stand naturally. If you stand stiffly at attention for the marking when that is not your normal posture, your skirt will be uneven when you lapse into your usual stance.

3. *Your helper*

Places pins 2 inches to 3 inches apart for straight hems, closer for curved hems, almost continuously for circular hems. Using the pins as a guideline, turns up and pins the hem tentatively to position. (Pins are placed at right angles to the fold.) Corrects any irregularities or jumpiness that may have occurred in the pinning.

4. *Both you and your helper*

Examine the skirt for evenness. Reset the hem in whole or in part if necessary. When satisfied with the appearance, remove the garment for finishing.

Turning Up the Hem

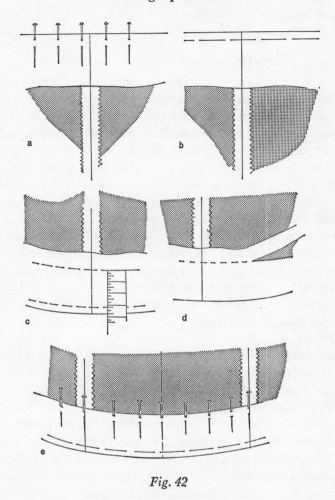

Fig. 42

1. Turn the hem to the inside of the skirt along the line of marking pins, correcting any irregularities.

If the fabric has a horizontal line at the hem and the skirt is full, it is advisable to follow the line of the fabric design rather than the slight curve that results from setting. (All body circumference lines are slightly curved.) In a plaid skirt, for instance, it would be better to sacrifice the truth of the setting for an optical illusion. The straight line will make the skirt look even. Were you to follow the accurate curve of the body setting that goes off the straight line, the skirt hem would look uneven.

2. If you plan to sew the hem immediately and if pinning will not bruise the fabric, then fix the foldline with pins placed at right angles and close to the fold (Fig. 42a). If pins will leave hole marks (better test your material) baste close to the fold with a fine needle and silk thread (Fig. 42b).

3. Measure and mark the depth of the hem. Using a gauge or a ruler, measure an even distance from the fold and mark with chalk, pencil, or pins depending on the color and texture of the fabric (Fig. 42c).

In a straight skirt the hem may range from 2 inches in opaque fabric to 12 inches in see-through fabric.

In anything other than a straight hem, the depth of the hem should be no more than can be made to lie flat against the inside of the hem. Sometimes this is done by easing (Fig. 43). Sometimes fullness is taken out at each seam (Fig. 44). If the edge has an unusual shape or if it is very flared or circular, a facing is used instead of a hem. Some circle skirts have only rolled hems (Fig. 45).

(Coat hems are generally 2½ inches to 3 inches, jacket hems are 1½ inches to 2 inches, dress sleeves have 1-inch hems, jacket sleeves have 1½-inch hems, coat sleeves have 2-inch hems. Flared hems on any of these are less.)

4. Trim the excess material (Fig. 42d).

5. Pin the hem to the garment at all seam lines, centers, and suitable intervals between (Fig. 42e). Distribute any fullness evenly between pins. As far as possible, match the grain of the hem and the grain of the skirt fabric. (Grain is a lengthwise or crosswise yarn of the fabric.)

EASING THE FULLNESS AT THE UPPER EDGE OF A HEM

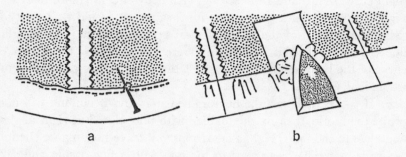

a   b

Fig. 43

Either machine or hand baste close to the raw edge. Pull up the thread to fit the skirt (Fig. 43a). Steam press.

Often rippling at the upper edge of the hem can be removed just with steam pressing. Use an upward motion of the iron from fold to raw edge (Fig. 43b).

Before doing any pressing it would be wise to skim through the section on pressing (page 287).

TAKING OUT HEM FULLNESS AT SEAMS

1. Turn the hem to the outside of the skirt.
2. Pin each seam close to and matching each corresponding skirt seam (Fig. 44a).
3. Stitch. Trim away excess material. Notch the seam allowances at the foldline to prevent bulk when the hem is folded up to its correct position (Fig. 44b). Grade the seam allowances to the foldline (Fig. 44b). Press open.
4. Note that the shape of the hem is the *reverse* of the shape of the skirt (Fig. 44c).
5. Turn the fitted hem to the underside and finish as one would any other hem.

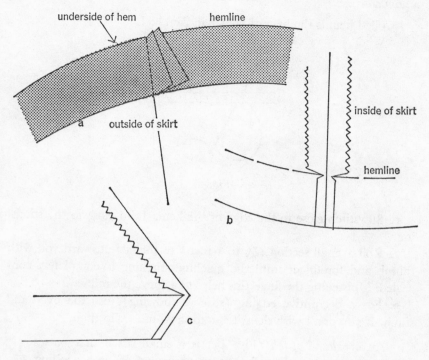

Fig. 44

A FACING INSTEAD OF A HEM

A skirt facing is cut in the same shape and on the same grain as the skirt at the hem edge. It is attached in the same way as any other facing.

A ROLLED HEM

A rolled hem is the hem of your handkerchief.

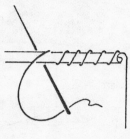

Fig. 45

1. Staystitch close to the edge of the hem. Trim close to the stitching.

2. Roll a small section (½ to 1 inch) of the edge toward you with thumb and forefinger until the machine stitching is completely concealed. Moistening the fingertips helps to achieve the roll.

3. For a decorative edging (stitches showing), use the overhand stitch. If you don't wish the stitches to show use a slipstitch.

> An *overhand stitch* (Fig. 45) is a small stitch that passes over and under the roll (but never through it) in a winding motion. When there are enough stitches on the needle, pull up the thread.

Finish with a Flourish

What goes on out-of-view is almost as important as what meets the eye of the beholder. For one thing, there is the matter of aesthetic integrity. *Fine craftsmanship is an organic part of anything beautiful.* Pride of workmanship is one of the great satisfactions in any creative work. That, in itself, would be enough to justify the extra work of finishing with a flourish. But that is not the whole story.

In sewing, that time-consuming finish becomes a *protection for the cut edges of the fabric.* A finish is needed for this purpose wherever there is an exposed edge: seam allowances, facings, as well as hems. The same finish may be used on all three. Or you may reserve your extra flourishes for the hem.

Because most ready-to-wear clothes sport seam bindings for hem finishes, many sewers are under the impression that this is the best, perhaps even the only, way to finish a hem. The truth is that some hems don't need binding, some are better off without it, and still others can be enhanced with more elaborate treatment. The choice depends on the fabric, the construction of the garment, and the imagination of the sewer.

Here are a dozen edge finishes to choose from. You may invent others. Indeed, your individual touch can become your signature.

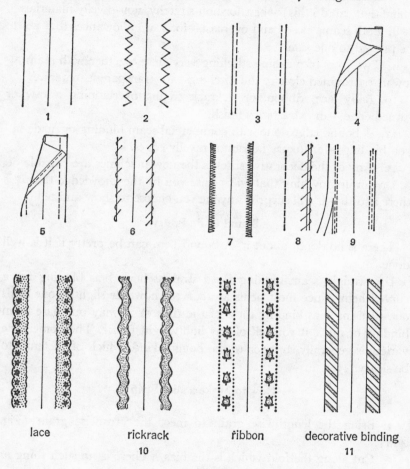

lace   rickrack   ribbon   decorative binding

10   11

Fig. 46

1. No special finish whatsoever—for firmly woven fabrics that don't fray; a finish used largely in tailoring.

2. Pinked edges—for firm materials.

3. A single row of straight machine stitching along the raw edge— suitable for knits and firm materials.

4. A turned-under edge pressed to position—for firmly woven materials.

5. A turned-under edge either hand or machine stitched—for thin materials, for washable fabrics.

6. Hand overcasting—for loosely woven or ravelly fabrics.

7. Machine overcasting (if you are lucky enough to have a machine that can do this)—best for non-stretchy, non-ravelly materials.

8. Both seams closed and overcast—for seam allowances that are to be pressed to one side.

9. Two rows of machine stitching very close together with seam allowances trimmed close to the stitching—for transparent materials.

10. Baby lace, ribbon, or rickrack edging overlapping a raw or turned edge—an extra fancy finish.

11. A bound edge done with commercial seam binding or made-by-you binding—for luxury fabrics or ravelly edges.

12. Any of the decorative stitches the new machines are capable of.

Dream up anything that will please you by the knowledge that it is there and that it will surprise anyone you choose to show and tell.

Bound to Be Pretty

There is no doubt about it. A bound hem can be pretty if it is well done.

Use straight seam binding for a straight hem, bias binding for a curved hem. Since most hems are curved, however slightly, one finds oneself using bias binding most of the time. You may purchase seam binding or make it yourself of any lightweight fabric. The homemade variety is generally superior to the bought kind, which often tends to be sleazy.

How to Make a Bias Strip

1. Bring the lengthwise grain to meet the crosswise grain (Fig. 47a).

2. Cut along the fold which is the bias. (There is no such thing as "near 'ems" when it comes to bias. It either is or isn't.)

A 45-degree triangle will quickly give you the bias. Lay one straight edge of the triangle along the lengthwise straight of goods, the other edge of the triangle along the crosswise staight of goods. The hypotenuse of the triangle is the bias. Trace it.

3. Rule off 1-inch strips parallel to the bias edge and cut (Fig. 47b).

4. Join as many strips as will give the needed length. Strips are joined on the straight grain (Fig. 47c).

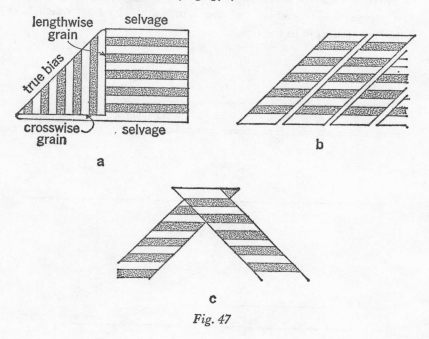

Fig. 47

Swirl-in Shape

A straight binding may be swirled into a curve with the steam iron.

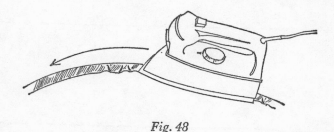

Fig. 48

1. Place the binding on the ironing board in approximately the desired curve. The binding can be eased into the exact shape when attached.

2. Keeping the side of the iron parallel to the edge of the binding, swirl the binding to shape. Stretch the outside edge while easing the inside edge. Follow the arrow in the illustration (Fig. 48).

How to Apply a Straight Binding

There are several methods of applying a straight binding. Which you choose will depend on (a) the fabric and (b) how much time you want to devote to the finish.

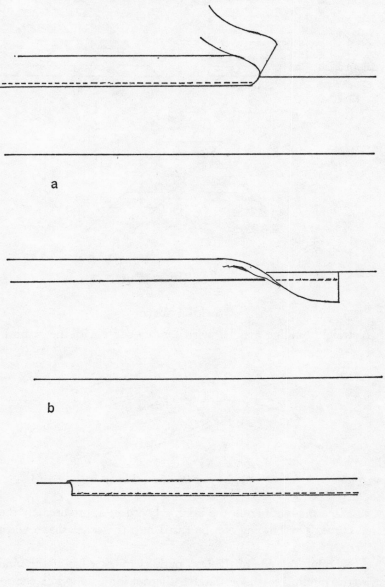

a

b

c

Fig. 49

METHOD I—TOPSTITCH

Overlap the straight binding on the edge of the garment and stitch (Fig. 49a). This is the method used on ready-to-wear clothing. It produces a flat finish (desirable) but in the hands of less-than-skilled machine operators comes off as a line of wavering machine stitching that often slides off the binding entirely (undesirable).

Attach to the garment with hemming stitches. There are a number of hemming stitches but the one most used on hems is the *vertical or straight hemming stitch* (Fig. 50).

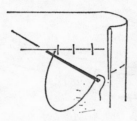

Fig. 50

Use a single thread. Work from right to left. Take a tiny stitch on the right side of the garment parallel to the hem and just off its edge. Lift only one thread of the fabric. Take a tiny stitch through the edge of the hem. Repeat. Start each new stitch on the garment directly under the stitch on the hem. The stitches on the wrong side are vertical while the stitches on the right side are horizontal.

METHOD II—SEAM-STITCH

Stitch the edge of the straight binding to the raw edge of the garment in a ⅛-inch seam in just the same way as if you were stitching together any two thicknesses of cloth in a seam. Fold the binding over the seam to conceal it (Fig. 49b). Press it flat. This makes a much neater and stronger finish without the hazards of the overlap-topstitch method.

Attach to the garment with hemming stitches.

METHOD III—THE DRESSMAKER'S HEM

For a couture touch, try the dressmaker's hem. Fold the binding in half lengthwise and press. Slip the raw edge of the hem into the fold of the binding completely enclosing the raw edge. Either machine or hand stitch to position (Fig. 49c).

Attach to the garment by the same method used for a tailor's hem. (See directions on page 71.)

How to Apply a Bias Binding

In commercial bias binding, both lengthwise raw edges are folded to the center of the underside and pressed. Do the same with the made-by-you binding.

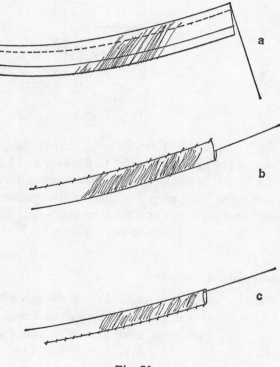

Fig. 51

1. Open out the binding.

2. Place the right side of the binding against the right side of the hem, raw edges matching, stretching and easing as necessary. Pin to position.

3. Machine stitch along the fold nearest the edge (Fig. 51a).

4. *For a seam-stitched binding,* fold the binding over the seam to conceal it. Attach the second fold of the binding to the garment with hemming stitches (Fig. 51b).

For a dressmaker's hem, fold the binding over the edge, enclosing it. Fasten the remaining fold of the binding to the line of machine stitching. Attach to the garment with running-hemming stitches (Fig. 52b) or catch stitches (Fig. 52c).

An Enduring (and Endearing) Attachment: The Tailor's Hem

Were you to develop one favorite way of attaching a hem, you would do well to choose the tailor's hem. It is the neatest, most invisible attachment of all. It is a method that, with variations, can see you through the miles and miles of hems you will be doing in a lifetime.

The true tailor's hem has no edge finish—simply the cut edge of non-ravelly material. Sticking to that would limit its use. Any other ridge-less finish is as good: a pinked edge, a line of machine stitching, an overcast edge. Even a bound edge can be attached in the same manner. In which case it becomes a dressmaker's hem, a fine couture touch, suitable for many materials.

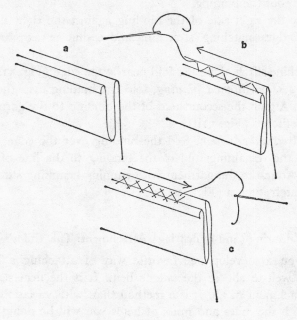

Fig. 52

1. Fold back the edge of the hem toward the hemline to a depth of about ⅛ inch to ¼ inch. Fold back the garment on itself. This places the folds of hem and garment opposite to each other (Fig. 52a).

2. Using a single strand of matching thread, lift one yarn of the garment, then one of the hem, alternating between garment and hem. Use either a running-hemming stitch (Fig. 52b) or a catch stitch (Fig. 52c).

> Work the running-hemming stitch from right to left. Make a series of small, loose stitches that weave between the garment and the edge of the hem (Fig. 52b).
>
> The catch stitch is a small backstitch worked from lower left to upper right on two imaginary parallel lines. In this case it would be garment to hem to garment, etc. (Fig. 52c).

You'll be happy to learn that it's not only cricket but it's actually preferable to put up a hem with the *least number of stitches* that will do so securely. Since the stitches are never visible (even on the underside) you do not need to perform as if you were in an embroidery contest.

With the tailor's hem, there aren't any telltale marks on the right side to indicate that a hem has been stitched to the garment. This is because the position of the hem and the garment for hand stitching provides sufficient length of thread between them to prevent that hard, rigid, quilted look so many hems suffer from.

On to the Next Project

By the time you have reached the hem, you are undoubtedly deep in dreams of your next project.

THE SIZE OF IT
Pattern Pointers

Fashion Comes in Standard Sizes

Figures are no more alike than thumbprints but fashion comes in standard sizes. There's the rub! It is true whether you are buying ready-to-wear or buying a pattern. To determine your size in ready-to-wear, you can try on dresses as long as your energy and patience (your salesperson's too) hold out. To determine your pattern size, you'll have to do a little arithmetic and a little experimenting.

There is this comfort: ready-to-wear sizes are variable. A size is anything (within loose limitations) a particular manufacturer and his staff decide it is. However, once you've decided your pattern size, you can be fairly certain *that* size will fit regardless of what make of pattern. That is, unless you grow taller or broader or skinnier.

Simply because it is the only practical way to deal with the problem of size for the millions of buyers of both ready-to-wear clothes and of patterns, these must be sold in standard sizes.

Standard is a statistic made up by averaging the measurements of groups of girls or women practically none of whom conforms to the standard in all of her measurements. Standard describes a mythical figure.

In sewing, the problem is to get a perfect fit for an imperfect figure from a standard size. To do this, one must start with a pattern that *most nearly corresponds* to one's measurements and alter the pattern as necessary.

In an effort to further accommodate the many variations among women and girls, patterns and clothes are now cut for figure types as well as for sizes. Hopefully if one chooses the correct figure type and size, one will come very near one's personal measurements.

Take Your Measure

In order to decide what your figure type and size are, it is necessary to take a few personal measurements. To do this, you will need a tape measure, enough string to encircle your waist, and the services of a good friend. The best measurements are taken over a slip and/or your bra and girdle if you wear them. All length measurements are taken *without shoes.*

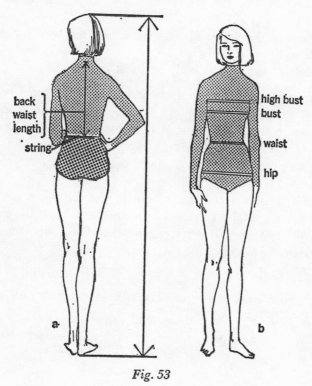

Fig. 53

LENGTH MEASUREMENTS

1. Measure your over-all height from the tip of your head (not your hairdo) to the floor (Fig. 53a).

2. Tie a length of string around the waist.

3. Have someone measure your back waist length from socket bone to waistline string (Fig. 53a). (To locate your socket bone, bend your head forward. The socket bone is the prominent bone on which your head is hinged.)

CIRCUMFERENCE MEASUREMENTS

All circumference measurements are snug but not tight measurements (Fig. 53b).

1. Measure the high bust. Bring the tape around the body directly under the arms.

2. Measure the bust. Bring the tape measure around the body across the fullest part of the bust. (Or where a bust would be if you had one.)

3. Measure the waist. (In the hollow of the waist or where you would like the waistline to be.)

4. Measure the hips around the fullest part.

> Note: the bust measurement is generally the measurement used in determining pattern size. However, if the difference between the high bust and the bust measurement is more than 2 inches, then use the high bust measurement as if it were the bust measurement to determine the pattern size. Make a bust alteration to fit.
>
> Or, choose your pattern size in the following manner: If you are small-boned and between sizes, choose the smaller of the two sizes. If you are large-boned and between sizes, choose the larger of the two sizes.

COMPARE YOUR MEASUREMENTS WITH THE MEASUREMENT CHART

Armed with the above measurements, you should now be able to decide your figure type and size. You'll need a lot less pattern alteration if you buy the right size within the right figure type.

Figure types are decided by the following:

1. Height

Misses	5'5" to 5'6"	the so-called average figure
Miss Petite	5'2" to 5'3"	an over-all shorter Miss figure
Women's	5'5" to 5'6"	a longer, larger, well-proportioned figure
Half-size	5'2" to 5'3"	a short-waisted, heavier than average figure
Junior	5'4" to 5'5"	a shorter-waisted Miss figure
Junior Petite	5' to 5'1"	a petite figure
Young Junior/Teen	5'1" to 5'5"	a not-fully grown figure

2. Degree of Figure Development

The Young Junior/Teen is for immature, developing teen and pre-teen figures. Women's and Half-sizes are for mature, more fully developed figures. All the rest for average developed figures of different stature. If you study the charts, you'll find only minor variations in bust, waist, and hip measurements of comparable sizes.

3. Length of bodice

Neck-to-waist measurement.

4. Styling

Misses and Miss Petite have similar sophisticated styling. Women's and Half-sizes are styled for heavier figures. Junior and Junior Petite provide a young fashion image. Young Junior/Teen caters to a *very young* fashion image.

The greatest range of styles is in the Misses group. If you are another figure type but crave the more sophisticated styling, choose the Misses size that comes nearest to your measurements and do a little more altering.

COAT AND SUIT SIZES

Buy the same size pattern for a coat or suit as you would for a dress. All necessary allowances are built into the pattern.

MATERNITY GARMENTS

Buy the same size as you did before pregnancy.

At Ease

Is there anything that matches the freedom we feel when shoes are kicked off and clothing stripped down to a bare minimum? So *un-attired*, one feels liberated because there are literally no restraints to movement. Thank the ingenious covering that Nature devised for you—your skin.

Some may come close (the knits and two-way stretches) but most fabrics of the clothes we wear have nowhere near the "give" of skin. That is why even those of us who love beautiful clothes find delight in shedding them.

How Much Ease? The Fabric, the Function, and You

You could confine your wardrobe to knits. Even close-fitting knits provide unrestrained comfort. However, confining yourself to any one thing can be dull. Besides, think of all those glorious woven fabrics that can be yours for the buying.

Next best to *moving with* a flexible fabric is *moving inside* a garment of an inflexible one. This means that clothes made of material with little or no "give" need to be made a little larger than the body beneath. This room-to-move-about-in is called *ease*. How much ease you need depends on the following factors:

1. The fabric.

Man-made fibers are often less resilient than natural fibers. Loosely woven fabrics have more give than firmly woven fabrics. Some weaves have a tendency to make fabric stiffer, for instance, the dobby weave of bird's-eye piqué.

2. The function of the garment.

Obviously you need more ease in active sportswear than in a ball gown designed to make you look pretty while gracefully gliding by.

3. The design of the garment.

Some styles are a lot less figure-revealing than others.

4. You, yourself.

Some girls can't stand the constraint of tight-fitting clothing. Others never feel alluring unless their clothes are practically plastered on them.

The pattern you buy has the ease built right into it. It is in the amount the pattern company considered appropriate for the size and in the amount the designer thought just right for the style. What can't be determined in advance by either of them is the material of which you've chosen to make the garment and how you like to wear your clothes.

A "Pinch" of Ease

Here is a good way to tell what your preference is. Try on a favorite dress (if you are making a dress) or a suit or coat (if you are making a suit or coat). Pinch out the excess fabric until the garment fits tight against the body at the bust, waist, and hips. Measure the amount of material in the "pinch." Add this amount to your actual body measurement. Then compare the total measurement of the pattern at a comparable place. (The bustline of a pattern is ½ inch above any vertical dart and on a line with a horizontal one. The hipline of the pattern is 7 inches to 9 inches below the waistline. When seams rather than darts do the shaping, look for the fullest part of the curved seam line. The waistline of the pattern is either a seam line or is marked in some way on the pattern.)

This is how it works.

Suppose the pinch is 3 inches at the bust, your bust measurement is 32½ inches, the pattern measures 35½ inches. Lucky you. You don't have to do anything to your pattern.

Suppose the pinch is ½ inch at the waist, your waist measurement is 23 inches, and the pattern measurement is 24½ inches. You will need to take 1 inch off at the waistline of the pattern.

Suppose the pinch is 2 inches at the hips, your hip measurement is 35½ inches, and the pattern measures 36½ inches. You will need to add 1 inch at the hips to make the skirt fit you as you would like it to fit.

It's a matter of simple arithmetic. A "pinch" may be as important a measurement in sewing as in cooking.

Sometimes, even if your total measurement (body plus preferred ease) differs slightly from the standard pattern size, the fullness of a particular design will take care of the small difference. That is why you can often wear a smaller size than actual body measurements indicate.

Understanding how ease works in a pattern and in a garment will help you to make clothes that really fit and are really comfortable.

The Size of It

Once you've determined your size, insist on the correct pattern size when you buy it. Should the pattern department be out of your size, order it. Don't be tempted to buy what they have and hope to alter it. It's not just a case of taking it in a little here and letting it out a little there.

Every pattern piece will need to be changed (graded) not only to keep the design in scale but to assure fit for your more standard-size body parts. It's even better to beg or borrow the right-size pattern from a friend if you're desperate to have that dress by tomorrow. Or you could select another style in the right size.

> *Grading* is the process of increasing or decreasing a pattern from one size to the next. The change is *gradual* rather than in one place, hence the term "grading." If you're a size 8 and the patterns you love generally start with size 10, or if you're size 16 and the patterns stop at size 14, you may want to investigate the system of pattern grading. Instructions for grading patterns will be found in *How to Make Clothes That Fit and Flatter* by Adele P. Margolis, Doubleday & Company, Inc.

FACTS ABOUT FABRICS

All the Print That's Fit to Be News

It may be a far cry from body painting, tattooing and scar patterns (Fig. 54a) to the latest print from Paris (Fig. 54b) but the impulse to ornament a solid expanse of color, often the very designs, and sometimes even the techniques remain the same.

Fig. 54

One Good Unit Deserves Another—and Another—and Another: Design Repeats

Long, long ago, some creative soul discovered that if one repeated a single motif over and over again, one could cover a larger area with design pleasant to look upon.

In every fabric where there is a design either as an integral part of its structure (weaving or knitting) or superimposed by printing, there is a place where the design motif starts all over again. This is known as a *repeat*. The repetition of these repeats is what produces the harmonious over-all effect.

Textile designers strive to disguise the point at which each repeat begins and ends so the flow of the design is continuous. So clever and so ingenious are they at this that frequently it is difficult to determine the beginning and the ending of the repeat. Determine it you must. To preserve the continuity of the fabric design, the repeats must be matched in your garment (Fig. 55a). The only exception to this would be a fabric of very small motifs in an over-all coverage (Fig. 55b) where the disturbance caused by darts and seams is minimal.

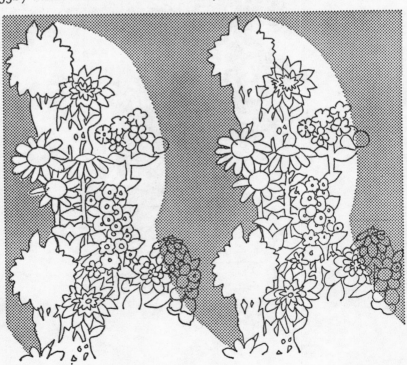

Fig. 55a

Fig. 55b

The ultimate in careful and sensitive cutting are the illustrations in
Fig. 56.

Fig. 56

The flowers on right and left fronts are so matched that when buttoned, the entire front forms the complete floral unit of the fabric design (Fig. 56a).

The flower motifs are so placed that there is no break in the over-all design despite the fact that part of a flower falls on the closing extension and the other part on the left front or part on a flap and part on the dress (Fig. 56b). The sleeves have been so cut that the spacing of flower motifs has been observed.

Whether printed, woven, or knit, all stripes, plaids, blocks, and checks must be matched.

The matching of the blocks is not only horizontal at the construction seams but vertical as well. The blocks on the pants begin where the jacket leaves off. The vertical line of the block follows from shoulder to ankle. Note how the patch pocket and flap have been so carefully positioned that they continue the fabric design both horizontally and vertically (Fig. 57a).

In a two-piece ensemble, the matching must be not only top to toe but inside and out (Fig. 57b).

Sometimes in an effort to dodge the intricate matching, part of a garment is cut on the bias. The collar and sleeve band of this design have been so cut. Happily, the bias cut also contributes to the design interest (Fig. 57c).

Every part of a garment which joins or overlaps another part must match or complete the unit. This rule applies not only to the major sections but also to the smaller parts: the under collar must match the upper collar; the facings must match the edges to be faced; the pockets, buttonholes, belts must match the areas in which they are located, etc.

Fig. 57

Going My Way?

As if this were not problem enough, the matter is further complicated by the fact that stripes, plaids, and motifs can be directional. (When they are non-directional there is no problem.) In a directional design, there is a one-way movement either up and down (Fig. 58a) or right and left (Fig. 58b).

a

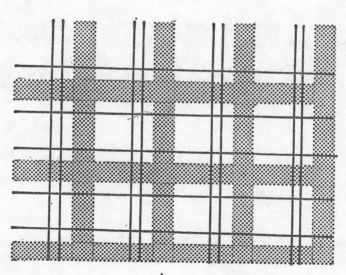

b

Fig. 58

Fabric Design on the Move

When the movement is up and down, place all pattern pieces going in the same direction—neck to hem (Fig. 59).

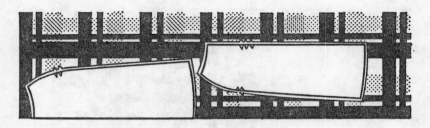

Fig. 59

When the movement is right to left, you have a choice. The stripes may move around the body all heading in the same direction (Fig. 60a) or can be arranged in a mirror image (Fig. 60b), one side the reverse of the other.

To have the stripes move around the body in the same direction (Fig. 60a), choose the stripe you want for the center, fold the material *lengthwise,* and place the pattern in a directional layout (Fig. 60c).

To achieve a mirror image (Fig. 60b), fold the material *crosswise,* matching stripes. Place the center line on the exact center of a vertical stripe (Fig. 60d).

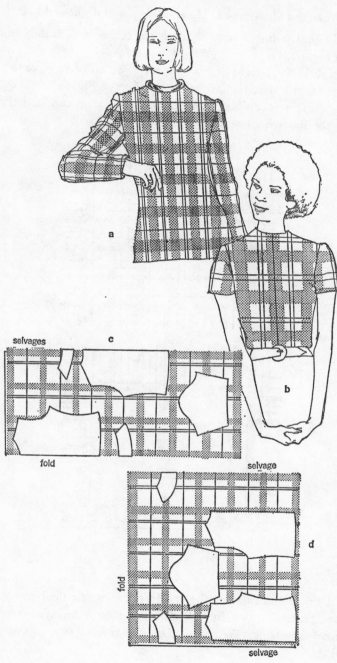

Fig. 60

When the Movement Is Up and Down *and* Right and Left

A plaid that is unbalanced in both directions is definitely not for novices (Fig. 61a).

If the fabric has a right and wrong side, you will just have to settle for the unbalance. Use the layout for Fig. 60a or Fig. 60b.

If the fabric is reversible, the crosswise unbalance can be balanced by using the following layout.

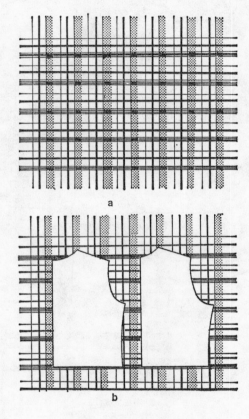

a

b

Fig. 61

On a single thickness of the fabric cut two identical pieces using the same pattern, going in the same direction on similar lengthwise and crosswise plaids (Fig. 61b). Use the reverse side of one as the right side.

This method is workable in diagonal materials too.

Mismatch on Purpose

One of the hallmarks of fine custom-made clothing or of expensive ready-to-wear is this meticulous matching of stripes, plaids, motifs.

With the charming perverseness that makes fashion so enchanting, along comes a vogue for mismatching (Fig. 62).

This must be done with great art and a sure instinct for color and pattern. Whatever else it looks, mismatching must look as if it were done with design aforethought—never as if one didn't know better.

Fig. 62

Are You Still of a Mind to Use a Striped, Plaid, or Motif-strewn Fabric?

The key pattern piece is the front. Place it first on the fabric. Note the position of the notches in relation to the fabric design but be mindful of the fact that it is the *stitching lines that must be matched,* not the cutting lines. Next, place the section that joins it, matching corresponding notches on similar lines or figures of the fabric. Continue in this way until every piece has been correctly placed to match those it must join.

Sometimes it is impossible to make every pair of seam lines match. For instance, you may be able to match the front sleeve cap to the front armhole but this may not necessarily make the back sleeve cap and back armhole match. The bodice side seams may match but the shoulder seams may not. Darts always interrupt the matching so that the underarm sleeve seams can match only to the elbow either from the wrist up or from the shoulder down but not both. What to do? *Make those seams match that will be most prominent* and hope for the best from the rest.

More Yardage Needed

It's elementary! To match design units you need more material than when a fabric is a solid color. How much more depends on the size of the repeat, the movement of line and color, and the number of pattern sections that need matching.

If the repeats are small, less material is needed than if they are large. If the fabric design is directional (one-way) more material is needed than if it is non-directional (two-way). If only two lengths need matching, less material is needed than if half a dozen lengths need matching.

Never mind the problems, the extra yardage, and the firm resolutions. You'll probably lose your heart to the next exciting print or plaid that comes along.

Built-in Design: Woven and Knitted Cloth

If you think you can escape all the foregoing perils by settling on a no-problem, solid-color fabric, it's not so. Fabrics have built-in designs according to the way they are woven or knitted.

It may be that a haphazard or random weaving or knitting of yarns can produce an adequate enough cloth but would it be an aesthetically pleasing one? From the very first, craftsmen found it more soul-satisfying to thread the yarns or to loop them in planned patterns. We've carried on the tradition ever since and for the very same reasons.

Weaving Came First

Weaving came first. It is really a very simple process which you may remember from childhood. (Remember those place mats and pot holders you made for your mother?)

A set of lengthwise yarns (warp) are placed side by side in a loom. A set of crosswise yarns (filler, weft, woof) are threaded over and under the warp yarns. In principle, weaving is the same today as when man first began to weave cloth. The advances are mainly in the manner of lifting and separating groups of yarns so the filling yarn can be shot through with one motion of a shuttle. What was once a slow hand operation on a small loom is now mechanically and speedily done on a huge loom.

Since the warp yarns must bear the stress of lifting and lowering, they are pulled taut when set in the loom. Because they must bear the weight of the filler yarns, they are often of tougher and stronger yarn.

The Basic Weaves

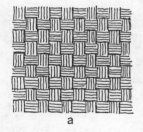 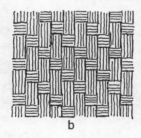 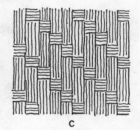

a   b   c

Fig. 63

THE PLAIN WEAVE—OFTEN CALLED THE LINEN WEAVE

The simplest weave is the plain weave (Fig. 63a). It is an under-one, over-one pattern. It is non-directional (two-way) and has no right or wrong side unless it is finished in a special way. In a solid color it is the easiest weave to use. All style lines show to advantage. The pattern pieces may be locked into position like a giant jigsaw puzzle without any concern for which is up and which is down.

THE TWILL WEAVE

In the twill weave (Fig. 63b) either the warp or the filler threads are interlaced in such a way that they progress one or more spaces to the right or to the left. This produces a diagonal design line.

Twill weaves are directional (one-way). They *do* have a right and wrong side. If the diagonal line proceeds from upper left to lower right on the right side, it will go from upper right to lower left on the wrong side.

When the diagonal lines are unobtrusive as in flannel, it does not present too much problem in the choice of pattern, layout, and cutting. However, when the diagonal lines are obvious, as in gabardine and some coat materials, the choice of style is limited. Layout and cutting require great care. Many patterns say quite plainly, "Not suitable for obvious diagonals." Better heed that advice.

THE SATIN WEAVE

The satin weave (Fig. 63c) is similar to the twill weave. The yarn interlaces in a progression too, but the intervals are longer. The ratio is anywhere from 4 to 1 to 7 to 1. Sometimes, in an attempt to avoid a twill effect, the yarns are held down in different places in each row.

Because the interlacing is minimal, yarns *float* on the surface of the cloth. When a silky fiber is used, a beautiful luster results. Silk yarns produce satin cloth. Cotton yarns produce sateen (polished cotton).

For a satin weave, a one-way layout of pattern pieces is imperative. First, because a directional weave requires a directional layout. Secondly, because light affects the color of the satin weave. It is one color going up, another going down.

Because of the long floats, satin-weave fabrics bruise easily. Pins and needles leave holes when they are removed, making corrections and alterations almost impossible. The floats may catch or break.

Pressing is perilous. Unless you are pretty sure of yourself as a sewer, don't attempt the satin weaves.

Variations on a Scheme: Recipes for Endless Variety

From these three basic schemes for producing cloth, it is possible to achieve an endless variety of fabrics by using:

1. Different kinds of yarns—strong as in coatings, fragile as in chiffon, random thick-and-thin as in raw silk, crinkled as in worsted, looped as in bouclé, slubbed as in shantung, etc.

2. Heavy yarns in one direction, lightweight yarns in the other. This produces a ribbed effect either lengthwise, crosswise, or diagonally as in grosgrain, faille, bengaline, ottoman.

3. Paired or multiple threads for a loosely woven, soft fabric like basket weave, monk's cloth, or hopsacking.

4. Combinations of fibers like silk and wool, linen and wool (the linsey-woolsey of the story books), cotton and synthetic, silk and synthetic and other blends.

5. Different colors for warp and filler yarns either random or organized as in tweeds.

6. Yarns woven at right angles to the surface of the cloth to produce a pile, as in velvet and velveteen, or to join double thicknesses as in a two-faced reversible fabric.

7. Novelty processes. Crepe and seersuckers are examples of this. Tightly twisted and/or plain yarns are shrunken to produce a crinkled effect.

These are but a few of the many variations, limitless it seems, that create the fabrics we love.

More Complex Weaves

The variations in the simple weaves may produce a complex effect but there are several weaves that really are more complex by virtue of their structure.

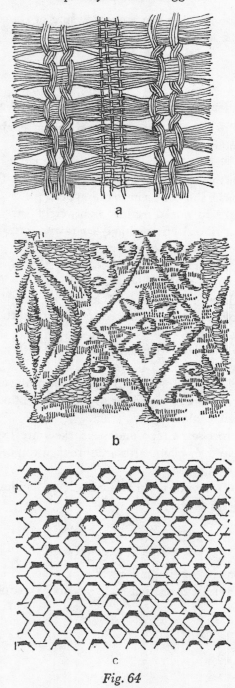

a

b

c

Fig. 64

The *leno weave* produces lacy fabrics. In this weave, the warp yarns are twisted around the filling yarns, often in a figure eight (Fig. 64a).

The *Jacquard weave* produces some of the most intricate and most beautiful fabrics—the brocades, the damasks, and the tapestries (Fig. 64b). Such cloth is woven on a loom that has a computerized control of each yarn (these may be in the hundreds) by a series of punched cards.

Dobby weaves are produced on a loom similar to the Jacquard but far less complicated. Bird's-eye piqué is an example of this weave (Fig. 64c).

Since these three weaves are highly decorative of themselves, choose simple patterns with few pieces. Because of the open work (leno weaves) and the floats (Jacquard and dobby weaves) these materials require immediate protection after cutting. Staystitch to prevent stretching. Overcast all cut edges to prevent raveling.

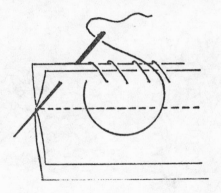

Fig. 65

Overcasting is a series of loose, slanting stitches worked over either single or double raw edges deep enough to keep the material from raveling. The stitches are even in depth and evenly spaced, "easy"—not drawn up tight. The thread encircles the raw edges (Fig. 65).

Supple, Shapely, Sensational: The Knits

No wonder they're so popular! All the ease of movement one could want (no need to add any), all the shape-without-stitching one needs (the figure does all the work), all the mobility desired (they remain unruffled and unmussed by travel). They're supple, they're shapely, they're sensational, they constitute a major part of today's wardrobes. So, aren't we lucky we can buy knits by the yard instead of going through the laborious task of creating them ourselves.

Whereas woven cloth is made by interlacing horizontal and vertical yarns, knitted fabric is made by *intermeshing* a series of continuous rows of loops in such a way that each loop interlocks with the preceding loop. A vertical series of loops is called a *wale;* a horizontal series of loops is called a *course*.

The fact that loops can straighten out when stretched and return to loops when released gives knits their great elasticity and flexibility.

Knit One, Purl One

Two stitches, knit (Fig. 66a) and purl (Fig. 66b) are the basis of knit construction. Of course you recognize them from all the sweaters you've ever worn.

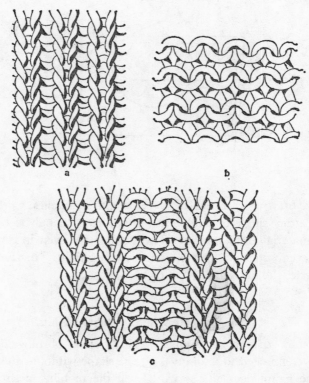

Fig. 66

The knit stitch (Fig. 66a) produces a flat surface. The purl stitch (Fig. 66b) produces a slightly raised surface. Alternating knit and purl stitches in the same row can produce a ribbed effect (Fig. 66c) that provides an excellent, snug fit. An intriguing variety of designs can be created from just these two stitches.

Filling Knits

In knitting, when the yarn runs horizontally across the fabric in a series of loops (Fig. 67a), it is called a *filling knit* (67b).

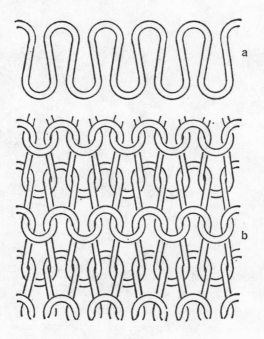

Fig. 67

The crosswise yarns are interlocked in a chain of stitches. When a link (loop) in the chain breaks, the fabric "runs" or "ladders." This is what happens to filling knit stockings. Care is required in cutting filling knits.

Filling knits are usually made on circular machines producing a tubular cloth. Jersey is a well-known, much-worn filling knit.

Double knits are filling knits made on a rib knitting machine.

Two sets of needles cast off stitches in opposite directions so they interlock. This produces a heavier cloth which looks alike on both sides. It is knitted flat, like woven cloth.

Warp Knits

When the loops run vertically, the fabric is a *warp knit*. In warp knits, the yarn follows a zigzag path and forms a loop at each change of direction (Fig. 68a). These loops interlock with other loops formed by adjoining warp yarns following a similar zigzag path (Fig. 68b).

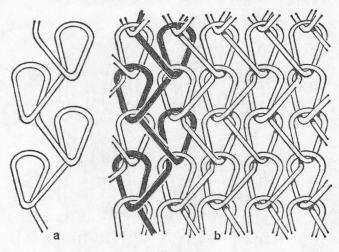

Fig. 68

Fabrics of warp knit aren't as sheer as the filling knits but they are much stronger (mesh stockings are an example of a warp knit). Because they don't run or snag, they are easier to cut.

Tricot is a warp knit often used in lingerie and as backing for laminated fabrics. You'll recognize it by the crosswise rib on the wrong side.

Raschel knits are warp knits which have a lacy appearance. They resemble the leno weave in that a yarn (in this case a chain or series of loops) holds the openwork in place.

Sliver Knitting

Fake furs are made by the *sliver knitting* process. This is a knit-pile construction just as velvet is a woven-pile construction.

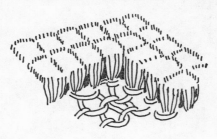

Fig. 69

Sliver knitting produces both the plain jersey backing and the pile at the same time. Bunches of loose fibers are locked in place by the looping action of the backing yarn over the knitting needle (Fig. 69).

Like woven materials, knitted fabrics are produced in great variety. This is achieved by using different fibers, different yarns, a variety of patterns, a variety of colors, ingenious and intricate methods of interlocking, and combinations of any of these.

Construction, a Clue to Use

Most knits are used on the vertical grain since they stretch more in a crosswise or diagonal direction. For this reason, it is a good idea to avoid crosswise or diagonal seams and flared or circular skirts. A good rule for selection of a pattern for a knit; the fewer the seams, the better.

This has been but a brief discussion of the more generally used methods of fabric construction. There are others like felting, bonding, laminating, to name but a few of the more familiar ones. There is also the whole subject of fabric finishes, which is important and interesting. If you love fabrics (and what sewer doesn't?) you may want to read a great deal more about textiles. The subject is a fascinating one.

How a fabric is constructed is a clue as to how it should be used to realize its possibilities to the fullest.

PART II

FASHION MULTIPLIED

Shirts, Skirts, Slacks, Shorts

THE MILEAGE IN MULTIPLES

The whole is equal to the sum of its parts—in mathematics. In fashion, the whole is greater than the sum of its parts. Consider the fashion mileage you can get from mixing and matching shirts, skirts, slacks, shorts. The combinations and permutations are endless. However you work the arithmetic, layers of separates add up to high fashion.

Furthermore, there is not a time of the day or night or season of the year or place upon this globe where "separates" could not see you through your fashion needs. Nowadays, there is hardly even a function where the dressing-in-parts formula would not work (Fig. 70).

Speedy Skirts

Just about one of the easiest and speediest articles of clothing one can make is a skirt. Since you have already learned how to insert a zipper and make a hem, you need only learn to make the waistband and you're set.

Successful Slacks and Shorts

Slacks and shorts are just as easy to make as skirts. There are a few more seams and a few more fitting problems, it is true, but exactly the same techniques are used as for a skirt. If you can make a skirt, you can make shorts and slacks.

Fig. 70

FOR THE FAINT-HEARTED

Ease into the shirt situation by sidestepping some of the sewing problems. Choose a collarless, kimono- or raglan-sleeved, zippered blouse (Fig. 71a). Simply sew the seams. No complicated techniques involved. A good first try.

a   b

Fig. 71

FOR THE INTREPID

Make a tailored shirt (Fig. 71b) and you will have come a long way in mastering many basic sewing techniques.

One Plus One Equals a Dress

Put skirt and shirt together at the waistline and you have a dress.

Panic or Panacea

There is a certain charm and freedom to planlessness but you'll get farther faster if you have a plan of action. With one, even complicated construction can be simplified. Without one, you'll be overwhelmed by the number of operations and the multiplicity of details.

A Plan for Action

The simplest plan of sewing is *unit construction.* By this system all that it is possible to do on one section of a garment is completed before going on to the next. A unit of work consists of all the sections that go to make a complete front bodice, a complete back bodice, a complete skirt front, a complete skirt back, the sleeves, the collar, and so on. Most pattern directions, particularly for simple designs, follow a unit work plan.

TO COMPLETE EACH UNIT

    1. Stitch and press all darts and seams.

    2. Apply any interfacings and/or underlinings.

    3. When the design calls for bound buttonholes, make them now. Machine or hand-worked buttonholes can be done after the garment is finished.

    4. If a zipper is needed, insert it.

    5. When the design shows pockets, tabs, etc., make and apply them.

    6. When the style features a collar, make it.

    7. An opening, a band, or a cuff is completed before the sleeve is set. A hem may be done after setting.

JOIN THE COMPLETED UNITS

When the units are completed as far as it is possible to do so, join them at the side seams and at the shoulders. Then proceed with all the circumference operations.

    1. Attach the facings.

2. Apply the collar.
3. Set and stitch the sleeves.
4. Stitch the waistline seam or attach the waistband.
5. Set and sew the hems.
6. Add final touches and any necessary handwork.

Some General Advice Before You Begin

Don't worry in advance. That way lies failure. Concern yourself with step 20 in the sewing sequence when you've finished step 19—certainly not before you've even begun step 1. You'll be defeated before you've begun if you're tense and anxious about the final steps. Besides, you'll be agreeably surprised to find how logical and simple the operation really is when you come to it at the proper time.

Do all of one kind of stitching at a time. Stitch *all* darts, stitch *all* similar seams, make *all* the pockets, work *all* the buttonholes before going on to another kind of operation. Getting into the swing of a particular action makes it more uniform, more perfect, easier, faster. Changeover to a new operation makes for loss of rhythm, momentum, and efficiency. Any gal knows that it is easier and faster to wash all the dishes before drying them than to wash and dry each dish separately.

Assemble all the equipment you will need for the amount you hope to accomplish at any one time. Have thread, needles, pins, thimble, scissors, yardstick at hand so you won't have to waste time hunting for them. Set up the ironing board, the iron and any pressing equipment needed. Press as you sew.

Learn to judge the widths commonly encountered in sewing. Play games with yourself. See how close you can come to the measurements—⅝ inch, the standard seam allowance, ¼ inch, an amount often taken in, let out, or trimmed back to—½ inch, 1 inch, 2 inches, the regular intervals on a ruler.

You can learn a lot by just looking. Examine better or higher-priced garments in the shops. Not that ready-to-wear is the answer for made-to-order clothes (your workmanship should be much better) but you can get good ideas on construction and finish.

All pattern directions presuppose some background in sewing techniques or that you will know where to get supplementary information should you need to. You will. Obviously, it would be impossible to include in a pattern envelope everything you should know to turn out a garment you'll be proud to wear. (Why bother making any other kind?)

Pattern instructions are minimal. Add to them any information you can acquire from sewing classes, articles, observation, discussions with friends who sew and from books like this one.

Anything Goes—If It Works!

The comforting thing about clothing construction is that there is nothing sacred. There is just no one way to do anything.

No one way to design. Make rules and along comes some design genius who defies them all.

No one way to sew. New techniques follow new styles, new needs, new technology, new fabrics.

No one-purpose needle or pin or thread or iron or anything. There are specific tools for specific purposes.

Following are some techniques that have stood the test of time. New ones are constantly developing. If you can invent some of your own— go ahead. Anything goes—if it works!

OUT OF SIGHT BUT
VERY MUCH IN MIND
The Interfacing

It's never "on stage" but it plays a very important supporting role. Though out of sight, it must be very much in mind. It's the *interfacing*.

If you remember your prefixes, you'll recall that *inter* means between. *An interfacing is a layer of supporting fabric which lies between the facing and the outer fabric.* It generally has the same shape and the same grain as the edge it interfaces. It is cut from the facing pattern—or one very like it.

Because a facing adds a second layer of cloth to all outside edges, it reinforces them as well as finishes them. But not enough. That is why we add an interfacing wherever the garment has a facing.

The interfacing adds firmness and sturdiness to areas subject to stress and wear because of the friction against the body (as in a neckline) or against another part of the garment (as in a jacket hem), or where there is much use (as in the opening and closing of a garment).

Interfacing Materials

An interfacing for a shirt or dress should bear some reasonable similarity to the material of the garment. For instance: a washable dress fabric needs a washable interfacing; a dry cleanable fabric, a dry cleanable interfacing. A lightweight material must have a lightweight facing. A medium-weight fabric takes a medium-weight interfacing, while a heavy cloth requires a heavy interfacing.

Self-fabric (if it is unfigured and not too limp) often makes a fine interfacing. It is the same weight and color and has the same degree of shrinkage.

Other dress fabrics also can be used for interfacing if they are appropriate for the material of the garment: organdy, organza, lawn, batiste, net, taffeta, etc.

However, there are some interfacing materials manufactured specially for this purpose. Those most often used for shirts and dresses are Siri, Si Bonne, Formite and others that resemble these three.

For a further discussion of interfacings, see Tailored to a *"T,"* page 236.

The Shirt Interfacing: Shape and Structure

A tailored shirt will have interfacing for the opening extension, the collar, and the cuffs.

When any of these has a shaped style line, a separate facing and interfacing are required (Fig. 72a).

When the style line is a straight one, the facing may simply be an extension of fabric that is turned under along a foldline. When this is so, the interfacing is cut in the shape of the facing but extends only to the foldline (Fig. 72b).

How the interfacing is applied depends on whether the shirt is to have machine-made or bound buttonholes.

In the washable fabrics of most shirts machine-made buttonholes are more practical because there is nothing to pull apart in laundering. Bound buttonholes are more generally used on fabrics to be dry-cleaned.

Fig. 72

How to Apply the Interfacing

TO A SHIRT WITH MACHINE-MADE BUTTONHOLES

You'll recognize the following couture method as the method used for facing the facing, page 44.

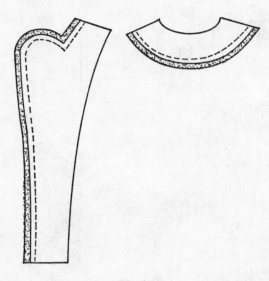

Fig. 73

1. Cut out the front and back facings and interfacings.

2. Place each interfacing over its facing, right sides together and raw edges matching.

3. Stitch the outer edges (Fig. 73).

4. Press the seam allowances open. Trim and grade them. Clip and notch as necessary.

5. Turn the facing-interfacing unit to the right side and press to position.

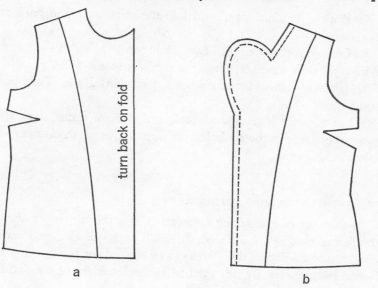

turn back on fold

a

b

Fig. 74

6. When the front facing is cut all-in-one with the garment, turn it back to position along the front foldline (Fig. 74a).

7. When the facing and garment are cut separately, treat the interfaced facing as one fabric and stitch it to the garment in the usual manner (Fig. 74b).

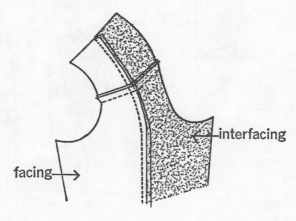

interfacing

facing

Fig. 75

8. With right sides together, stitch the shirt front and back at the shoulders.

9. Open out the front and back facing-interfacing at the shoulders. With right sides together, stitch the shoulder seams (Fig. 75).

10. Press the shoulder seams open, trim, and grade. Turn back to position.

When the shirt is completed (collar, underarm seams, sleeves, etc.) make the machine buttonholes through all three thicknesses—shirt, interfacing, facing.

TO A SHIRT WITH BOUND BUTTONHOLES

In this type of interfacing application, it is the garment rather than the facing that gets interfaced. In addition to all else an interfacing does, it also reinforces those areas to be slashed for the opening of the bound buttonholes. By this method the outer edges of the facing are finished differently and last of all.

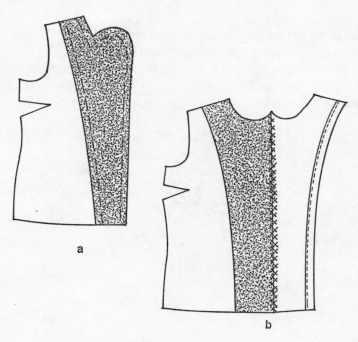

a

b

Fig. 76

1. Cut the interfacing slightly narrower than the facing so the outer edge won't show beyond the facing.

2. Place the interfacing against the *wrong side* of the shirt. Baste to position (Fig. 76a). When the facing is cut all-in-one with the shirt, lightly catch stitch the interfacing along the foldline (Fig. 76b). Treat the interfaced shirt as one fabric.

3. Make the bound buttonholes. Directions for making them will be found on page 306.

4. When the facing and garment are cut separately, stitch the facing to the interfaced shirt. When the facing is cut all-in-one with the garment, turn it under along the foldline. Press each to position.

5. To finish the outside edge, turn under ¼ inch along the entire outside edge of the facing. Either machine or hand stitch (Fig. 76b). It is possible to slip the interfacing into the turn-under and secure it with the stitching at the same time the edge is being finished. However, this is not necessary since it is not likely to be seen if it is sufficiently narrower than the finished facing.

6. When the shirt is completed, finish the underside of the buttonholes on the facing. See page 316.

Collar Interfacings

HOW TO APPLY THE INTERFACING TO A PETER PAN COLLAR (OR ANY VARIATION THEREOF), A CONVERTIBLE COLLAR, A TAILORED COLLAR

In thin or transparent materials, interface the collar rather than the under collar (its facing). This will place the interfacing in such position that when stitched and turned to the right side, the seam allowances won't show.

In opaque materials, it is the under collar that gets interfaced.

When the Collar and Under Collar Are Cut Separately

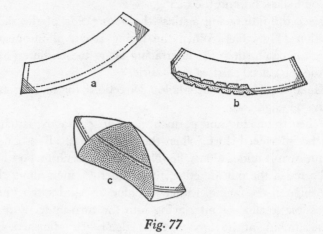

Fig. 77

1. Cut out the collar and the under collar. Remember to make the collar just a wee bit larger so that the joining seam may be rolled to the underside.

2. Cut out the interfacing. Trim off its corners to about ¼ inch beyond the seam lines (Fig. 77a). This will eliminate the interfacing from the corner, thereby preventing corner bulk when the collar is turned to the right side. This is a good way to handle the interfacing in all corners—lapels, extensions, cuffs, welts, flaps, etc.

3. Apply the interfacing to the collar or the under collar as the fabric requires. Baste to position. Handle the interfaced collar or under collar as one fabric.

4. Stitch the collar to the under collar including the interfacing. Leave the neck edge open. Take care in stitching any corners.

5. Press the seam allowances open. Press the corners open on a point presser. Trim and grade the seam allowances, making the under collar seam allowances narrower than those of the collar. Free the corners of bulk. Clip and notch curved edges as necessary (Fig. 77b).

6. Turn the collar to the right side. Carefully work out the corner by pushing *gently* from the inside. The blunt edge of an orange stick is perfect for this purpose. Don't use a sharp instrument. Don't push too hard. Don't pick at it with a pin.

7. Press all outside edges, rolling the seam to the underside.

8. Understitch the enclosed (encased) seam allowances to the under collar either by hand or by machine (Fig. 77c). End the stitching 1 inch each side of the corners.

All of your sewing skill goes into the making of a collar or any other part of a garment in which an upper layer and its facing are involved. Important to the construction are the following techniques and a piece of pressing equipment called the point presser.

HOW TO STITCH A CORNER

In very sheer materials, stitch the seam to the corner ending with the needle in the fabric, raise the presser foot and pivot a 90-degree angle, lower the presser foot and proceed with the stitching in the new direction.

In lightweight fabrics, stitch the seam almost to the point of turning, take one stitch *across* the corner, continue stitching the other side.

In heavier fabrics, follow the procedure for lightweight fabrics but *take three stitches* to round the corner. It is impossible to get a sharp corner in any but lightweight fabrics. You will have to raise the presser foot after each stitch to set the needle in position for the next stitch.

THE POINT PRESSER

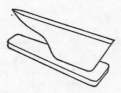

Fig. 78

You are probably wondering how you can possibly press the seam allowances open when corners are involved. The answer to this problem is the point presser, that wonderful piece of equipment no sewer should be without.

Slide the point of the point presser under any seam and into any corner that needs to be pressed open.

HOW TO FREE THE CORNERS OF BULK

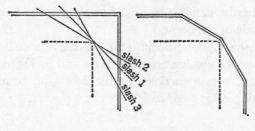

Fig. 79

It takes three slashes to free a corner of bulk: one diagonally across the corner as close to the stitching as is safe, a second slash diagonally into the seam allowance on one side, a third slash diagonally into the seam allowance on the other side.

If you have any doubts that your stitching will hold at the corner, reinforce it with a second row of tiny machine stitches directly over the first.

ROLL THE JOINING SEAM TO THE UNDERSIDE

Whenever any two layers of fabric are to be stitched together, enough material must be allowed on the upper one so that the seam that joins the two can be rolled to the under side—out of sight. There are two ways in which this may be done.

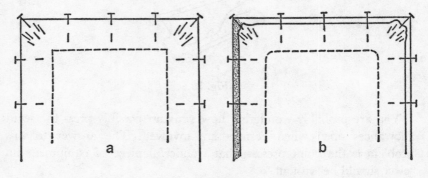

Fig. 80

Method I (Fig. 80a)

1. Cut the upper layer slightly larger than the under layer. How much depends on the thickness of the fabric—all the way from ⅛ inch for thin fabrics to ⅝ inch for thick ones.

2. Pin the corners together diagonally, edges matching.

3. Push a little bubble of fullness into each corner on both sides of the pin. Pin the bubble to position.

4. Pin the material at the ends, at the center of each side, and as many places between as seem necessary to hold the material in place. Either stretch the shorter length to match the longer length or ease in the fullness of the longer length so it matches the shorter length.

5. Stitch all seams an even distance in from the edges.

Method II (Fig. 80b)

1. Cut both layers the same size. Borrow some of the seam allowance of the upper layer to make it larger.

2. Set the raw edges of the upper layer down from the raw edges of the under layer. How much depends on the thickness of the fabric and how much seam allowance you have. Work in the fullness. Pin in the same way as for Method I.

3. Stitch the two thicknesses a seam allowance in from the edge of the under layer.

When the Upper Collar and Under Collar Are Cut All in One

When the upper collar and under collar are cut all in one either the upper or the under collar may be interfaced. It depends on how transparent or how opaque the material is.

TO INTERFACE THE UNDER COLLAR

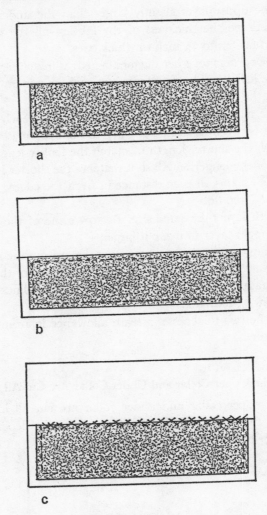

a

b

c

Fig. 81

1. Cut the interfacing from the under collar pattern. Note that it extends only to the foldline.

2. Place the interfacing over the wrong side of the under collar. Pin or baste to position.

3. Machine stitch ¾ inch in from the three raw edges. Trim the interfacing close to the stitching so none of it will be caught in the seam (Fig. 81a).

4. To fasten the fourth edge along the fold: either machine stitch ⅛ inch in from the foldline (Fig. 81b) or catch stitch lightly along the foldline (Fig. 81c).

TO INTERFACE THE UPPER COLLAR

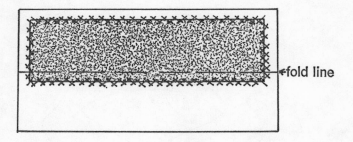

Fig. 82

1. Cut the interfacing from the collar pattern plus a seam allowance along the lengthwise fold. Trim the seam allowances from the neck and side edges.

2. Lightly catch stitch all edges of the interfacing to the collar (Fig. 82).

TO COMPLETE THE INTERFACED ALL-IN-ONE COLLAR

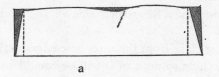

a

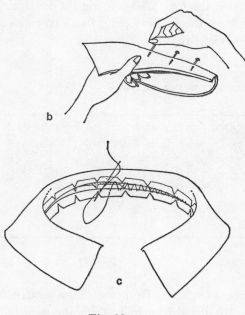

b

c

Fig. 83

1. With right sides together, fold the interfaced collar lengthwise along the foldline.

2. Starting at the neck edge and tapering to nothing at the corners, set back the raw edge of the upper collar from the raw edge of the

under collar. This is done so that some of the collar seam allowance may be used for the extra length necessary to roll the joining seam to the underside.

3. Across the ends, stitch a seam allowance in from the under collar raw edges (Fig. 83a).

4. Press the seam allowances open using the point presser to get into the corners of the collar. Trim the seam allowances and grade when necessary. Snip the seam allowances diagonally at the corners to free them of bulk.

5. Turn the collar to the right side carefully working out all corners with a blunt-edged instrument.

6. Press all outside edges.

How to Put the Roll in the Rolled Collar

It's a familiar story to you by now: an outside curve takes more length than an inside curve.

When a collar has a roll, the upper layer, being the outside curve, must have enough length to negotiate the turn. Ideally, this length should be added in the cutting. With heavier materials, this is a must. However, in lightweight materials some length can be salvaged from the neck seam allowance. With the upper collar on top, roll the completed collar over the hand. Place pins along the roll line at right angles to the neck edge (Fig. 83b). Baste the neck edges together slightly below the seam line (⅝ inch in from the raw edge of the under collar).

In an alternate method, the extra length can be achieved by rolling the collar to position *after* it has been stitched to the garment and facing. The upper and under collar neck seams will then no longer be one directly over the other. Hopefully, one seam allowance of the upper layer will be close enough to a seam allowance of the under layer so they can be lightly (and permanently) basted together to hold the collar in place (Fig. 83c).

How to Interface a Standing Collar

There are several ways to make a standing collar really stand. Use the one that is suitable for the fabric and the degree of desired stiffness.

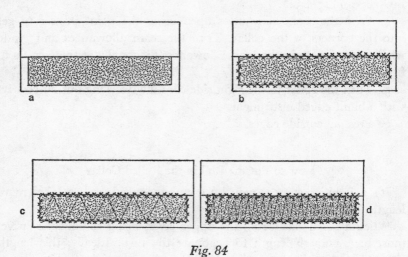

Fig. 84

THE IRON-ON METHOD

1. Trim away the seam allowances of the under collar pattern.

2. Using this new pattern cut the interfacing of iron-on material.

3. Place the interfacing in position on the wrong side of the under collar. Press it on (Fig. 84a).

THE STIFF-INTERFACING METHOD

1. Cut a length of stiff interfacing material from the under collar pattern minus seam allowances.

2. Place the interfacing in position on the wrong side of the collar. Lightly catch stitch all edges (Fig. 84b).

THE STIFFENED-INTERFACING METHOD

1. Cut a length of interfacing material from the under collar pattern minus seam allowances.

2. Make diagonal rows of machine stitching until the interfacing is the desired degree of stiffness (Fig. 84c). The smaller the stitches and the more closely spaced the rows of stitching, the stiffer the interfacing will be (Fig. 84d).

3. Place the interfacing in position on the wrong side of the under collar. Catch stitch all edges.

Once the interfacing is applied, the standing collar can be completed in the same way as any other collar.

The Collar Joins the Garment

By comparison with all the work necessary to make the collar, attaching it to the shirt is comparatively simple.

The garment must be ready for the collar:

the completed front and back are joined at the shoulders.

the facings and interfacings are joined at the shoulders.

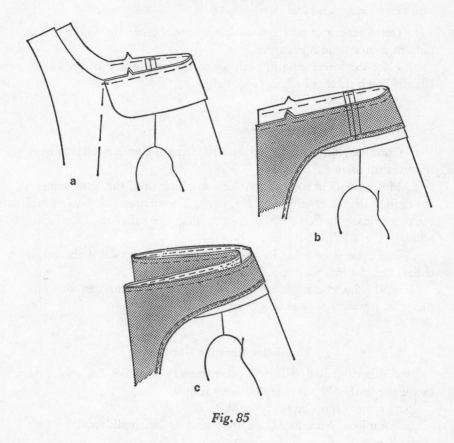

Fig. 85

QUICK-AND-EASY METHOD

1. Pin the completed collar to the neck edge in the same relative position in which it will be worn, that is—the right side of the shirt is up, facing you; the right side of the collar is up, facing you. Match the neck edges at the center back, the shoulders or notches, and the points at which the collar joins the front neck edge or the lapel. Clip and stretch the collar as necessary to make it fit the neckline of the shirt (Fig. 85a).

2. Baste the collar to the shirt. Take several backstitches in place (called over-and-over stitches) to fasten the collar at the point where

it joins the front. This will prevent it from slipping when the collar is machine stitched to the neckline.

3. Place the right side of the facing against the right side of the shirt with the collar sandwiched between the two (Fig. 85b). Once more, match center backs, shoulder seams, notches. Ease, stretch, clip as necessary to make it fit. When the collar neckline and the garment neckline are two opposing curves, it is much easier to join them when one or the other has been clipped first practically to the seam line. Pin or baste the facing to position.

4. Stitch through all the layers joining collar, facing, and interfacing in one seam. If the fabric is too heavy to join all four thicknesses in a single seam, try the following:

    (a) Complete the collar but do not baste the neck edges together.

    (b) Pin the neck edge of the under collar to the neck edge of the garment. Pin the neck edge of the upper collar to the neck edge of the facing. Match center backs, notches, shoulders, seams, and points at which the collar joins the garment at the front. Baste to position.

    (c) Stitch the under collar to the garment and the upper collar to the facing in one continuous seam (Fig. 85c).

In Method I

5. Grade all seam allowances. Clip and notch as necessary.

6. Turn the facing to the inside of the shirt. Press.

In the alternate method

5. Press the neck seam allowances open. Clip and notch as necessary.

6. Turn the facing to the inside of the shirt. Lightly baste the neck seam allowances together.

Both methods

7. Tack the edge of the facing at the shoulder seams and at any other seams and darts. *Never hem the facing to the garment.* Besides being extra work, hemming produces an outline of the facing on the right side of the garment that detracts from the style lines of the garment.

A *tack* (swing tack, suspension tack) is made of several long, loose stitches that link together any two separate parts of a garment.

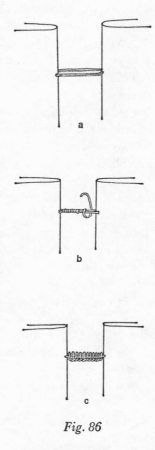

Fig. 86

Take a tiny stitch on one part, then another directly opposite on the part to be joined. Pull up the thread to the desired length. Repeat, making several such stitches (Fig. 86a).

Fasten the thread.

When a swing tack is in a hidden position (such as this one), this is sufficient. When a swing tack is in an exposed position, it is "prettied up" and strengthened by wrapping thread around it (Fig. 86b) or by working blanket stitches over it (Fig. 86c).

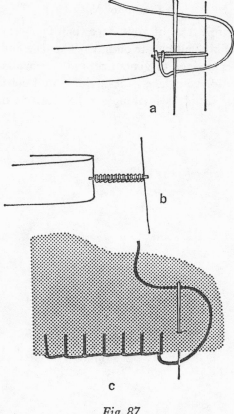

Fig. 87

To make the blanket stitch fasten the thread. Loop it over the swing tack with the loop toward you. Pass the needle (held vertically) behind the tack and bring it out through the loop, pointing it toward you (Fig. 87a). Pull up the knot. Work succeeding stitches close together until the tack is entirely covered.

This knotted loop of thread has many uses. It forms thread eyes, loops, belt carriers (Fig. 87b). When worked over the edge of a fabric it makes a decorative finish (Fig. 87c).

A Frame for Your Face

It's that portrait area of you—face, hairdo, neckline, collar—that people see first and concentrate on most. The face and hairdo we must leave to the beauticians to glamorize and the artists to immortalize. But that frame for your face—the neckline and collar—there's something we sewers can do something about: learn to handle them perfectly.

SOMETHING UP YOUR SLEEVE

Pay no attention to old wives' tales of how hard it is to set and sew a sleeve. That "something up your sleeve" is the knowledge that when you don't know what you are doing, everything is hard. When you do know, anything is easy.

The Eye of the Arm and the Cap of the Sleeve

Perhaps you've never seen a real dressmaker's form but most every sewer has seen a picture of one (Fig. 88a).

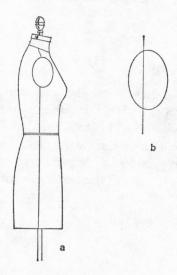

Fig. 88

Do you see the oval that shows where the arm would be if the form had one? It does look somewhat like a great eye, doesn't it? The pros named it the *armscye* for the eye of the arm. Most of the rest of us refer to it as the armhole.

Were you to draw a line from the shoulder seam to the side seam you would divide the armscye into front and back (Fig. 88b). As you can see, the split is not equal: there is more front than back.

Sleeves Come in Pairs

Lay the bodice front, bodice back, and sleeve side by side on a flat surface. Place the front of the sleeve toward the front bodice, the back of the sleeve toward the back bodice (Fig. 89).

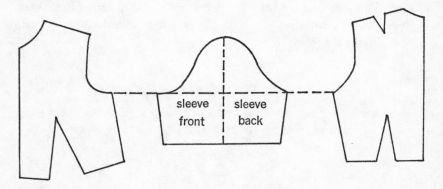

Fig. 89

That portion of the sleeve above the horizontal line in Fig. 89 is the *sleeve cap*. The vertical broken line separates the cap into front and back. The front cap is drafted to fit the front armhole, the back cap to fit the back armhole. Glance back at Fig. 88b and note that the division of the armscye produces a deeper curve on the front armhole than the back. The cap must fit these different curves and lengths.

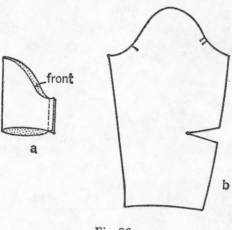

Fig. 90

If you are ever in doubt as to which is the front and which is the back of a fitted sleeve, fold the sleeve in half lengthwise. The front cap is always the deeper curve (Fig. 90a).

In a below-elbow-length sleeve, there is another way to tell front from back. The elbow darts or gathers or easing are always in back (Fig. 90b).

FRONTS AND BACKS ARE NOT REVERSIBLE

There is a right sleeve and a left sleeve, therefore a right front and a left front, a right back and a left back. The notches on the pattern tell you which is which. In setting the sleeve into the armhole, you must make very sure that you match the right front sleeve with the right front bodice and the left front sleeve with the left front bodice. Reverse the sleeves and they won't fit the armhole! What's worse, they won't fit you.

Sleeve Ease

The armhole and sleeve cap are further divided into overarm and underarm (Fig. 91).

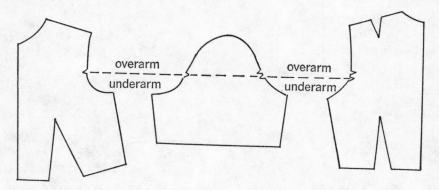

overarm
underarm

overarm
underarm

Fig. 91

Notches are placed at those points where the seam lines that arch over the shoulders swing into underarm curves. Change of direction occurs at the points where arm and body meet, both front and back.

The underarm curves sweep down from the notches to the underarm seams. The curves are identical on both sleeve cap and bodice. Therefore, easy to match when setting the sleeve.

In a fitted misses' dress, the armhole generally drops 1½ inches below the notch to the underarm seam. This is to provide comfort in wearing and room for movement. Many great couturiers set the sleeve higher than this on the underarm. They hold that a high setting provides greater ease of movement (no unsightly pulling up of the garment when the arm is raised) and greater trimness to the garment.

Sleeveless dresses, too, are built up under the arm. Since there is no sleeve to restrict the motion in any way, the underarm curve can be brought up as high as is comfortable. In patterns that show the style with and without sleeves, note the two underarm stitching lines. Choose the upper seam line for the sleeveless version.

The overarm curves sweep upward from the notches to the shoulders of both cap and bodice. Unlike the underarm, these curves do not match in length and shape. The sleeve cap is slightly longer than the bodice, giving it a somewhat different curve. This difference in length (generally 1½ to 2 inches) and shape represents the *ease*. Ease is a must—as necessary in a sleeve as it is in a bodice or skirt and for the same reasons—comfort and ease of movement. It is a very great temptation to eliminate the ease in order to make the sleeve setting easier. But, *sleeve ease must be retained* or the sleeve will not fit well or feel comfortable.

Since this part of the cap is on a near-bias angle, most fabrics can be eased into the armhole fairly readily. For those that are difficult to ease—hard-to-budge, rigid, firmly woven, or stiff fabrics—try the sleeve setting below.

Sleeve Set

This method of setting a sleeve is the reverse of the generally accepted procedure but works like magic.

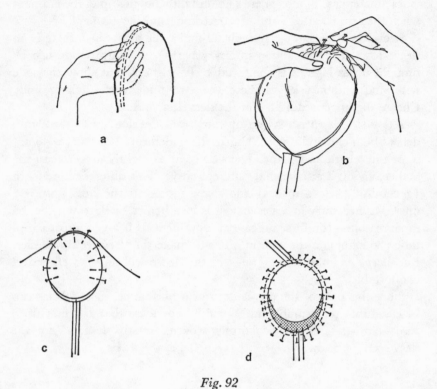

Fig. 92

1. Stitch the underarm sleeve seam. Press it open.

2. Gather the cap from the front notch to the back notch. Place the first row of running stitches just inside the seam line. Place the second row ¼ inch away in the seam allowance. Pull up the gathering until the sleeve cap cups over your hooked fingers (Fig. 92a). Don't worry that you are pulling up too much cap for the armhole. Adjustments can be made as the sleeve is being set.

3. With right sides together, insert the sleeve into the armhole.

Work on the wrong side with the sleeve up so you can distribute the fullness evenly across the cap. Hold the sleeve in the outside curve it will assume when worn (Fig. 92b).

4. Start the setting *at the shoulder*. Match the shoulder seam of the bodice with the shoulder marking of the sleeve cap. Place a pin at right angles to the seam line.

5. Working down on each side, distribute the fullness evenly across the cap down to the notches. Place the pins at right angles to the seam line (Fig. 92c). Use your fingertips or the point of a pin for separating the gathers.

6. Pin the underarm into the armhole matching the underarm seams of both sleeve and bodice.

In hard-to-ease fabrics (like piqué or taffeta), distribute the fullness so the cap drops slightly below the notches and the underarm of the sleeve drops slightly below the underarm of the bodice. The drop may be as much as a seam allowance but no more (Fig. 92d). Using the underarm of the sleeve as a pattern, cut away the bodice to match the sleeve. This is also a good method to use when an adjustment in fitting has altered or reduced the size of the armhole.

Pinning vs. Basting

It is true that basting a sleeve into the armhole makes it easier to judge the fitting. However, if you are sure of the fit, pinning eliminates an extra operation. One can simply pin and stitch.

Where precise matching of stripes, plaids, checks, motifs are called for, pins hold more securely than basting as a preparation for the stitching.

An ideal method for setting a sleeve is to have someone do it for you from the right side. Or, do it yourself over a dress form.

1. Turn under the seam allowance of the gathered cap.

2. Overlap it on the armhole, distributing the fullness. Pin to position.

3. Slip-baste the cap to the bodice.

Stitch the Sleeve into the Armhole

SURE SEWERS

Work with the sleeve side up so you can continue to control the ease.

Starting the stitching at one notch, stitch around the sleeve until you return to the starting point *but do not stop*. Continue the stitching until you get to the opposite notch (Fig. 93a). This reinforces the underarm, an area that gets much wear and tear.

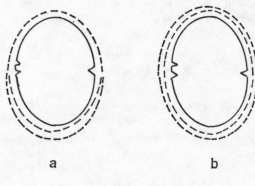

a   b

Fig. 93

UNSURE SEWERS

Start the stitching at the underarm seam and stitch until you return to the starting point. Examine the stitching line from the bodice side. If the stitching is somewhat wavering, make a second row of stitching very close to the first, correcting it as you sew (Fig. 93b). This time, work with the bodice side up so you can see what needs correction. This method ensures stitching perfection as well as underarm reinforcement.

Clip and Cut

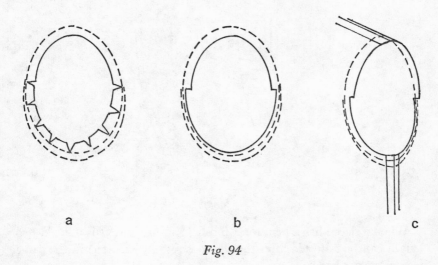

a   b   c

Fig. 94

The sleeve is meant to fit at the armhole seam and not at the cut edge, which is shorter. So, clip the seam allowances at the notches almost to the stitching. Clip the underarm seam allowances every half inch (Fig. 94a). If you skip the clipping, your sleeve will be too tight on the underarm.

Since you have two rows of stitching for strength on the underarm, you can safely trim the seam allowances close to the underarm seam (Fig. 94b).

Press the remaining seam allowances into the cap of the sleeve where they serve as a tiny prop for the cap (Fig. 94c).

A small pair of trimming scissors (3 inches or less) are good for the large amount of snipping, clipping, and trimming one must do in construction.

The Sleeve Hem

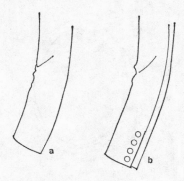

Fig. 95

When a sleeve has a hem for a finish (Fig. 95a), that is done last so length can be adjusted after the sleeve is set. It is treated in the same way as a skirt hem.

When a sleeve has some style detail at the hemline (Fig. 95b), that is done first before the sleeve is set. It is so much easier to handle just a sleeve in the machine rather than sleeve plus rest of garment.

It is a good plan in all your sewing to *complete what you can on smaller units before joining them to the rest of the garment.*

The Shirtwaist Sleeve and Its Band

If the sleeve finish is a fitted band or cuff then an opening must be provided that permits one to pull the sleeve on over the hand. The opening may be simple to complicated. Easiest to construct is a hemmed space between the ends of the band (Fig. 96a) that is folded into a pleat on closing (Fig. 96b). The most complicated to construct is the tailored placket (Fig. 96c). (Follow pattern directions carefully.) A frequently encountered placket is the continuous lap (Fig. 96d). This is a narrow strip of binding stitched to both sides of the opening slash. Less work but equally attractive is the faced opening (Fig. 96e).

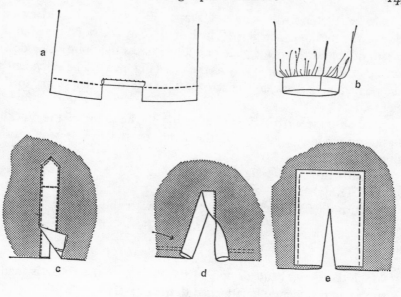

Fig. 96

A Pleasant Placket: The Faced Opening

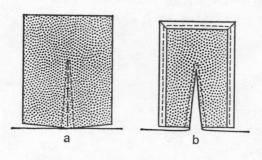

Fig. 97

1. Mark the slash line (opening) on the sleeve.
2. Cut a strip of self-fabric for a facing.
3. Place the facing, centered, over the slash line. The right side of the facing is against the right side of the sleeve. Pin or baste to position.

4. The stitching will be in a V-shape (Fig. 97a). Stitch along one side of the marking, starting ¼ inch from it at the start, taper to almost nothing at the point, take one stitch across the point, then down the other side in the same way as the first (Fig. 97a). The stitch across the point makes it easier (indeed, possible) to turn the facing to the right side.

5. Slash between the lines of stitching to the point of the V. The slash must come right up to the point or the facing won't turn smoothly.

6. Turn the outside edges of the facing to the wrong side. Edge stitch (Fig. 97b).

7. Turn the facing itself to the inside. Tack lightly at each corner.

Prepare the Sleeve Band

Make the sleeve band or cuff in the same way the collar is made. Leave open the edge to be attached to the sleeve.

Prepare the Lower Edge of the Sleeve for the Band

To prepare the lower edge of the sleeve for the band, either gather it (Fig. 98a) or pleat it (Fig. 98b).

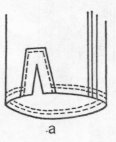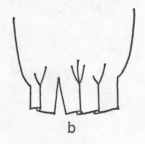

.a　　　　　　　　　　　b

Fig. 98

Attach the Band to the Sleeve

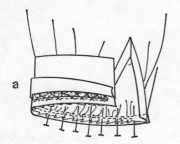 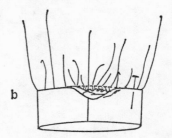

Fig. 99

1. With right sides together, place the open edge of the upper sleeve band to the edge of the sleeve. Starting at the placket, match the edges and the notches. Place pins at right angles to the seam line, distributing the fullness evenly (Fig. 99a).

2. With the gathered or pleated edge of the sleeve up, stitch the band to the sleeve. Stitch slowly taking care that the pleats and gathers stay in position.

3. Turn under the seam allowance of the free edge of the band facing. Place the fold along the stitching line (Fig. 99b). Pin to position.

4. Slipstitch (a couture touch) or hem to position. There are several hemming stitches but the easiest one for this type of construction is the *slant hemming stitch*.

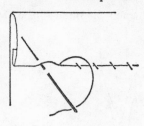

Fig. 100

Slant hemming is a series of small diagonal stitches worked through the garment and hem simultaneously. In this case the stitches will go through the seam allowances and the folded edge of the facing. Both needle and stitch are slanted (Fig. 100).

This is the fastest, strongest, and (generally) the most conspicuous of the hemming stitches. However, it can be safely used to finish the underside of the band because the stitches will not go through to the right side and, hopefully, will not show.

Set and Sew the Cap

When all of the style details have been attended to at the wrist edge of the sleeve, set and sew the cap of the shirtwaist sleeve by the same method used for setting and sewing the cap of the fitted sleeve.

To the Point: About Those Needles and Pins You Are Using

One well-known big-name designer uses his pins just once and then discards them. He holds that sliding a pin through material even a single time disqualifies it for use forever after. Extravagant, to be sure, but very much to the point. Pins and needles should have fine, sharp points that slide easily into the fabric without bruising it. They should be large enough to handle but small enough to avoid harm to the fabric.

Since the first primitive seamstress threaded her bone needle with a coarse sinew, there have been a multitude of needles devised for every conceivable purpose. No matter what needs sewing on—be it a bead, a mattress, a sail, a handkerchief, an upholstered sofa, a chiffon dress, a fur collar or a hole in a sock—you can be sure there is a needle for the job.

Unfortunately, the packets of needles most easily obtainable—the "sharps" and "betweens" are the hardest to thread. They have such tiny eyes. The ideal needle for most general dressmaking and tailoring is in reality an embroidery needle—the crewel. It is like a sharp but longer. Its larger eye, designed to take the thicker embroidery thread, is a cinch to use with sewing thread.

Crewel needles come in sizes 1 (coarsest) to 10 (finest). Many packets contain an assortment of the more frequently used sizes—5 to 10. There are two crewel needles that could see you through most of your hand sewing needs—number 10 for fine fabrics and number 8 for the heavier ones. If you can find a packet of each, it would be well to keep a supply on hand.

As for pins, a number 16 rustproof dressmaker pin is a good medium-sized pin. You may want to have a smaller one (size 14) for sheer fabrics or a larger one (size 17 or 20) for heavier cloth. You could even indulge yourself in a packet of those brightly colored plastic-head pins. They're so decorative and they slide so easily into material.

TAKE CARE

Discard all bent pins and needles. The former function imperfectly and the latter stitch inaccurately. The burr which often develops at needle or pin-point catches, snags, and damages material.

The black paper package in which needles are sold protects them from rust. Keep them there.

Above all, avoid those outsize needles and pins that seem to appeal to so many sewers. On fine fabrics they are absolutely murderous. Shun them as you would any other lethal weapon.

Hanging by a Thread

The thread you use often makes a difference in the strength and appearance of a seam. Sewing thread should match the cloth of the garment in color, weight, and fiber.

Cotton thread is used for cotton fabric. (They are both vegetable fibers.) Silk thread is used for silk and woolen fabrics. (They are all animal fibers.)

Nylon, Dacron, or polyester threads are used for fabrics of manmade fibers. (They are all synthetic fibers.)

The new cotton-covered polyester threads have the properties of both natural and man-made fibers. In truth, mercerized cotton thread can be used on most fabrics quite successfully.

Obviously, you would not sew a sheer fabric with a heavy thread: it would show as well as produce a bumpy appearance. Nor would you use a lightweight thread on a heavy fabric: it would not hold. Choose a weight of thread compatible with the weight of the fabric. Thread may be strengthened by running it through beeswax. This is also a good way to prevent tangling and knotting.

Ideally, the color of the thread should exactly match the color of the fabric. This is hard—sometimes impossible—to find. Next best is a color that blends with the color of the cloth. A shade darker works up better than a shade lighter.

For hand or machine sewing, thread the needle with the end cut from the spool. Don't tear thread. Those wispy filaments left by an uneven tear make it difficult to thread the needle.

SIZING YOU UP IN SKIRTS, SLACKS, AND SHORTS

If you are going to be sized up in your skirts, slacks, and shorts, better make sure you are wearing the right size.

Trim Fit Starts with the Right Size

While the size of shirts and dresses are usually selected by the bust measurement, skirts, slacks, and shorts are generally selected by the waist measurement. The latter are presented in the same range of figure types as the former.

If your hips are much larger in proportion to your waist than the standard size, select the size by your hip measurement. Hip-hugger pants and skirts are selected by the hip measurement. Up to a seam allowance added to the hips and tapered to the waist can accommodate larger than standard-size hips (Fig. 101a). (Continue the alteration to the hem to make the change proportionate.)

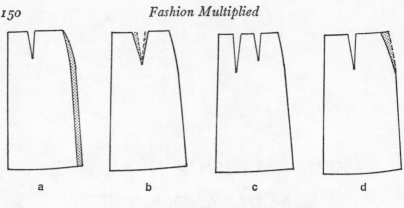

Fig. 101

A ⅝-inch seam allowance on four seams totals 2½ inches. If the hips are larger than that in proportion to the waist, it is better to select the pattern size by the hip measurement and make the skirt or pants fit at the waist by enlarging the darts (Fig. 101b), making more darts (Fig. 101c), and/or by tapering the side seams (or any others) from hips to waist (Fig. 101d).

The Long and Short of It

A straight skirt with no design detail at the hem may be lengthened or shortened at the hem (Fig. 102a). A straight skirt with design detail at the hem should be shortened or lengthened at the place indicated on the pattern to preserve its style line (Fig. 102b).

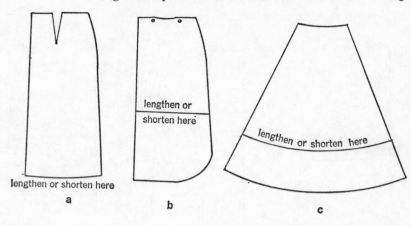

Fig. 102

To preserve the sweep at the hem of a flared skirt shorten or lengthen at the place indicated on the pattern (Fig. 102c). To shorten at the hem reduces the fullness. To lengthen at the hem increases it. If either of the last two is desired, alter the pattern to suit.

HOW TO LENGTHEN OR SHORTEN A PATTERN

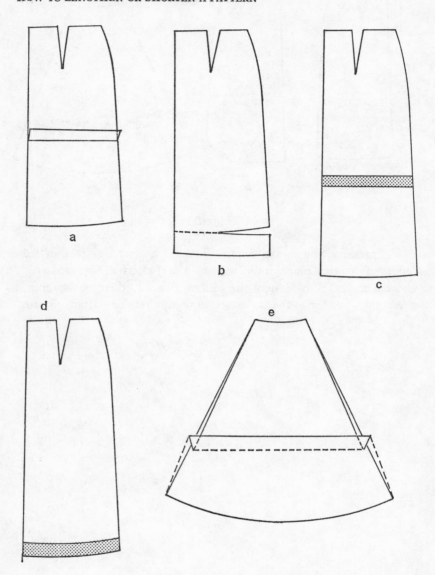

Fig. 103

To shorten a pattern, tuck it (Fig. 103a) or cut some off the lower edge (Fig. 103b).

To lengthen a pattern, slash and spread it to the desired amount. Fill in the space with tissue paper (Fig. 103c). Scotch-tape to position.

Another way to lengthen a pattern is simply to extend it at the lower edge (Fig. 103d).

Correct any jog that results from the change by drawing a new line that begins at the waist and ends at the hem (Fig. 103e).

Made to Measure

You need a few measurements in order to decide the right size of the pattern and to make any needed changes.

Tie a fairly heavy string around your waist. Push it into the hollow of your waist or where you would like your waistline to be. A skirt fits best when it settles into the natural waistline. However, there are aesthetic considerations. If you are long-waisted, you may want to raise the waistline somewhat. If you are short-waisted, you may want to lower it.

Now, measure the waistline with a tape measure. Don't hold your breath or pull the tape too tight. Sure a small waist is pretty, but you'll have to get it smaller by diet and exercises, not by tape measure. Remember that your skirt must fit comfortably or chances are you won't wear it.

Tie a second string around the fullest part of the hips. Measure the circumference. Note the number of inches below the waistline the hip measurement is taken. The fullest part of the skirt must be this distance below the waistline. Lengthen or shorten the pattern accordingly. *This change is made in the area between waist and hips, not below the hips or at the hem.*

Made to Fit: The Waist-to-Hip Area

The crucial area in fitting a skirt is waist-to-hips (Fig. 104a). The rest of the skirt is merely an extension of the seams from hips to hem.

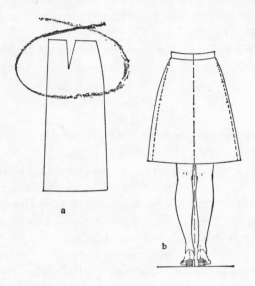

Fig. 104

When there are any fitting problems below the hip line, look for the cause above it. It could be that for your figure, this area of your skirt (or pants) is not long enough or short enough, not wide enough or narrow enough. Perhaps there is too much or too little shaping by darts and seams. When skirt seams swing forward or backward, poke out or hike up, look for the origin of the trouble in the waist-to-hip area.

To prevent skirt-fitting problems, first cut to measure.

Suggested Sequence for Fitting the Skirt

1. Pin the waistband in position.
2. Pin the center front and center back of the skirt to the center front and center back of the waistband.
3. Pin the side seams at the hips. Make certain that the center-front and back vertical grain lines hang at right angles to the floor and that the horizontal grain lines both front and back are parallel to the floor (Fig. 104b).

4. Pin the side seams, fitting the curve of the hips.

5. Check the front and back darts or seams for correct shaping. Unsightly bulges indicate the darts are too large. Spanning across the abdomen and buttocks indicate darts that are too long or incorrectly placed. Repin the darts, making the needed corrections.

6. Continue pinning the side seams from hips to hem. Should the side seams tend to swing forward or backward, unpin the seam, check the grain line, check the darts, correct as necessary, and repin.

The only way to truly avoid fitting problems in a skirt is to wear an unfitted one. But you can't do that forever. Somewhere along the line one does yearn for a good fitted skirt. Better learn how to handle the problem of fit.

NOW YOU SEE IT, NOW YOU DON'T
The Waistband

Waistbands: Usual or Unusual

Something has to hold up a skirt or pants—a bodice, a belt, a band.

The usual waistband is made of the same fabric as the skirt. But, a lifetime of self-fabric waistbands can be pretty dull stuff. Why not try for something a little different? Consider the decorative possibilities of a contrasting color, of print-against-plain, of plaids, stripes or checks, of grosgrain, satin or velvet ribbon, of a contrasting texture. Variety can be fun.

And why must a waistband always be visible? Why not conceal it on the inside of the skirt or pants?

The Grain of the Fabric as Part of the Design

Most waistbands are cut on the lengthwise grain of the fabric to match the grain of the skirt or slacks. A bias waistband not only avoids the chore of matching plaids, checks, and stripes, the change of direction actually adds to the design interest. The crosswise grain has its advantages too: there is less stretch. It also permits you to salvage a handsome selvage for a decorative finish.

Upper and Under Bands: Straight and Narrow or Contour

A waistband is composed of two parts: an upper band (the part

that shows) and an under band (the part next to the body) that
doesn't show. The under band, like the under collar, is really a facing.

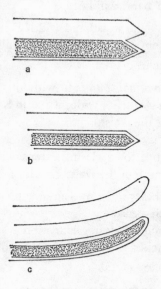

Fig. 105

As with other facings, it may be cut all in one piece with the upper
band (Fig. 105a). Or upper and under bands may be cut separately
(Fig. 105b).

It's easier and faster to construct the band if it is cut all in one
piece. However, there is much to be said for cutting the upper and
under bands separately. They can be shaped like a contour belt for excellent fit (Fig. 105c). If the fabric is too heavy or too bulky for a
complete waistband, the under band can be made of some lighter
weight material—lining, French belting, or grosgrain ribbon.

How to Determine the Width and Length of a Waistband

The width of the all-in-one-piece waistband is equal to twice the
finished width of the waistband plus two seam allowances. For instance: the width of a 1-inch waistband will be:

> 2 inches—the doubled band
> 1¼ inches—two ⅝-inch seam allowances
> _____
> 3¼ inches—total

The width for separate upper and under bands is equal to the finished width of each band plus two seam allowances. For example: the width of each 1-inch band will be:

    1 inch—the waistband width
    $1\frac{1}{4}$ inches—two $\frac{5}{8}$-inch seam allowances
    —————
    $2\frac{1}{4}$ inches—total

Straight-and-narrow waistbands fit without shaping. When a waistband is more than $1\frac{1}{2}$ inches wide, it requires a shaped side seam to fit the indentation of the waist.

The length of the waistband is equal to the waist measurement, plus ease, plus an allowance for a closing extension, plus seam allowances. For example: the length of the waistband for a 23-inch waist will be:

    23 inches—waist measurement
    $\frac{1}{4}$ inch—ease
    $1\frac{1}{2}$ inches—closing extension
    $1\frac{1}{4}$ inches—two $\frac{5}{8}$-inch seam allowances
    —————
    26 inches—total

The $1\frac{1}{2}$-inch closing extension may be an overlap (Fig. 106a) or an underlay (Fig. 106b). You may eliminate the closing extension by running the zipper up to the top of the band (Fig. 106c).

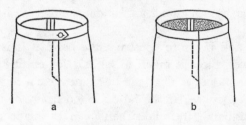

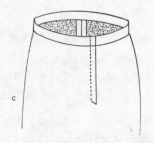

Fig. 106

Sewing sequence for a waistband with an extension: stitch the darts and seams of the skirt (or pants), insert the zipper, attach the band.

Sewing sequence for a waistband without an extension: stitch the darts and seams, attach the upper band, insert the zipper to the top of the upper band, apply the under band.

Bias Is Better

Bias waistbands fit best of all. Their moldability makes them settle comfortably into the natural indentation of the waist.

The length of the bias waistband should be less than your actual waist measurement because the bias will stretch. That's the nature and the virtue of bias. The heavier the fabric, the fuller the skirt, the more the pull on the waistband and the more the bias will stretch. Subtract 1 inch from the waist measurement to compensate for the stretch. If the fabric is very heavy or the skirt very full, subtract 1½ inches to 2 inches. Because the stretch in length reduces the width, make the bias waistband a little wider than a straight band.

In all other respects, the bias waistband is handled like the straight-and-narrow waistband.

A Stiffened Band

Most people like a little stiffening in a waistband. Choose an interfacing material of the degree of stiffness you prefer. Cut a length of it from the under band pattern. Apply it in the same way as suggested for the collar and the sleeve band.

It Knows Its Place

No waistband, however well or attractively made, will fit right if the waistline seam to which it is attached is not the *exact curve of your waist.*

The ideal waistline is presumed to tilt forward slightly (Fig. 107a).
Ready-to-wear clothes and all patterns are built on this principle.

Fig. 107

What if your waistline does just the reverse—tilts backward (Fig.
107b)? Many waistlines do.

For a skirt to fit the waistline (whatever the tilt) without wrinkling,
pulling, or straining, *the exact line of the waistline seam* must be located.

1. Try on the skirt. It should be large enough to rest comfortably at
the waist and hips without riding up. Where necessary, let out or take
in the seams and darts to make the skirt fit as it should.

2. Tie a heavy string snugly at the waist (or where you would like
your waistline to be).

3. Place a row of pins along the bottom of the string around the entire waist. This is easy enough to do for yourself if you have to, though
it's helpful to have someone mark the waistline for you.

4. Remove the skirt. Replace the pin markings with a line of guide
basting.

5. Trim the excess to a seam allowance.

Follow the same procedure for the waistline of pants.

Seeing Is Deceiving

Standard waistlines in ready-to-wear clothes and commercial patterns are symmetrical—that is, right and left sides are balanced. You may discover upon examination of the waistline marking that your waistline is not symmetrical—right and left sides are different.

If the difference is slight, ignore it. It may be the result of inaccurate marking. However, if the difference is pronounced, you must respect it. A waistband attached to *your* waistline, however unbalanced, will look right while one attached to the symmetrical pattern waistline will look all wrong on you.

Here Is an Easy Way to Attach a Waistband

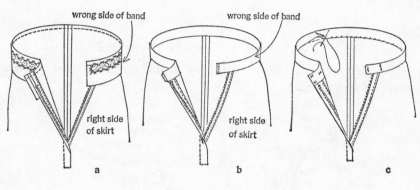

Fig. 108

1. With right sides together, pin the upper band to the skirt (or pants) along the seam line. When there is an extension, it projects beyond the opening (Fig. 108a).

2. Stitch the upper band to the garment. Grade and clip the seam allowances.

3. Press the seam allowances open first, then into the band.

4. Fold an all-in-one band in half lengthwise, right sides together. Stitch across the ends (Fig. 108b). When cut separately, stitch the under band to the upper band along the length and across the ends.

5. Press the seam allowances open over the point presser. Grade the seam allowances and free the corners of bulk.

6. Turn the band to the right side. Fold the all-in-one band lengthwise along the foldline. Make sure that the waistband is even in width from seam to fold along its entire length. Pin or baste to position. When an under band has been stitched to an upper band, roll the joining seams to the underside.

7. Press, then baste to position. Be sure to observe this order. If you baste first and then press, the basting marks will leave an imprint on the material.

8. Turn under the seam allowance of the loose edge of the under band and hem or slipstitch it to the garment along the stitching line (Fig. 108c).

9. Make a machine buttonhole on an overlap extension. Sew on the button.* Finish off the underlay extension with hooks and eyes or snaps.†

How to Make a Topstitched Waistband

The procedure for this construction is the reverse of that for the standard waistband.

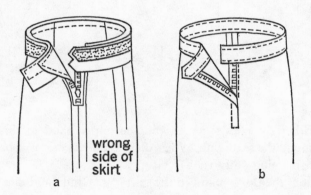

Fig. 109

---

* See page 165 for directions.
† See page 167 for directions.

1. Stitch the right side of the under band to the wrong side of the skirt or pants (Fig. 109a). Grade and clip the seam allowances. Press them open, then into the band.

2. Fold the all-in-one-piece band or turn the separate band-and-facing waistband so the right sides are together. Stitch across the ends.

3. Press the seam allowances open over the point presser. Grade them. Free the corners of bulk.

4. Turn the band to the right side (outside).

5. Fold the all-in-one band lengthwise along the foldline, keeping it even from seam to fold. Pin or baste to position. When upper and under bands have been joined by a seam, roll it to the underside. Press and baste to position.

6. Turn under the seam allowance of the loose edge. Overlap the folded edge of the band on the *right side* of the garment, covering the seam line. Pin or baste to position.

7. Topstitch through all thicknesses (Fig. 109b).

8. Sew on the fastenings.

How to Make an Inside Waistband

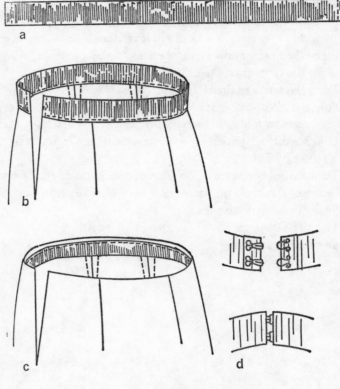

Fig. 110

1. Use a length of 1-inch to 1½-inch grosgrain ribbon or French belting. Cut it to the waistline measurement, plus ease, plus two seam allowances—one for each end.

2. Turn under the seam allowances at each end and stitch (Fig. 110a).

3. Swirl the grosgrain ribbon into a slight curve with the steam iron. It will fit better if contoured. To swirl: lay the ribbon on the ironing board in a curve. Keeping the side of the iron parallel to the

edge of the ribbon, stretch the outside edge while easing the fullness of the inside edge.

4. With right sides up, overlap the ribbon on the skirt at least ¼ inch above the waistline marking (into the seam allowance) (Fig. 110b). This will provide an allowance for rolling the seam to the underside. Stitch.

5. Trim and clip the seam allowance under the ribbon for a flat and easy turning.

6. Turn the waistband to the inside of the skirt, rolling the seam to the underside. Press to position (Fig. 110c).

7. Tack the band securely to all seams and darts on the underside.

8. Sew hooks and eyes to the ends of the band for fastening (Fig. 110d).

How to Sew on a Button

Try on the skirt and pin the waistband closed.

Using a safety pin (this won't fall out as a straight pin may), pin through the buttonhole opening. Close the safety pin. "Unbutton" it. This locates the position for the button.

a   b

Fig. 111

There are two types of buttons: those with holes called sew-through buttons (Fig. 111a), and those with stems or shanks of either self-material or metal loops (Fig. 111b).

The shank (or stem) is the bridge between the upper and under parts of a closing. It floats the button on the surface of the garment. Without it, the garment would bunch rather than button. So important is this bridge that when a button doesn't have a shank or stem, one must be created.

THE SEW-THROUGH BUTTON

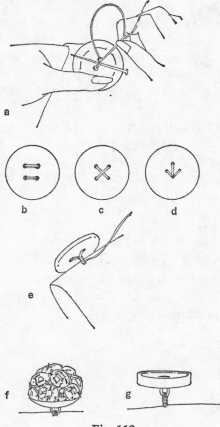

Fig. 112

1. Use a not-too-long single thread. Double threads tend to pull up unevenly. Use buttonhole twist, heavy-duty thread, or thread that has been drawn through beeswax to strengthen it and prevent knotting.

2. Fasten the thread with several tiny backstitches on the right side at the position indicated for the button.

3. Place a matchstick, toothpick, or thick pin (or any similar object) over the button (Fig. 112a). All sewing is done over the object to provide enough thread for the stem. Make the stem as long as the several layers of fabric are thick—outer fabric, interfacing, facing—plus a tiny bit for ease. The length of the stem will determine what you use for your prop. This is also an easy way to keep all the threads equal in length.

4. Bring the needle up through one hole and down through a second hole. Catch a bit of the fabric at the base of the button but do not go through to the underside. Bring the needle up through the third hole and down through the fourth (when there is a third and a fourth). Repeat about four times.

The thread may form parallel bars (Fig. 112b), a cross (Fig. 112c), or a flower-like design (Fig. 112d). The first two are used more generally.

5. Remove the matchstick (etc.) and raise the button to the top of the stitches.

6. Wind the thread around the stitches to form the stem (Fig. 112e). Start the winding right under the button and end it near the fabric where it can be anchored with several tiny backstitches.

THE SHANK BUTTON

When the button has a shank, all you need to do is sew through the loop taking enough stitches to fasten it securely (Fig. 112f). (In a heavy overcoat, create a thread stem in addition to the metal shank [Fig. 112g].)

How to Sew on Snaps

Snaps are used in areas where there is not too much strain. They are composed of two parts: a ball and a socket.

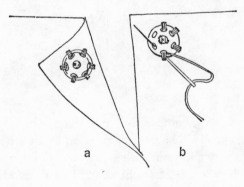

a   b

Fig. 113

1. Mark the exact placement of the snaps.
2. Sew the ball on first on the underside of the overlap (Fig. 113a). Sew with overhand stitches through the small holes at the edge. Carry

the thread under the snap from hole to hole. Make sure that the stitches do not come through to the outside. They should never show.

> *Overhand stitches* are small stitches, close together, made over and over an edge.

3. Press the ball against the opposite edge to locate the exact position of the center of the socket. Mark with chalk or a pin. On some fabrics, chalking the ball and pressing it against the opposite side works well.

4. Center the socket over the marking and sew with overhand stitches through the small holes at the edge (Fig. 113b).

Snaps come in sizes from small to large. If the fabric can take it, the large snaps hold well on a skirt or pants.

How to Sew on Hooks and Eyes—Regular or Heavy Duty

Hooks and eyes are used in areas where there *is* strain. Like snaps, they come in sizes from small to large. Large or heavy-duty hooks and eyes are used in areas where there is great strain. They must be sewn on very securely.

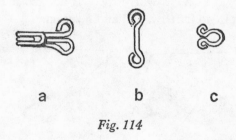

a   b   c

Fig. 114

Hooks and eyes are composed of two parts: the hook or bill (Fig. 114a) and the eye. There are straight eyes (Fig. 114b) for edges that overlap (like the waistband with extension), and round eyes (Fig. 114c) where the edges meet (as in an inside waistband).

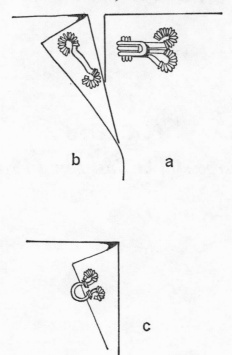

Fig. 115

1. Mark the position for the hooks and eyes carefully.

2. Set the hook close to the edge for a true closing. Sew it first, working the overhand stitches around the first ring.

3. Slip the needle through the fabric and bring it up at the second ring.

4. Sew the second ring working overhand stitches around it.

5. Slip the needle through the fabric and bring it up at the hook end. Work overhand stitches just under the bill. It is just as important to anchor the bill as to secure the rings (Fig. 115a).

6. Fasten the thread with tiny backstitches. Cut the thread.

7. Stitch the eye with overhand stitches around the rings. In addition, sew a few additional stitches near the edge to hold the eye in place (Fig. 115b).

A round eye is extended slightly beyond the edge (Fig. 115c).

For a couture touch use covered snaps and covered hooks and eyes. See directions on page 357.

POCKETS
Purposeful or Just Plain Pretty

Whether you really mean to use them or to have them just for show, pockets can be an asset to a shirt or skirt (or dress or pants or suit or coat, for that matter). You can hide the pockets in seams (Fig. 116a), splash them on a surface (Fig. 116b), or maneuver them into a slash (Fig. 116c).

Even if your pattern doesn't have a pocket you can add one—or many. Pockets often become *the* decorative feature of an otherwise simple garment. Just remember to keep the lines of the pocket in harmony with the lines of the design.

Fig. 116

A Pocket in a Seam

No one may know the in-a-seam pockets are there until you plunge
your hands into them (Fig. 117a). Or, you may advertise their presence with topstitching (Fig. 117b).

Fig. 117

THE RIGHT SIZE, THE RIGHT SHAPE

If the pocket is meant for use, make it large enough to get your hand into it easily and deep enough to let your hand settle comfortably.

You will need a pair of pouch-shaped pieces for each pocket: an upper pocket directly under the top of your hand and a lower pocket resting against the palm of your hand (Fig. 118a).

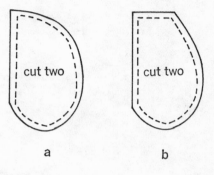

a   b

Fig. 118

When a pocket joins a waistline as well as a vertical seam, it should have a flattened top that is included in the waistline seam (Fig. 118b).

THE RIGHT MATERIAL

The opening of the in-a-seam pocket will reveal the material of which it is made. Anything seen, as this is, becomes part of the design of the garment. Therefore, what material you choose for the pocket should fit in with the total concept of the design.

A flash of color or pattern adds design interest. Why not use a contrasting color or figured material for the pockets and collar and cuff facings? This could add drama to an otherwise simple style.

The more usual treatment of the in-a-seam pocket is to preserve the continuity of color and texture. There are several ways in which this can be done.

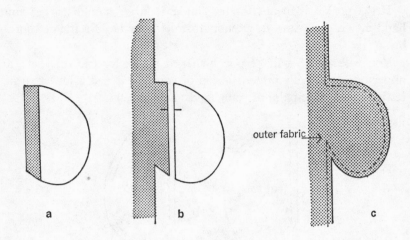

Fig. 119

1. If the fabric of the garment is light or medium weight, cut the pockets of the same material.

2. Or, cut the under pocket of the outer fabric and the upper pocket of lining material.

3. For heavy material, cut both upper and under pockets of lining material. Face the edges that join the garment with strips of outer fabric deep enough so the lining won't show when the pocket opens (Fig. 119a).

If you enjoy playing with patterns you might even consider doing one of the following:

1. Scotch-tape a tissue paper extension to the seam allowance of the pattern at the pocket opening (Fig. 119b). Make it equal in size to the facing of Fig. 119a. Now garment-plus-pocket facing can be cut as one piece. Of course the pocket itself should be made correspondingly smaller.

2. Add the entire underpocket pattern to the garment with Scotch tape. Cut the two as one pattern (Fig. 119c). Overlap the seam allowances at the joining.

In both cases, cut the garment-plus-extension of the fashion fabric and the rest of the pocket of lining material.

How to Set and Stitch the Pocket into the Seam

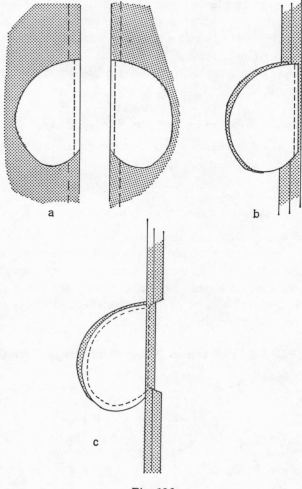

Fig. 120

1. With right sides together stitch the straight edges of the pocket to the garment, matching the markings for the opening. Use only ⅜ inch of the usual ⅝-inch seam allowance. This will give ¼ inch for rolling the pocket seam to the inside (Fig. 120a).

2. With right sides together, stitch the seams of the garment below and above the pocket. Take the regulation ⅝-inch seam allowance (Fig. 120b).

3. Clip the seam allowances at the corners where the garment and pocket seams meet. Grade the pocket seam allowances.

4. Press the garment seam allowances open. Press the pocket along the original seam line with seam allowances pressed toward the front.

5. Stitch the pocket sections together with the standard ⅝-inch seam allowance (Fig. 120c).

When a pocket extends to the waistline, baste and stitch it into the waistline seam.

A Patch Can Be Pretty if It Is a Pocket

While a pocket in a seam is generally inconspicuous, a patch pocket is brazenly exposed. As such, it becomes a very important part of the design.

Why Not Design Your Own Patch Pockets?

Play with paper cut-outs until you get just the right size, shape, placement, and number of pockets. (One good pocket may deserve another. Chanel did it!) Trace the chosen pocket on fresh paper. Add seam allowances and a hem. Decide whether you want it on straight grain, cross grain, or bias for its decorative effect. Consider a trimming of braid, ribbon, or topstitching. Let yourself go!

Patch Pocket Construction: Whatever the Design of the Pocket

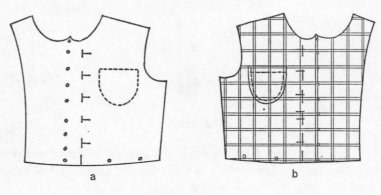

a   b

Fig. 121

1. Mark the position of the pocket carefully on the right side of the garment with guide basting (Fig. 121a).

2. Cut out the pocket. If striped, checked, plaid, or printed fabric is used, be sure to match pocket and garment (Fig. 121b).

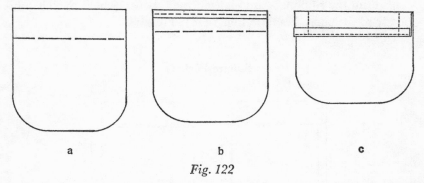

a   b   c

Fig. 122

3. Mark the foldline of the hem (Fig. 122a). It may be helpful to mark the seam allowances also.

4. Choose an appropriate finish for the hem edge of the pocket (Fig. 122b). Keep it as flat and unobtrusive as possible.

5. Turn the hem of the pocket to the outside (right side) along the foldline. Pin to position and stitch (Fig. 122c). Fasten the stitching securely at the hem edge.

Rounded Pockets

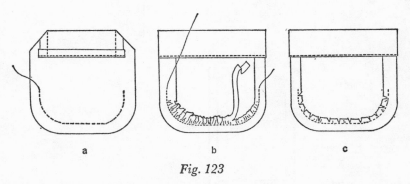

a   b   c

Fig. 123

1. Place a line of gathering stitches around the curve of the pocket about 1/4 inch away from the seam line (Fig. 123a).

2. Make a diagonal slash across each corner. Grade the seam allowances (Fig. 123a) and press them open over the point presser.

3. Turn the hem to the inside (wrong side of the pocket) working out the corners carefully (Fig. 123b).

4. Draw up the gathering stitches. Turn the seam allowances evenly to the wrong side. (Fig. 123b).

5. Trim the rippling seam allowance to about ⅜ inch. Notch sufficiently so the curve lies flat (Fig. 123c). Press.

Square Pockets

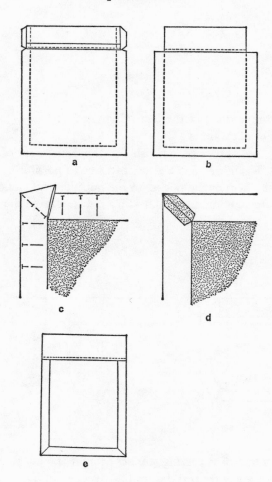

Fig. 124

1. Make a diagonal slash across each corner of the hem. Clip the seam allowances at the end of the hem. Grade them (Fig. 124a).

2. Press the seam allowances open over the point presser. Turn the hem to the inside, carefully working out the corners (Fig. 124b).

3. *Miter* the seam allowances of the remaining corners. To miter a corner turn the seam allowances to the outside. Pinch the corner into a dart. Pin the dart diagonally across the corner (Fig. 124c). Stitch the seam. Trim the seam allowances and press them open (Fig. 124d).

4. Turn the corners to the inside (wrong side), working them out carefully. Keep the seam allowances even (Fig. 124e).

5. Press the pocket.

How to Apply the Patch Pocket

Pin the pocket to position on the right side of the garment. Place the pins at right angles to the sides (Fig. 125a). Baste if necessary.

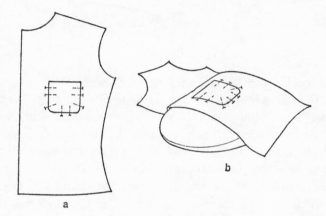

Fig. 125

Hints on Pocket Placement

If the garment is unfitted, lay it on a flat surface. Place the pocket over it (Fig. 125a).

If the garment is fitted, place the pocket area over a curved pad to simulate the body curve. Position the pockets (Fig. 125b). Pockets so placed will lie flat when worn. Pockets positioned on a flat surface will not have sufficient length to lie flat when worn over the body curve.

The best curved pad over which to work is the tailor's ham. A tightly rolled up towel is a fair substitute.

The Topstitched Pocket

When visible stitching is consistent with the design of the garment attach the pocket to it by topstitching. This is generally a single line of stitching close to and an even distance in from the edge (Fig. 126a). Begin the stitching at one corner and stitch to the opposite one.

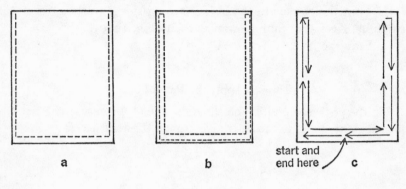

a   b   start and end here   c

Fig. 126

If the pocket will be subjected to much wear, double topstitch it (Fig. 126b). This is easy on a two-needle sewing machine. On a single-needle sewing machine, start the stitching at the bottom of the pocket rather than at one end. Stitch to one end, take a few stitches across the end (both to reinforce the end and to place the needle in position for the second row of stitching). Stitch around the pocket to the other end, stitch across the end and down the second side to the start of the stitching. Pull the threads through to the underside and tie them in a square knot. *To tie a square knot* bring the thread first right over left, then left over right. Follow the arrows in Fig. 126c. Keep the rows of stitching an even distance from each other throughout. Take the same number of stitches across each end.

For either single or double topstitching use a regulation stitch size and matching or contrasting thread.

TOPSTITCHING IN FROM THE EDGE FOR A DECORATIVE EFFECT

A very pretty patch pocket can be made by topstitching in from the edge (Figs. 127a and 127c).

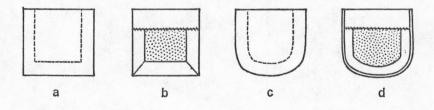

a   b   c   d

Fig. 127

For this effect, a straight-sided pocket needs a much deeper seam allowance (Fig. 127b) and a curved pocket needs a facing (Fig. 127d).

The topstitching can be used to attach the pocket to the garment in which case it is done like the single topstitched pocket. When the topstitching is used merely decoratively, it is done before the pocket is applied. The pocket is then applied to the garment with slipstitching (the stitch used for the slipstitched pocket below).

When the topstitching truly attaches the pocket to the garment use a regulation size machine stitch—whichever is suitable for the fabric. When the topstitching is used just decoratively the stitches may be as large as will make them interesting on the fabric.

The Slipstitched Pocket

For designs that look better without visible stitching, slipstitch the pocket to the garment. Properly done, the slipstitch method floats the pocket on the surface of the garment.

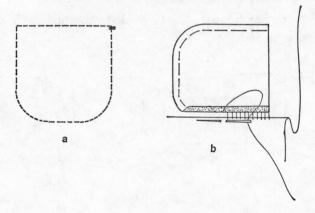

Fig. 128

1. Pin or baste the pocket in position.
2. Reinforce the starting corner by taking several small over-and-over stitches on the underside of the garment (Fig. 128a). Bring the needle up to the right side.
3. Fold back the pocket against itself, making the fold slightly in from the finished edge of the pocket. Fold back the garment against itself (Fig. 128).
4. Slip the needle along the folds alternating between the pocket and the garment (Fig. 128b). The lower stitch starts directly under the ending of the upper stitch. The upper stitch begins directly over the end of the lower stitch.
5. Continue slipstitching around the edge of the pocket.
6. Finish off by making several small over-and-over stitches on the underside.

No doubt you recognize this method as the one used for attaching a decorative facing to the right side of the garment, page 46.

The Lined Pocket

Pockets on washable shirts and skirts need not be lined. Pockets on medium to heavy-weight, non-washable materials (those used for dress clothes or tailored garments) do need to be lined.

Here is an easy way to line a pocket.

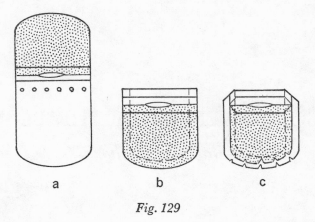

a   b   c

Fig. 129

1. Stitch the lining to the hem of the pocket, leaving a small opening at the center of the seam (Fig. 129a). Press the seam allowances open.

2. Fold the pocket along the foldline of the hem with right sides of pocket and lining together.

3. Stitch around the remaining sides of the pocket (Fig. 129b).

4. Grade the seam allowances, free all corners of bulk, notch all curved edges (Fig. 129c).

5. Turn the pocket to the right side through the opening. Carefully work out all corners. Close the hem opening with slipstitching. (No one will ever know how you managed all this unless you tell.)

6. Press the pocket, rolling the joining outside seams to the underside. (Of course, you would have made an allowance for this in the stitching.)

7. Pin the pocket to position on the garment and slipstitch or topstitch.

Bound, welt, and flap pockets are usually associated with tailored garments. These are all dealt with in Part III, Tailored to a *"T"*.

BORROWED FROM THE BOYS
Slacks and Shorts

Slack Happy

It's a fair exchange. If the boys can borrow from us our fancy fabrics and our frills, we can borrow from them the comfort and practicality of pants. So right are they for our active lives that it looks as if we have borrowed them for keeps!

Blue jeans, dungarees, clam diggers, pedal pushers, hot pants, Jamaica shorts, Bermuda shorts, deck pants, toreadors, jodhpurs, breeches, trunks, gaucho pants, frontier pants, Capri pants, classic trousers, palazzo pajamas, "at homes" of lace, velvet, brocade, lamé, chiffon; even those hybrids known as culottes—part skirt, part pants. Skinny, straight, flared pants; long, short, in-between pants. Just so they are pants. Too good a thing to let the males alone corner the market.

Finicky About Fit

It's not the sewing that is the problem with making your own pants. It's the fitting. Anyone who can stitch a seam can make slacks or shorts, but making them fit is another matter. While good fit is important in everything one makes, it is imperative in pants.

Men and boys don't appear to be too troubled about wrinkles in the rear or baggy seats. But we girls are pretty finicky about the fit of our pants.

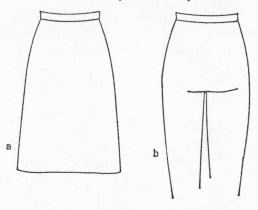

Fig. 130

Whatever one's problems are in fitting a skirt, they are magnified when fitting pants. In a skirt, the mass (speaking of design, now, not you) of the waist-to-hip area is balanced by the length and width of the lower skirt (Fig. 130a). In pants, the lower area is divided by the vertical lines of the pant leg (Fig 130b). This may make your legs look slimmer, but, by comparison, the upper part looks larger than it really is. What to do?

1. Choose a style that is best for your figure. Try on some slacks or shorts to get an idea of what is most becoming. You'll soon find which styles reveal your bad features and which conceal them. Find a similar pattern.

2. Fit meticulously. Make the necessary pattern changes from your personal measurements. Manipulate the fabric to fit the figure.

Style Lines Streamline

Fortunately, pants are generally designed to minimize a hippy look. In a skirt, the shaping from waist to hips is accomplished by darts and seams with a considerable amount of the shaping allocated to the curved side seams. In slacks and shorts, the side seams are kept fairly straight while most of the shaping is placed at front and back. This in itself produces an illusion of straightness which is slimming.

If the ordinary darts and seams don't work well on you, try a style with control seams over the buttocks and over the abdomen (Fig. 131a). This style provides wonderful opportunity for straight-line fitting. Since pants are pressed into a crease along such a line anyway, the style is fashionable and what you've hidden in that seam remains your secret. If you can't find such a pattern, you can create one from any standard pattern. Directions follow.

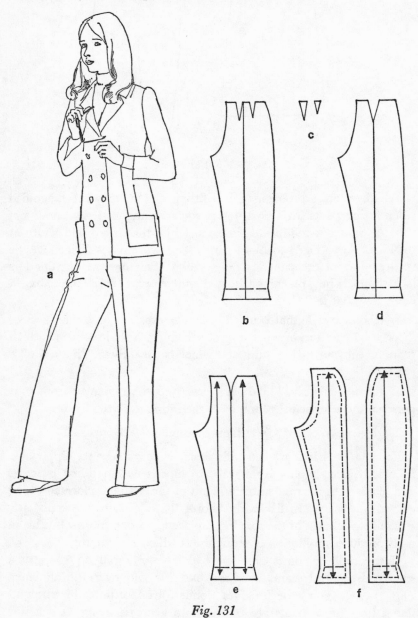

Fig. 131

1. Fold the pattern in half lengthwise. Unfold and draw in the line of the fold (Fig. 131b).

2. Trace the pattern dart or darts on another piece of paper. Cut them out (Fig. 131c).

3. When there is one dart, center it over the dividing line. If there are two darts, combine the amount in one and treat it in the same way. Trace the dart on the pattern (Fig. 131d).

4. Correct the angularity of the new line at the dart point with a gently curved line (Fig. 131e).

5. Draw a grain line in each half of the pattern parallel to the original grain line (Fig. 131e).

6. Cut the pattern in two along the dividing line. Add a seam allowance to both cut edges (Fig. 131f). You could write yourself a note to this effect in big red-penciled letters so you wouldn't ignore the message. Better yet, Scotch-tape a tissue paper seam allowance to the pattern.

Note how the shaping by darts has been converted to shaping by seams. Such a pattern means extra cutting and extra stitching but this is a small price to pay for the extra perfection of fit.

Cut to Fit

While the design of the pants is your first consideration, the second concern is making the standard-size pattern fit your not-so-standard figure. This is even more important in pants than in a skirt. You may salvage a skirt in the seam allowances but you get no second chance to change a crotch, say, once the pants are cut.

Personal Measurements

To determine what changes must be made in the pattern, one needs to have a few personal measurements: waist, hips, thigh, length of pants, depth of crotch. For some styles, you may even need the knee, calf, ankle, and instep measurements (Fig. 132a).

Use the same *waist* and *hip* measurements as for the skirt.

The *thigh* measurement is taken at the fullest part of the upper leg. Note how far below the waistline you are taking this measurement. Add 1 inch for ease.

Measure the *length* of the leg on the side seam from the waistline.

To measure the *crotch* depth, sit on a hard chair. Measure the distance from the waistline to the chair (Fig. 132b).

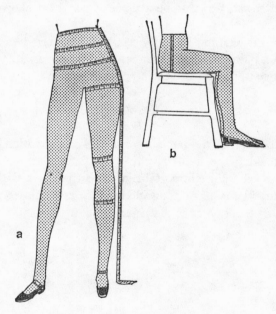

Fig. 132

Compare Measurements

Now examine your pattern and compare with your measurements. Decide where and how much the pattern needs changing. Don't bother with small changes of ⅛ inch or less. They can be absorbed in the seam allowances. Don't forget that you now have four seam allowances (at least) on which you can make changes—center front, center back (crotch seams), and both side seams. Divide what you need by four and make slight changes on each seam. When you make a change on one seam line, you must make a corresponding change on the seam line that will join it.

CROTCH CHANGES

Make crotch changes first. The crotch position on the pattern: a line drawn across the widest part of the crotch at right angles to the grain line (Fig. 133a).

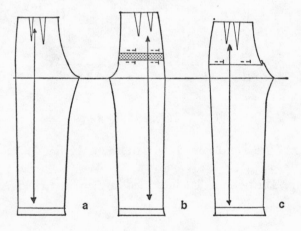

Fig. 133

Too short? Slash the pattern and spread to the desired amount. Fill in the spread with tissue paper (Fig. 133b). Scotch-tape to position.

Too long? Tuck the pattern to the needed amount. Pin or Scotch-tape to position (Fig. 133c).

These are to be made after the crotch changes.

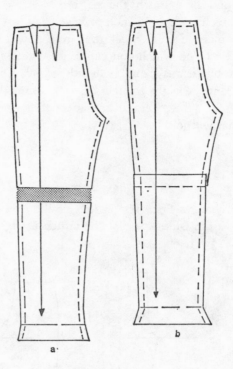

Fig. 134

Too short? Slash and spread the pattern on the line indicated in the pattern (Fig. 134a).

Too long? Tuck on the line indicated in the pattern (Fig. 134b).

WAIST CHANGES

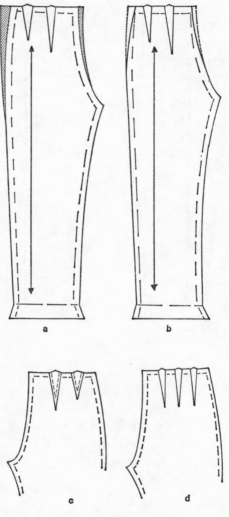

Fig. 135

Too small? Add to the waistline and taper to the hips (Fig. 135a).
Too large? Take off the waistline and taper to the side seams
(Fig. 135b). *Or,* make the darts larger (Fig. 135c). *Or,* create a new
dart (Fig. 135d).

HIP CHANGES

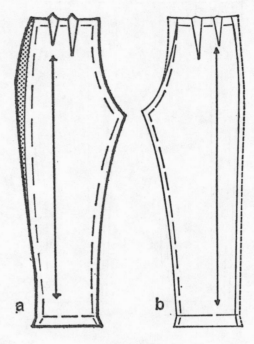

Fig. 136

Too narrow? Add to the side seam and taper to the waist (Fig. 136a).

Too wide? Take off the side seam and taper to the waist (Fig. 136b).

THIGH CHANGES

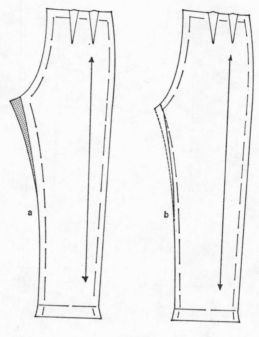

Fig. 137

Too narrow? Add to the inner leg seam (Fig. 137a).
Too wide? Take some away from the inner leg seam (Fig. 137b).

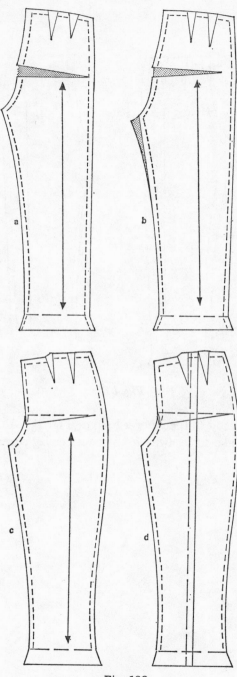

Fig. 138

Large buttocks? Slash and spread on the back crotch seam, taper to the side seam (Fig. 138a). If necessary, add to the inner leg seam (Fig. 138b).

Flat buttocks? Tuck on the back crotch seam, taper to the side seam (Fig. 138c). If necessary, tuck vertically as well (Fig. 138d).

The same kind of corrections are made on the front crotch seam for a protruding or very flat abdomen.

Testing! Testing!

So now you have altered your pattern in accordance with your personal measurements. You think your fitting problems are over? Alas! One can't depend on mathematics alone to guarantee good fit. All arithmetic can give you is length and width and a general idea of the required shaping. That's not enough.

Becomingness, ease of movement, posture, direction of seam line, individualized shaping can only be truly tested in cloth. Not the cloth of your pants. That would be too risky a test since only minor changes can be made at that stage. *A trial muslin* will save you a lot of grief.

Hints on Fitting the Trial Muslin

Baste the leg seams first. Baste the crotch seam. Clip the crotch seam allowance. Baste the waistband in place. It is hard to judge the fit of pants without suspending them from something.

Examine the pants for becomingness and fit. Decide what needs correction.

The front and back vertical grain lines should hang at right angles to the floor. So should the side seams. Check the shaping by darts and seams. As with the skirt fitting, if there is trouble below the hipline, look for the remedy above it. If the waist-to-hip area fits well, the pants will fall straight from the hip to the ankle at front, back, and side.

The darts are an important part of the shaping. You may shorten or lengthen them, diminish or enlarge them to fit the curves of your hips, abdomen, and buttocks.

The waistline should fit snugly. There is somewhat more ease over the hips than there is in a skirt. (Chances are you will probably wear your slacks or shorts when lightly girdled, if at all.) The thigh area should not bind. The crotch must not be too tight.

Knit and stretch fabrics are fitted with less ease because of their elasticity. Suede, leather, canvas, duck, denim, etc. need more ease because of their non-stretchability.

Plan a front or back zipper installation. A side-seam closure has a tendency to make one look hippy.

When there are wrinkles, release the nearest seams and darts and repin to fit (Fig. 139a).

Determine the waistline. If it needs building up, add a strip of muslin. If it needs dropping, trim some away (Fig. 139b).

If the crotch is too tight, let out the inner leg seam. If necessary, add a strip of muslin (Fig. 139c).

If the seat is too baggy, take in some of the pants back on the inner leg seam. Or, pin a horizontal tuck across the buttocks. Perhaps you will need to do both (Fig. 139d).

It's all so logical. Add, subtract, take in, let out, build up, trim away, do whatever is necessary to provide a smooth fit.

Unless you are a loner by choice and particularly partial to the try-on-and-take-off method, find a sewing buddy who will help with the fitting. Under your direction, of course. When you have perfected the fit in the trial muslin, mark all the changes on it with red pencil. Lay the original paper pattern over it and trace all the alterations. Use the corrected pattern rather than the muslin for the layout and cutting. It is more accurate and more reliable.

Basic Pants Pattern

If you like pants and wear them a lot, it is a good idea to make a basic pants pattern.* By superimposing the style pattern on your basic pants pattern, you can tell at a glance what needs changing and how it should be done.

* For instructions on how to make a basic pants pattern and detailed help in fitting, see *How to Make Clothes That Fit and Flatter* by Adele P. Margolis, Doubleday & Company, Inc.

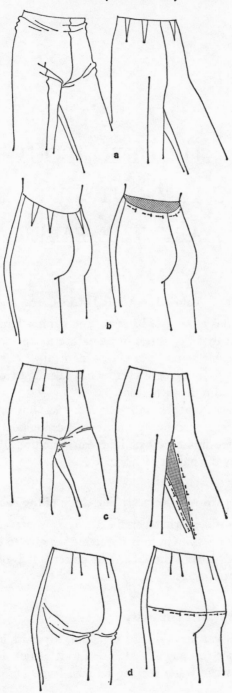

Fig. 139

THINGS TO THINK ABOUT BEFORE
YOU LAY OUT, CUT, AND
MARK THE FABRIC

Fabric Has a Mind of Its Own

Every material has a mind of its own. You cannot force it to do what it does not want to do or is not in its nature to do. For instance, one can't handle marble as one can clay. Or metal as one can wood. Or paper as one can fabric. Or even some fabrics as one can others. Fabric has a mind of its own, also.

All artists learn to *work with the material, not against it.* Great artists may discover previously unknown possibilities in the material but even they are limited by its inherent structure. The artist-sewer, too, is limited by the nature of her cloth.

Regard with Respect: The Grain of the Fabric

Whatever the fiber, whatever the texture, whatever the weave or knit, all cloth has *grain*. Grain is the name we give to either a lengthwise or crosswise yarn of the fabric. In patterns it is often referred to as the "straight of goods."

ALL FABRICS HANG WITH THE GRAIN

Therefore, all garments do. In fact, they'll persist in hanging with the grain whether you pay any attention to it or not. It's one of those scientific verities like water seeking its own level. Disregard the grain and you may end up with an effect you hadn't planned, didn't anticipate, and can't abide.

So necessary to the appearance and fit of a garment is the grain of the fabric that a wise sewer learns at the very start of her sewing career to regard with respect the grain of her fabric. That will make the difference between a great garment and a great disaster.

Prepare the Fabric for Cutting

As set up in the loom, the vertical and horizontal yarns are always at right angles to each other. That is how the loom works. That is how the fabric comes off the loom—grain perfect.

Were one able to buy the raw fabric (assuming one would want to) directly as it is taken off the loom and were it carefully cut to your length along the filler thread, then you would have material in perfect condition for the layout and cutting. Obviously, we don't buy our fabrics fresh off the loom, nor do we use them in an unfinished state, nor are sales people generally so accurate in cutting. So we have problems.

Problem Number One: Fabric Finished Off-grain

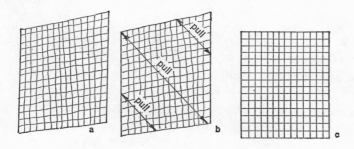

Fig. 140

Often in the finishing process, fabric is pulled off-grain in just about the same way that you might press a handkerchief out of its rectangular shape (Fig. 140a). Just as you can pull or press your handkerchief back into shape, so can your material be corrected in the same way.

Pull the grain in the opposite direction (on the bias) (Fig. 140b) until the yarns are restored to their original rectangular position (Fig. 140c). If pulling dry fabric doesn't straighten the grain, dampen the cloth first or steam press it to position on the wrong side. Caution: don't dampen silk. It water spots. You will have to pull and press the dry silk material to position as best you can.

Problem Number Two: Fabric Printed Off-grain

Fig. 141

Sometimes fabric is printed off-grain (Fig. 141). This does not happen often since there are frequent checks. But it does happen often enough to make some yardage imperfect. Sometimes this escapes detection, so you may occasionally run across such a piece of material. Generally, the imperfection is spotted, whereupon the factory rejects it. That doesn't mean it isn't sold, and, unfortunately, used. Such fabrics find their way into the mill-end stores and onto bargain counters where they turn out to be not such bargains after all.

Fabric printed off-grain presents a real problem for the sewer. If you straighten the grain, the printed design may march itself downhill. If you follow the print, the fabric will hang lopsided because it is cut off-grain. What to do? Of the two evils, the lesser is to follow the printed design and hope for the best. Moral: examine fabric carefully before buying.

Problem Number Three: Fabric Cut Off-grain

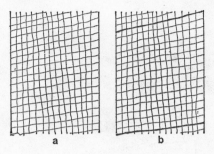

a   b

Fig. 142

This is the problem most frequently encountered in piece goods: the fabric is cut off-grain. Unintentionally, of course. The cut may be made straight across the material but if that has been pulled off-grain to begin with, the cut will also be off-grain (Fig. 142a). The heavy line in Fig. 142b shows the true grain.

How to Restore Fabric to True Grain

Before one can proceed with the layout and cutting of any garment, the true grain must be restored. The same is true of everything that goes inside the garment—interfacing, underlining, lining, interlining.

To restore the vertical and horizontal yarns to their original rectangular position, it is necessary to straighten *both horizontal cut ends*.

You're in luck if the fabric has a prominent yarn, rib, line, or stripe. Just cut along one of these.

Next best, though just as easy and just as quick, is to tear the material on the horizontal grain. Many fabrics tear easily without any ill effects. You had better test, however. Make a short snip through the selvage and into the fabric with the point of a pair of sharp scissors. Tear.

FOR HARD-TO-TEAR WEAVES

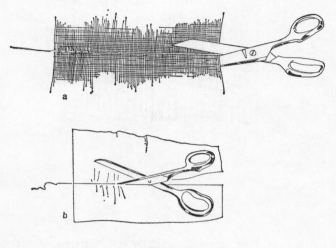

Fig. 143

In hard-to-tear weaves, straighten the horizontal grain by the following method.

Pull a crosswise yarn, hold the fabric up to the light so you can see the space left by the drawn yarn, and cut (Fig. 143a). Don't attempt to do the whole row in one fell swoop. You'll never make it. The thread will break. Pull a short distance, then cut, repeat until you are clear across the width.

Sometimes the material gathers along the pulled thread. Cut a few inches between the gathers (Fig. 143b). Repeat until the whole width is straightened.

In either case, you know you've been successful when you can lift one horizontal yarn across the entire width.

This should not be a lengthy process. If it takes you forever, you're doing something wrong. Start again.

Have you noticed that we have been talking solely about the horizontal grain that needs straightening? We need not concern ourselves about the vertical grain. That has already been established by the loom along the selvage, which is the vertical grain.

Knit Goods Have Grain Too

Did you think you would avoid the whole business of straightening the grain by sticking with knits? It won't work. Knit goods have grain too.

In knitted fabric *a lengthwise rib is the vertical grain*. One can't assume that the fold of a tubular knit is the lengthwise grain any more than one can assume that a straight cut across woven material is the horizontal grain. The knitted fabric may have been folded off-grain.

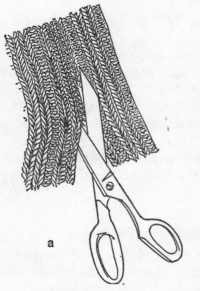
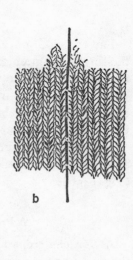

Fig. 144

Find a lengthwise rib and follow it throughout the length of the fabric. If you have sharp eyesight and a steady hand, or if the knit has a prominent rib, cut along it directly (Fig. 144a). When the ribs are not so easy to follow by eye, study a few inches at a time and mark with a line of guide basting (Fig. 144b). Cut beside the thread.

Don't worry about losing that convenient fold which you had hoped to use for your layout. You shouldn't use it any way. The crease can never be pressed out. Make a new fold where necessary.

The *horizontal grain of knitted fabrics* is a crosswise course. When this is prominent, it's easy enough to cut along it for the horizontal grain. When it is not, the horizontal grain must be established at right angles to the vertical grain.

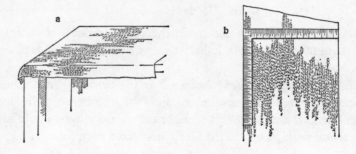

Fig. 145

Lay the cloth on a flat surface (table, desk, cutting board) with the lengthwise grain along one straight edge. Place the fabric in such manner that you can use a corner to determine the right angle (Fig. 145a). Weight the material with books or any other safe, weighty object to hold the fabric in position. Using tailor's chalk, trace along the horizontal edge.

Or better yet, use a drafting tool—a right-angle triangle, an L-square, a T-square. Square the horizontal grain off the vertical grain (Fig. 145b).

A Precautionary Measure: Buy More

As you can see, you may lose inches of your precious material by the time you have straightened both ends. Knowing this, it would be wise to buy a little more fabric than the amount suggested in the pattern.

Prepare the Pattern: The Hang of It

The designer uses the grain of the fabric for style, for fit, and for the hang of the material.

Because of the taut setting of the lengthwise yarns in the loom, the lengthwise grain is straighter, stronger, and more stable than the horizontal grain. Most garments are cut so they hang with the lengthwise grain (Fig. 146a), that is, the up and down of the pattern lies along the lengthwise yarns (Fig. 146b).

Fig. 146

Fig. 147.

Sometimes for decorative purposes a pattern is placed so the length-wise grain runs across it rather than up and down (Fig. 147a). Because the firmer warp yarns tend to make the fabric have less "give" on the cross grain, it is best used in small areas—a yoke, for instance (Fig. 147b) or where one would prefer a stiffer effect—a bouffant or dirndl skirt, for example (Fig. 147c).

The line that cuts diagonally across the warp and filler threads is the bias (Fig. 148a). The bias is the hypotenuse of a 45-degree triangle.

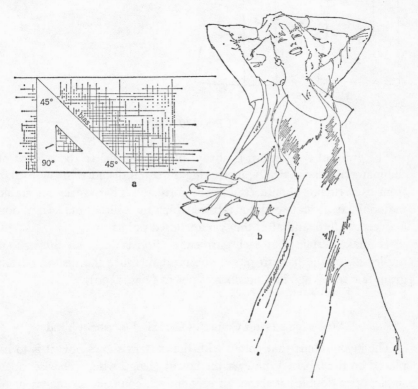

Fig. 148

Bias can be stretched, blocked, shaped. It produces molded, body-clinging, figure-revealing fit (Fig. 148b). Very sexy!

Every pattern piece no matter how small or how large must fit into the general plan. It has its grain marked on it. Sometimes this is indicated by a line with an arrowhead at each end. Sometimes there is a direction: lay on straight of goods (another name for the grain).

Examine the grain line on your pattern. If it does not run the entire length of the pattern piece (Fig. 149a), you must elongate it so it does (Fig. 149b).

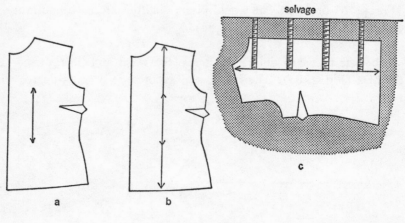

Fig. 149

The grain of the pattern is always placed parallel to the selvage of the material. Theoretically, measuring an equal distance in two places from a given line should establish it correctly. That works for stable materials. It doesn't work for fabrics which may slither out of position between, before, and after the two anchored points.

To make certain that each garment section is *on grain* throughout the length of the pattern piece, one must measure the distance from grain line to selvage in a number of places (Fig. 149c).

"Near 'ems Don't Count": On-grain Placement Vital

The layout chart that comes with the pattern shows how it is to be placed on the fabric. Whatever the layout (lengthwise, crosswise, open single, open double) it shows an economical, compact arrangement of all pattern pieces *on-grain*. You must place them exactly that way—respecting the grain. Don't trust your eye. For accuracy, get out that yardstick or ruler (a tape measure is too unreliable) and really measure each pattern piece from grain line to selvage in as many places as will ensure correct placement throughout. Near 'ems don't count.

Two by Two: The Noah's Ark Principle of Cutting

Wherever possible, cutting is by two's. One either cuts two-of-a-kind or two halves (to be joined by a seam for a whole) or a half-pattern placed on a fold of fabric (to become a whole when unfolded).

Half a pattern is better than a whole pattern for large or balanced sections. It ensures that both sides of the garment are cut alike. It saves time. Folded fabric is not so unwieldy as fabric opened to full width.

When cutting by two's note which two's are in pairs—a right and left, like sleeves (Fig. 150a), and which are just duplicates, like patch pockets (Fig. 150b).

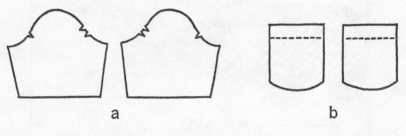

a   b

Fig. 150

Printed Side of Pattern: Face Up or Face Down?

When a pattern is cut by two's or on a fold it doesn't matter whether the printed side of the pattern is face up or face down. You'll get what you need either way. Sometimes a shaded area on the layout chart is used to indicate that the pattern is placed face down. This is simply because the pattern pieces fit more compactly (like a jigsaw puzzle) if laid in a particular way (Fig. 151a).

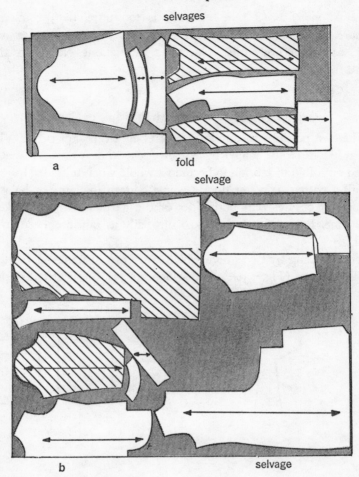

Fig. 151

When a complete pattern is cut singly on a full width of the fabric, it is placed with the printed side up. This is how it will appear in the finished garment.

If a pattern needs to be used more than once or reversed (like the sleeves in Fig. 151b), it is very helpful to trace and cut out an extra one. This can be used to complete the entire layout without lifting the original pattern from the material for replacement.

When a whole pattern rather than the usual half makes the layout easier, trace another half (the shaded area of the back in Fig. 151b). Scotch-tape it to the original pattern.

Each pattern piece has an identifying letter or number. Match it with the one on the layout chart. Note by its shape how each piece is placed on the fabric—face up or face down. Notches are a good clue too.

Pattern Puzzles: The Layout

Pattern pieces vary in size. So do fabric widths. To fit the one on the other makes for a variety of possible layouts. It's like playing with a giant puzzle. The game is to place the pieces in such fashion as to use the width and length of the material most economically.

Fabric Arrangements

Here are the fabric arrangements that are used.

LENGTHWISE FOLD

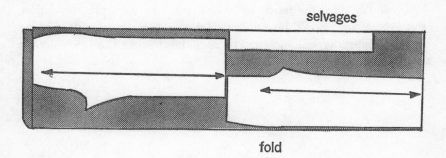

Fig. 152

With right sides inside, fold the fabric in half lengthwise, matching the selvages and the straightened ends (Fig. 152).

CROSSWISE FOLD

Use for pattern pieces too wide to fit half the width of the fabric.

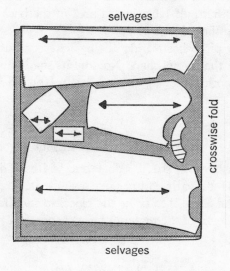

Fig. 153

With the fabric opened to its full width, fold it in half crosswise, right sides inside (Fig. 153). Match the selvages and the straightened ends.

Obviously were the fabric to have a one-way nap, pile, or design, this type of fold would be ruinous. Half the garment would be going up and the other half down. For such fabrics use the open double layout.

OPEN DOUBLE

Use for fabrics that have nap, pile, or directional design.

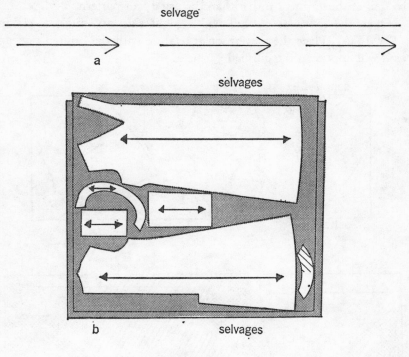

Fig. 154

Mark the direction of the fabric design or nap with chalked arrows along the selvage (Fig. 154a). Measure the amount of fabric needed for the complete one-way layout. (This calls for a trial layout.) Cut at the determined length along the crosswise straight of goods. Swing the fabric around so both layers are going in the same direction. (The arrows will indicate this.) Place the two thicknesses together open full width, right sides inside (Fig. 154b).

OPEN SINGLE—FULL WIDTH

Asymmetric and bias designs provide a complete pattern for a section of the garment rather than the usual half-pattern.

Open the fabric to its full width, right side up, single thickness (Fig. 155a). Place the pattern on the fabric with the printed side up as it will appear in the finished garment.

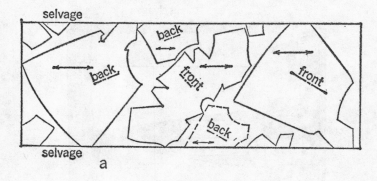

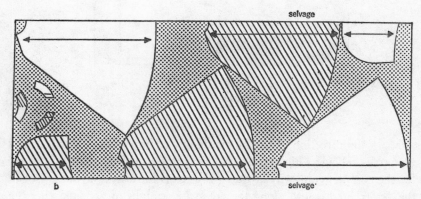

Fig. 155

Sometimes the pattern pieces are so wide, that each section must be placed individually on the full width of the fabric (Fig. 155b).

A DOUBLE FOLD

Sometimes each of several pattern pieces needs to be on a fold. For instance, the center front and center back of a skirt that need to be so placed.

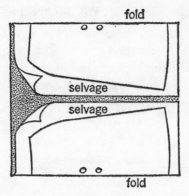

Fig. 156

Measure the widest part of the pattern. Mark this measurement in from the selvage in a sufficient number of places to provide an accurate foldline. With right sides inside, fold along the marked line (Fig. 156). When the fabric has a visible weave, stripe, plaid, or check, fold along it instead of measuring.

COMBINATIONS

One part of the garment is laid on one type of fold, another part on a different fold.

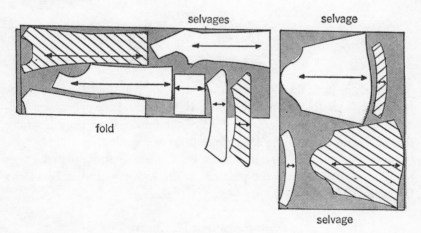

Fig. 157

You can only fold fabric one way at a time. Pin the pattern on the fabric in one layout. Cut it out. Then pin and cut out another (Fig. 157). Repeat as many times as necessary.

How Do You Know Which Layout to Use?

Happily for you, this has all been worked out for you. Included in your pattern is a chart indicating a number of possible layouts. Choose the one planned for your size, the view of the design you are making, and the width of the fabric. Circle the chart with colored pencil so you have no trouble remembering which layout you are using (Fig. 158).

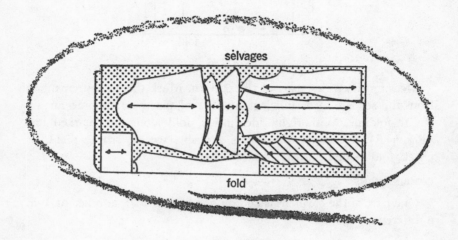

Fig. 158

Fabric Face-saving

When you have decided which layout is for you, fold the fabric appropriately (if fold there must be), right sides inside whenever possible. This not only protects the face of the fabric, it places the wrong side of the material in the correct position for marking.

Place the selvages together and pin. Place the straightened edges together and pin. Place the pattern on the fabric as indicated in the layout and pin.

Hints on Pattern Placement

When the layout chart shows a complete pattern piece, half of which is shaded, it means the pattern is cut on a fold in that space. A complete shaded pattern indicates it is to be used a second time (Fig. 159a).

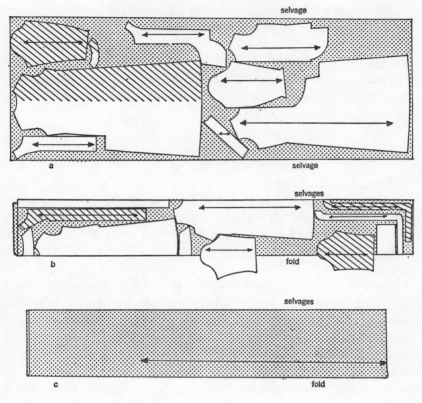

Fig. 159

When a pattern piece is shown extending beyond a folded edge (Fig. 159b), it means this piece must be cut in that space after all the other pieces have been cut and the remainder of the cloth is opened. Rather than re-establishing the grain line in this cut-away piece (you may not have enough material were you to pull threads to straighten the fabric again), establish a grain line in the space parallel to the selvage *before* you begin your cutting (Fig. 159c). Use tailor's chalk to do the marking.

In a one-way layout all the pattern pieces are placed going in the same direction—neck to hem.

Place the pattern pieces close together so they dovetail. If you are too generous with spaces between them, you may not have enough material for the entire layout. A trial placement of the pattern is very much in order.

When you are working with plaids, stripes, checks, you have a line in the fabric to go by instead of measuring the grain. To make sure that upper and under layers are cut on the same stripes of the material, pin the two layers together every few inches or so matching the lines. It's easier to do this when the fabric is folded with the right side outside. Right-side-outside also makes it easier to match the plaids, checks, etc.

Pinning the Pattern to the Fabric

Place the folded fabric on a firm surface—a table, a cutting board, the floor if necessary. A bed will not do: it is not firm enough; nor is a carpet. If the surface is not long enough to accommodate the entire length of cloth (and who has one that does?) support what is not on it by a chair or an ironing board. This keeps it from trailing on the floor.

Start at one end of the fabric and place each pattern piece on it following its position on the layout chart. As the pattern is pinned, fold the completed end and pull up more cloth. Repeat the procedure until the entire layout is pinned.

Pin the straight of goods parallel to the selvage first. When that is set, smooth the pattern toward the outer edges and pin the rest.

Keep the pattern and the fabric as flat as possible trying not to raise them from the cutting surface any more than necessary.

Use one hand as an anchor and the other to pin.

The pins must go through the pattern and both thicknesses of cloth.

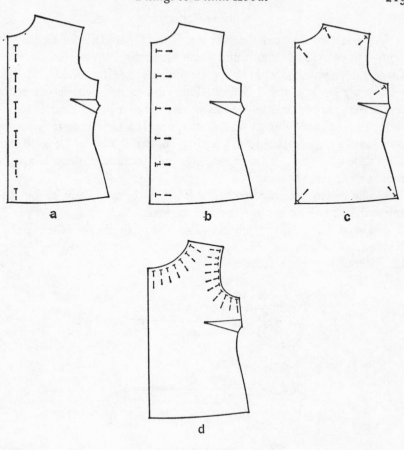

Fig. 160

Pins may be placed parallel to the cutting edge (Fig. 160a) or at right angles to it (Fig. 160b). Pin the corners diagonally (Fig. 160c). Curves take more pins than straight edges (Fig. 160d). Use enough pins to provide a true cutting edge; every few inches will do. Don't use too many: they may make the fabric heave.

When you have finished pinning, you had better go back and compare the layout with that on the chart. Check off each piece that you have pinned to the cloth to make sure you have them all. This is the last chance to catch any errors before cutting. Now you are ready to cut out the fabric. At last!

Cutting Concerns

In a sense cutting out the garment is the Great Divide. Up to this point you can change your mind about anything—any step of the way. Once you've put shears to cloth, your decisions are irrevocable. There's no turning back. Cutting is final. This knowledge is enough to scare any sewer, experienced as well as novice. And it does! Fear is something that anyone who sews must conquer. It's far better to get over this hurdle than to horde a length of material forever because one hasn't the courage to cut. After all, it's only fabric and there is always more to lose your heart to.

1. Cut when you are fresh and alert and least likely to be distracted. You will be less apt to make mistakes.

2. Use a sharp pair of scissors (Fig. 161a) or shears (Fig. 161b). Bent shears (Fig. 161c) are best. The lower blade slides along the table without lifting the fabric.

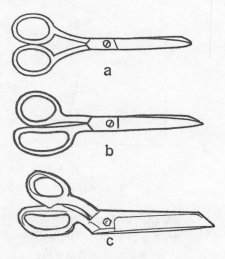

Fig. 161

Don't use pinking or scalloping shears for cutting. They do not give an accurate cutting line. They make it too difficult to judge seam allowances when sewing. They make cutting through the pattern and double thickness of cloth too difficult. Save the pinking or scalloping shears for an edge finish.

3. Keep the cloth and the pattern smooth, flat, and still on the cutting surface. Move around the layout so you are in a comfortable po-

sition for reaching and cutting rather than turning the material to meet you.

4. As in the layout, start at one end of the fabric while the other end is supported or rolled up. The weight of the fabric can be a drag —literally.

5. Use long, firm strokes for the straight edges, short strokes for the curved edges.

6. It may slow up the cutting process a bit but it is safer to cut the notches outward beyond the cutting edge of the pattern (Fig. 162a). Two or three notches may be cut as one shape (Fig. 162b).

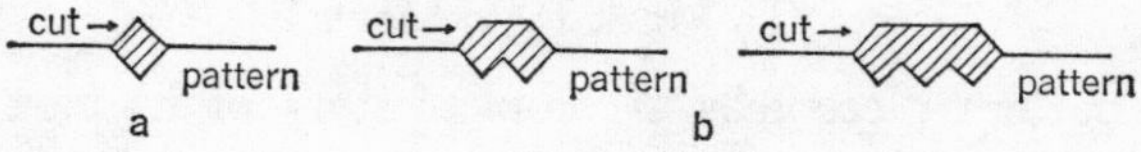

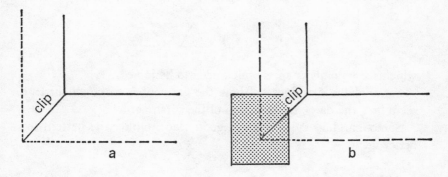

Fig. 162

Notches are those little triangular or diamond shapes on the cutting line of the pattern. They come singly, in pairs or in groups. Sometimes they are numbered in the order in which they are put together. When you find one notch (or more than one) you will find its twin on another section of the garment. The two must be matched. With notches you don't have to puzzle out which section goes with what. The notches tell. They speed up the assembling of a garment.

Fig. 163

7. Where the pattern reads *clip* or *slash*, it is the fabric not the pattern that is to be clipped or slashed. This should not be done until the seam line is first reinforced or stitched. The reinforcement may be

small staystitching (Fig. 163a) or a lightweight facing (Fig. 163b). A patch of organza or a strip of seam binding are often used for this purpose.

8. As each section is cut out, lay it flat or hang it on a hanger. If you must fold it for storage, make as few loose folds as possible. Keep the pattern side out for protection and for easy identification.

There is no doubt about it, cutting out the fabric is one of the hard, backbreaking, tedious parts of sewing. Be comforted by the thought that once the garment is cut out, you're well on your way.

To Mark It, to Mark It!

Every pattern piece tells a complete story of its part in the construction (Fig. 164). Even were you to lose that fateful sheet of pattern directions, you could still put your garment together with all the information you will find on the pattern itself.

Some of the markings are for identification: the name of the pattern company, the number of the pattern, the name of the pattern piece, its number or letter.

Some of the markings show how the pattern is to be laid on the fabric and cut out: the fold of the fabric, the grain line, the cutting line.

Some of the markings show how the garment is to be assembled: the notches, special markings like

$$\bigcirc \quad \circ \quad \triangle \quad \square$$

which show points or spots which need to be joined.

Some of the markings tell how the garment is to be stitched: the seam line, the darts, the direction of the stitching.

Some markings tell where is a good place to alter the pattern for a better fit.

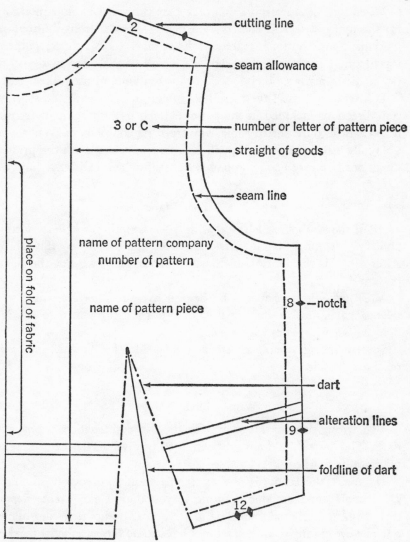

cutting line

seam allowance

3 or C — number or letter of pattern piece

straight of goods

seam line

name of pattern company
number of pattern

name of pattern piece

8 — notch

place on fold of fabric

dart

alteration lines

9

foldline of dart

12

Fig. 164

When you get into more complex patterns you will find markings for the many style and construction details—center front, buttonhole placement and buttons, extension folds, dart tucks, pleats, gathers, topstitching, and so on. The symbols for all of these are made up of perforations, arrows, notches, solid or broken lines, printed directions.

It is wise to "read" these symbols in conjunction with the step-by-step directions included in the pattern. Each pattern company strives to be a little different in some way from its competitors. When you are really a skilled sewer, you will be able to dispense with the printed directions but as of now, you had better study them carefully.

Leave Your Mark

All of the symbols which deal with the *assembling, stitching, fitting,* and *style details* must be transferred from the pattern to the fabric. After all, it is the fabric which will be your garment, not the tissue pattern.

Mark everything that will be helpful to you. The more time you take to mark, the less time it will take to put the garment together. No figuring out what goes with what.

Some markings are placed on the wrong side of the fabric and some on the right side.

Wrong-side Markings

The wrong-side markings are for the big construction seams and darts. The darts should always be marked precisely. The seams may or may not be marked.

Do mark the seam line when seams require precision stitching. *Don't* mark the seam line *if* fitting to your figure may create departures from the original seam line *or if* you can judge the seam allowance by eye. Many sewing machines have some measurements marked on the throat plate. If yours doesn't you can make your own marking with masking tape or with a fine line of nail polish. It is a help to have the measurements right on the machine.

MARKING MATERIALS

Wrong-side markings may be made with tailor's chalk, dressmaker's carbon paper, or basting thread.

Tailor's chalk is safe and quick. It is easy to apply and easy to brush off. Here's how to use it:

1. Make perforations in the pattern in enough places to mark a dart, seam, or spot marking. Use any suitable sharp instrument, an orange stick, a pencil, an embroidery stiletto. Be careful not to mar the fabric.

2. Place a pin through each perforation being sure to make it go through both thicknesses of fabric (Fig. 165).

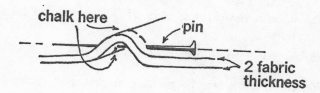

Fig. 165

3. Chalk the area caught by the pin on both upper and under sides.

Dressmaker's carbon paper is a great marking device but must be used with caution. (Note: dressmaker's carbon is *not* typewriter carbon.) It is used in conjunction with a tracing wheel. A blunt one is the best kind; it won't tear the pattern.

Do not use dressmaker's carbon on white, light-colored, or sheer materials. It will leave a permanent, visible mark on the fabric. Nor is it effective on vari-colored or textured materials: it simply doesn't show. Better test the marking on a scrap of your material before proceeding. Where you can use dressmarker's carbon, it is a wonderful stitching guide.

How to mark with dressmaker's carbon paper (Fig. 166).

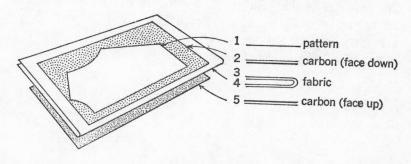

Fig. 166

1. Unpin a small section of the pattern. Always do a small section at a time. Unpinning the entire pattern to position the carbon is too risky. You may not get it back again precisely. Besides, it doesn't come in sheets sizes large enough to do it that way.

2. Slip a sheet of dressmaker's carbon paper of a contrasting color between the pattern and the fabric. Place the coated side against the fabric.

3. Slip a second sheet of carbon paper under the lower thickness of cloth with the coated side against the fabric. In effect, you are enclosing the fabric with the carbon paper so both sides can be marked simultaneously.

4. Carefully replace the pattern and pin in just enough places to hold all in position.

5. Using the tracing wheel, carefully mark the seam line. Use a ruler for the straight lines; it's easier to trace with one. Trace the curved lines freehand carefully following the line on the pattern.

6. Unpin the pattern, remove the carbon, slide it along to a new section and repeat. Make sure the new marking is a continuation of the old.

Right-side Markings

Some markings are necessary on the right side of the garment while the work is in progress—the position of the pocket, a buttonhole, or a button, the center front, a foldline for a facing or a pleat, etc. You can't take chances with anything that may mar the beautiful surface of the cloth. Who wants to start with the cleaning fluid before a garment has even been worn?

The safest right-side marking is basting thread of a contrasting color. It can be easily removed when it has served its purpose and leaves no trace that it has been there.

When it is a line you want to indicate, use *guide basting:*

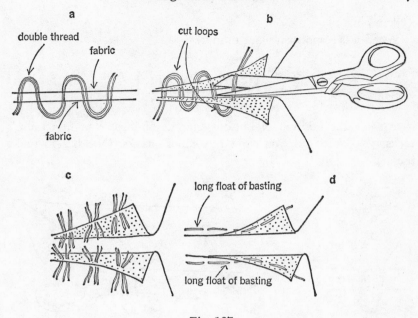

Fig. 167

1. Using a double thread, make a line of basting through the pattern and both layers of the fabric.

2. Leave 1-inch loops of thread between stitches (Fig. 167a).

3. Open the layers of the fabric carefully and cut the thread between, leaving small tufts (Fig. 167b).

4. Clip the stitches that appear on the surface of the pattern to release them (Fig. 167c).

5. Carefully remove the pattern.

6. Since the tufts of thread may pull out, immediately replace them with a line of guide basting (Fig. 167d).

7. Remove the tufts.

TAILOR'S TACKS

When it is a spot you want to mark—

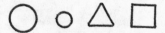

—to show the position of buttons, snaps, joinings, etc.—use tailor's tacks. (No, Virginia, you can't buy tailor's tacks. One has to make them.)

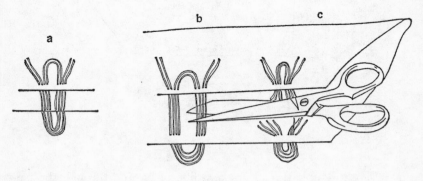

Fig. 168

1. Use a double thread of contrasting color.
2. Puncture a perforation in the pattern at the spot to be marked so the thread is not involved with the tissue.
3. Take a stitch through both thicknesses of the cloth leaving a 1-inch end.
4. Take another stitch in the same place making a 1-inch loop.
5. Repeat steps 3 and 4 making a double loop. Cut the thread leaving a 1-inch end (Fig. 168a).
6. Carefully separate the two layers of cloth until a stitch appears on each outer side. This will hold the tufts in place.
7. Clip the thread between the layers (Fig. 168b). This produces tufts on the right side of the fabric called tailor's tacks (Fig. 168c).
8. Carefully remove the pattern.

Other Markings

Thread may be used in place of a notch on fabrics that ravel. Use a double thread of contrasting color. Make several loops on the very edge of the fabric.

Combinations of Markings

Sometimes it is a good idea to mark the fabric with dressmaker's carbon paper on the wrong side and transfer the markings to the right side with guide basting or tailor's tacks.

Sewing Is Not What It "Seams"

Did you think that sewing means dashing off to your sewing machine as quickly as possible and stitching away madly? Not so! There are really not that many yards of machine stitching in an entire garment. Stitching is but the tip of the iceberg. It's that submerged seven-eighths—the planning, the care, the precision—that is so vital to the beauty of the garment. Sewing is literally not what it "seams."

PART III

TAILORED TO
A "T"

TAILORED TO A "*T*"

Just about the nicest thing anybody can say about your sewing is that it is "Tailored to a *T*." Done to a turn. Fashioned skillfully, gracefully, precisely. It is a goal to which every confirmed sewer aspires.

Don't let the vision of that strictly man's-tailored suit of hard-surfaced worsted put you off. Even the men are departing from it. A whole new breed of tailored clothing has emerged—men's as well as women's—more imaginative in design and made of softer, more easily handled materials: the woolens, double knits, velveteens, cottons, silks, synthetics, and blends.

As is only natural when the styles and fabrics change, some of the traditional tailoring methods must be changed too. Retained however, are the subtle but firm shaping, the miraculous pressing, some of the fine features of construction, and the heritage of a flawless fit.

If you can make a dress you can make a coat or suit. (A coat is easier.) The techniques used for dressmaking are also used in tailoring. The additional techniques required for tailoring supply all the skills needed for advanced dressmaking.

So, tackle your first coat or suit and tailor it to a *T*.

THE SHAPE OF THINGS TO COME
The Understructure

Undercover Support

Have you ever wondered what goes on under cover of cloth that gives a garment its distinctive shape? It's not as mysterious as it seems.

There are two ways to support the lines of a design. One way is to *let the body do all the work of propping-up*. Obviously, you can only get out of that kind of garment the shape you put into it. The second way is to *build the shape right into the garment* via a substructure. By doing this, you can have any shape you want.

The substructure is really a framework on which the fashion fabric is draped or hung. (In this respect it is like the girders of a building which support the finished structure.) When a garment has such support it is said to be structured. When it lacks such support it is said to be unstructured. You will also hear the first type referred to as "hard" tailoring, the second type as "soft" tailoring. Which method you choose depends on the fabric and the fashion.

The vast majority of suits and coats are still structured garments. Even if the soft, unstructured tailoring appears right for a particular garment, you must still know what you are leaving out and how to compensate for it.

Tailoring Is a Many-layered Thing

The fashion fabric is like the icing on a layer cake. It is the come-on, the decoration. The substance lies in the many layers of substructure.

Layer I—The Facing

As we have seen in our previous discussions, all outside edges of a garment need some sort of finish; you would hardly wish to wear one with raggedy, raw edges. In most instances, *the finish is a facing*.

When the edge is a straight one, the facing is simply turned back as in a hem (Fig. 169a), a front closing (Fig. 169b), or a collar (Fig. 169c).

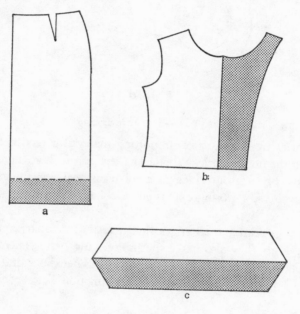

Fig. 169

When the edge is a shaped one, a second layer of fabric cut on the same grain, generally of the same material (though any suitable material is acceptable), to the same shape and near-same size (Fig. 170). The facing is stitched to the garment in such a way as to conceal the joining seam.

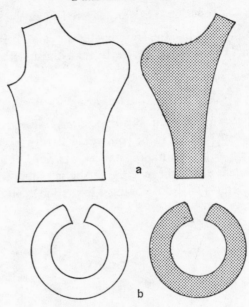

Fig. 170

Layer II—The Interfacing

An interfacing is a layer of supporting material placed between the facing and the outer fabric. Whenever there is a facing, there also will be (or should be) an interfacing: a collarless neckline, the armhole of a sleeveless dress, a closing extension, a collar, cuff, lapel, flap, welt, hem, etc.

Interfacings reinforce all edges that are subject to stress and wear. By adding body they also make the fabric hang better (hems), stand better (collars and cuffs), fit better (collarless necklines and sleeveless styles), look prettier (welts, flaps), and function better (closing extensions).

In dressmaking, the interfacing is limited to the same size, shape, and grain as the facing. In tailoring, the interfacing assumes more size and importance.

THE INTERFACING IN TAILORING

In tailoring, the interfacing is extended to include the shoulder-armhole-and-bust area in front and the shoulder-and-armhole area in back.

The simplified and often abbreviated interfacing patterns included in some commercial patterns are not sufficient to produce the subtle, firm shape of professional tailoring. Nor do they support the exact lines of the design.

Check the interfacings in your pattern. If they are not enough to achieve the desired effect, make your own interfacing patterns. While this may be a little extra work, it pays off by providing elegant shaping and support.

How to Make Your Own Interfacing Pattern

1. On the style pattern, draw the over-all outline of the interfacing.

2. Either cut the original pattern apart (when you don't intend to use it again) or trace the interfacing pattern onto a fresh piece of paper (when you do intend to use the pattern again).

The Over-all Outline of the Front Interfacing

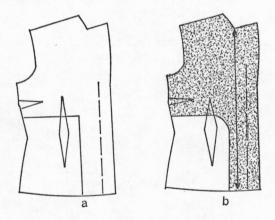

a   b

Fig. 171

1. Carry the interfacing across the shoulder and chest to the arm-hole and across the bust to the side seam (Fig. 171a).

2. Bring the interfacing 3½ to 4 inches down from the armhole on the side seam (excluding darts) or as far down as may be necessary to include any underarm shaping.

3. Make the remainder of the interfacing from the cross line to the hem ½ inch wider than the facing, itself, so the inner edges of both are graded.

4. With a curved line, correct the corner where the horizontal and vertical edges of the interfacing meet (Fig. 171b).

5. Trace the grain line and the notches.

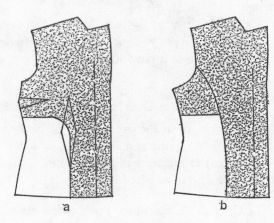

Fig. 172

Should the width of the above interfacing bring the inner edge close to a dart or seam, carry the interfacing all the way over to the center of the nearest dart (Fig. 172a) or to the nearest seam (Fig. 172b). These are logical stopping places.

The Front Shaping

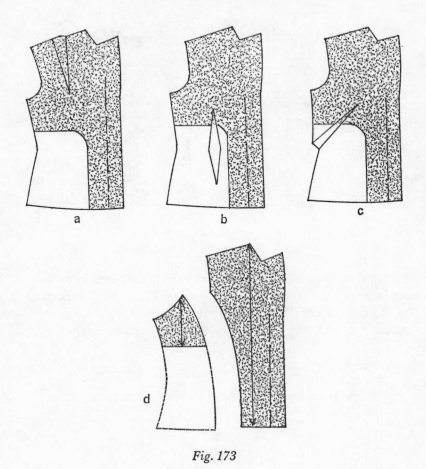

Fig. 173

1. Include any darts that lie completely within the over-all outline (Fig. 173a).

2. Include 1½ to 2 inches of the tops of any vertical darts (Fig. 173b) or any angled darts (Fig. 173c).

3. Include any shaping seams that lie within this area. Cut as many sections of interfacing as there are sections of outer fabric (Fig. 173d).

When the Facing Is Cut All in One with the Garment

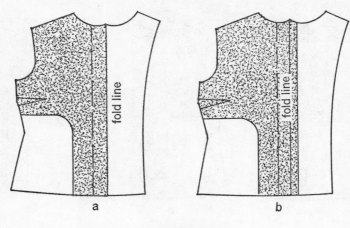

Fig. 174

When the facing is cut all in one with the jacket or coat, cut the interfacing only to foldline for a crisp edge (Fig. 174a) or extend it ½ to ⅝ inch beyond the foldline for a soft edge (Fig. 174b).

Keep in mind that it is the garment that gets interfaced, not the facing.

The Over-all Outline of the Back Interfacing

Fig. 175

1. Bring the back interfacing 3½ to 4 inches down on the center back and a distance down on the side seam to match that of the front interfacing.

2. Join these two points with a flattened S-curve from the center back to the underarm seam (Fig. 175).

The long, bias sweep of the S-curve provides "give" for the forward movement of the arms. A no-stretch straight line would restrict such action. Often the back interfacing is cut on the bias to provide even more ease of movement.

THE BACK SHAPING

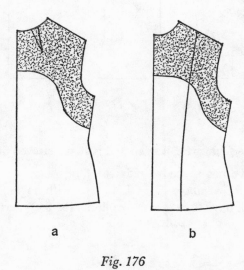

a   b

Fig. 176

1. Include any darts that lie within this over-all outline (Fig. 176a).

2. Include any seams that lie within this over-all outline (Fig. 176b). Cut as many sections of interfacing as there are sections of outer fabric.

An Underarm Section

When there is an underarm section rather than an underarm seam, follow the same general outline as for the front and back interfacings but divide the area into its several parts (Fig. 177).

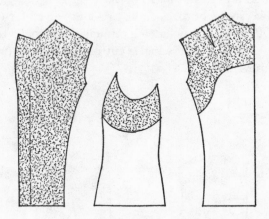

Fig. 177

Interfacings for Raglan and Kimono-sleeved Styles

A set-in sleeve has a ready-made stopping place for the extended interfacing at the armhole. This is not so with raglan and kimono sleeves. You will have to set your own limits for the interfacings.

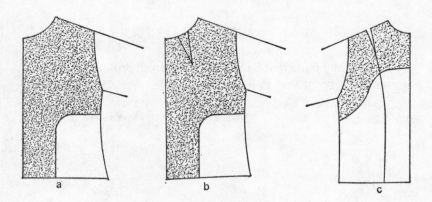

Fig. 178

1. Measure the length of your shoulder from neck to shoulder socket bone. Add ½ inch to this length for the shoulder width of the garment. (A tailored garment is worn over blouses, sweaters, dresses and needs a little more room.)

2. Mark the new shoulder point on the pattern.

3. Draw a curved line from the shoulder point to the underarm seam (Fig. 178a) on both front and back patterns. The rest of the interfacing is the same as that of the set-in sleeve.

4. Include any darts (Fig. 178b) and seams (Fig. 178c) that lie within this over-all outline. Cut as many sections for the interfacing as there are in the pattern for the outer fabric.

5. Trace the grain line and the notches.

Yoke Designs

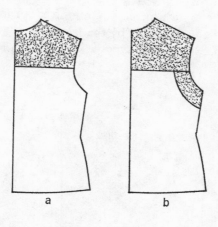

a   b

Fig. 179

If a garment has a yoke design, interface the entire yoke (Fig. 179a). Sometimes an underarm section is added (Fig. 179b).

Layer III—Total Support: The Underlining or Backing

Some fabrics either alone or interfaced may not be able to sustain the lines of the design. They need *total support*. Total support is supplied by an *underlining*, often called a backing.

An underlining is cut from the same pattern as the outer fabric and applied to its underside. When the two fabrics are joined, a new fabric is created that has the surface appeal of the original plus the character of the underlining. For instance: chiffon underlined with crepe is no longer chiffon and no longer crepe; it is crepe-backed chiffon and can be used in an entirely different manner than either crepe or chiffon. A loosely woven wool underlined with Siri or Si Bonne is no longer a limp wool but a firm one which can be used for designs that call for firm fabric.

Undoubtedly it may seem more logical to use a firm material to begin with. But then fashion isn't really logical. Think what fun a surprise or unorthodox use of fabric can be. By the use of an underlining any effect becomes possible and the choice of fabric for design is limitless.

Either or Both

If you underline a garment do you also need an interfacing? That depends on (a) the design and (b) the fabric.

For a sweater-like or Chanel-type jacket an underlining is sufficient (Fig. 180a).

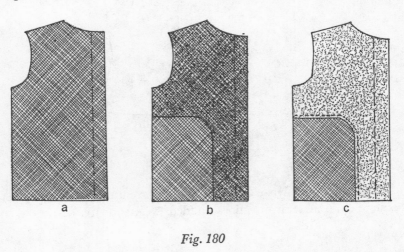

a   b   c

Fig. 180

A loosely woven or lacy fabric may be underlined first to conceal the interfacing (Fig. 180b).

A closely woven but supple fabric may be firmed up by a combination of interfacing and underlining joined as one layer (Fig. 180c).

Interface the part you normally would; underline the rest. Join the two by overlapped seams (see page 254).

Sometimes several different kinds of supporting material are used in one garment, each performing a specific function in a particular part of the garment. Often an entire shell is constructed and placed under the fashion fabric (Fig. 181).

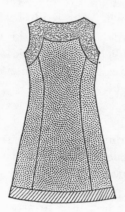

Fig. 181

What to Use? The Interfacing and Underlining Materials

Were you making a costume for a pageant or a play you would use anything that could produce the look you wanted. You wouldn't balk at a substructure of bone, steel, wire, wood, or whatever. (Once upon a time all of these *were* used. Just thumb through your history books and examine the pictures of the period costumes.) Fortunately, you don't have to go to such lengths for tailoring—or dressmaking, either. You should, however, retain the same freedom to use any materials— if they work! The only test is will *this* supporting material produce and hold the lines of *this* design in *this* particular fabric.

Theoretically, any fabric can be used as an interfacing or under-lining. Many dress materials are so used: organdy, organza, lawn, muslin, crepe, taffeta, net, etc. However, there have been a number of supporting materials especially developed for such purposes.* So great a variety are commercially available for the home sewer as to be bewildering. You probably know the names from the extensive ad-

* For a complete list of materials commercially available see *The Complete Book of Tailoring* by Adele P. Margolis, Doubleday & Company, Inc.

vertising with which each company makes its extravagant claims. Experience with these materials will soon disclose which you prefer.

Supporting materials are divided into three classes: the wovens, the non-wovens, and the fusibles (iron-ons). They vary in character—limp to stiff. They vary in weight—light to heavy. They vary in width —18 inches to 72 inches. They vary in price. They vary in cleanability: some are washable, some are dry cleanable. Some come in an array of colors, some come in neutrals.

Interfacings are generally compatible in weight with the fabrics they interface. That is, lightweight fabric—lightweight interfacing, medium-weight fabric—medium-weight interfacing, heavyweight fabric—heavyweight interfacing.

Underlinings, however, may be of any weight or any texture that will give the desired effect.

Interfacing and underlining materials are used interchangeably. What is underlining in one garment may be interfacing in another. What is interfacing in one can be underlining in another. There are no rules. It's a case of using your judgment.

Woven interfacings are best used in areas that require suppleness or that are to be blocked, that is, shaped over a mold or press pad. Of the wovens, the best known and most frequently used are hair canvas, Siri, Formite, and Si Bonne. There are many on the market more or less similar to Si Bonne.

Non-woven interfacings are fine for belled, bouffant, or stiff details. In this group are Pellon, Evershape, Keyback, Interlon, and Kyrel. They are not suitable for areas that need to be blocked.

The fusibles are good for small areas. Use them to stiffen standing collars, cuffs, belts, and as a reinforcement for areas to be slashed like buttonholes and bound pockets. There are many iron-ons available: Pellomite, Sta-Flex, Keyback, Adheron, Interlon, Pressto, Weldex. There also is the fusion material called Stitch Witchery.

Hair Canvas: The Classic Interfacing Material for Tailoring

The classic interfacing material for tailoring is *hair canvas*. It comes in light, medium, and heavy weights and in a variety of fibers—cotton, wool, linen, synthetic, and blends.

What makes hair canvas so very special is the goat's hair or horse hair woven into its filler yarns. The hair gives the canvas its springiness, its resilience, its ability to cling to wool. Cut to take advantage of its crosswise roll (Fig. 182), it is ideal for a lapel, a rolled collar, or cuff.

Fig. 182

The softest hair canvas is made of wool. Use this for the soft fabrics: the cashmeres, the camel hairs. Use this, too, for the soft, wrapped styles.

The stiffest hair canvas is that made of synthetic fiber. Use it *only* in places where considerable stiffening is necessary.

The most generally used hair canvases are those of medium-weight linen or cotton. The texture of these falls somewhere between the two extremes. They are firm yet pliable. They provide the shaping of most jackets and coats.

THE CLASSIC TAILORED COLLAR

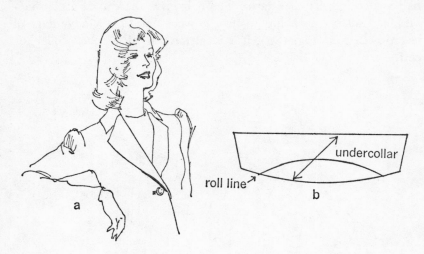

Fig. 183

The collar associated with classic tailoring is a neck-hugging, notched, set-on collar (Fig. 183a). The best interfacing for this collar is *tailor's linen*. When cut on the bias from the under collar pattern (Fig. 183b), it molds well and fits beautifully.

For a similar collar on a dropped neckline (more usual in women's tailoring) use hair canvas.

TOO MUCH OF A GOOD THING—WHICH TO CHOOSE?

Since there is such a variety of interfacing and underlining materials to choose from, it isn't always easy to make a decision as to which to use. The safest thing to do when you shop for interfacing and underlining material is to take with you a sample of your fabric and a picture of the design. Slip the interfacing or underlining under the fashion fabric. Study the effect. Decide whether the weight, finish, texture, degree of flexibility, softness, firmness, or crispness will produce the design of your pattern.

Layer IV—Winter-proof for Warmth: The Interlining

A coat or suit may be winter-proofed for warmth by the insertion of an interlining between the interfaced garment and the lining. Lamb's wool is the material most often used.

A PATTERN FOR THE INTERLINING

Even if the pattern doesn't call for it, it is possible to interline a coat or jacket. Use the lining pattern (Fig. 184a) and make the following changes:

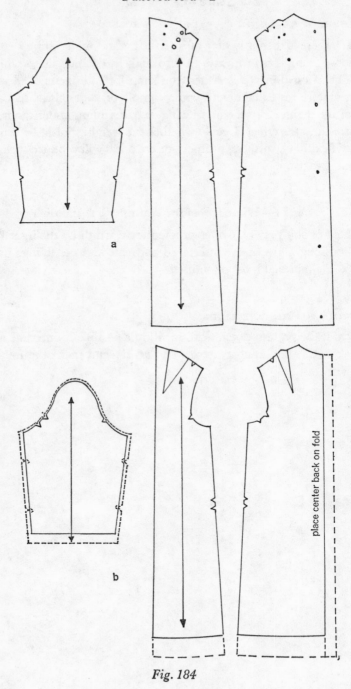

a

b

place center back on fold

Fig. 184

1. Eliminate the center-back pleat.

2. Extend the lines of the front-shoulder dart-tuck until they converge to form a dart.

3. Trim away the seam allowances at the front facing, the back facing, and the hem.

4. Allow only ¼-inch seam allowances at the shoulder, the armhole, and the sleeve cap for overlapping seams.

Fig. 184b shows the interlining pattern derived from the lining pattern.

WARMTH VIA A QUILTED, KNIT, OR PILE-FABRIC LINING

Another presently fashionable way to add warmth is via a quilted, knit, or pile-fabric lining. Such bulky linings double as lining-interlinings. They contain features of both. The pattern is like the one for the interlining. The construction and insertion are like that of the lining except for the outside edges. Obviously, it is important to reduce the bulk of such linings wherever possible.

1. Choose a style that has enough fullness to accommodate the bulkiness.

2. Eliminate the center-back pleat of the lining pattern. Convert the front-shoulder dart-tuck into a dart.

3. Trim away the seam allowances of all outside edges. Finish them with seam binding. Attach the binding to the garment.

4. Make the sleeves of an easy-to-get-into silky material.

5. Avoid turn-unders and double thicknesses wherever possible.

Layer V—The Last of the Layers—The Lining

The lining is the last of the layers. It is conceivable that by now there are many layers of surprising goodies that constitute the inner workings of your garment, none of which you would want anyone to see. That's what a lining is for. It's a cover-up!

The Lining as Cover-up

While this is not meant to be an encouragement for botched work, one has to admit that a lining—be it for dress, skirt, coat, or jacket—does conceal construction, perhaps errors, certainly shortcuts, and shaping secrets.

Fig. 185

Most linings are made of silky materials so they will slide on and off easily. That silky feel adds a touch of luxury. Why not also add a splash of color, a dash of pattern, or a toasty-warm texture (Fig. 185)?

The lining must not interfere with the already considerable shaping of the garment. It is designed, stitched, and inserted in such a way as to permit freedom of movement. Therefore, you will find considerable ease in a lining: a pleat at the front shoulder for shaping the bosom instead of the usual dart, a pleat at center back released above and below the waist, and a little extra length at all hems.

The Gentle Persuasion

In deciding how much or how little substructure to use in any garment, be mindful of the fact that anything that goes into the inside of a garment adds to its shape, its body, its weight, and its warmth. Don't get so carried away by the idea of an understructure that you overload your garment with it. Many fabrics need only the gentlest persuasion to keep them in line. It is a joy to wear something that doesn't feel like a suit of armor or weigh a ton. Strike a happy balance.

Does She or Doesn't She? Only Her Tailor Knows for Sure

The fact that so much is going on inside your beautiful garment makes it imperative that the inner construction be as unobtrusive as possible. That handsome fabric and those interesting style lines are the stars of the show. They must not be upstaged by all that undercover stuff. No one but you must know what constitutes the inner construction.

Where the Darts Lie Buried

Lumps and bumps are dead give-aways of where the seams and darts lie buried—that is, if they are joined in the usual manner. They dissolve into nothingness if you follow the methods described below for stitching all seams and darts in the interfacing, underlining, and interlining.

Tailored to a "T"

Keep Your Secret: Join Seams by Overlapping Seam Lines

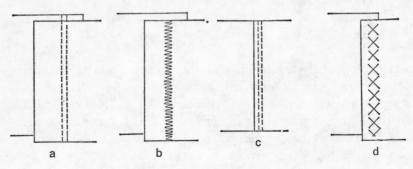

Fig. 186

1. Mark each seam line carefully.

2. Overlap the seam line of one section on the seam line of the other. Pin to position.

3. Stitch. Make two rows of straight stitching—the first directly on the seam line, the second right beside it (Fig. 186a). Or, if your machine can do zigzag stitching, stitch directly over the seam line (Fig. 186b).

4. Trim away the seam allowances on both sides close to the stitching (Fig. 186c).

5. There may be times when the joining is better done by hand stitching. Use the catch stitch or the cross-stitch (Fig. 186d).

JOIN SEAMS OVER TAPE

This is an excellent method for stitching a shaping seam or one that needs special reinforcement.

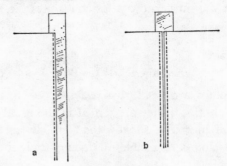

Fig. 187

1. Mark each seam line carefully.
2. Trim away the seam allowance.
3. Cut the required length of tape or a narrow strip of interfacing.
4. Bring one seam line to the center of the strip. Stitch (Fig. 187a).
5. Bring the second seam line to meet the first. Stitch (Fig. 187b).

JOIN DARTS BY OVERLAPPING SEAM LINES

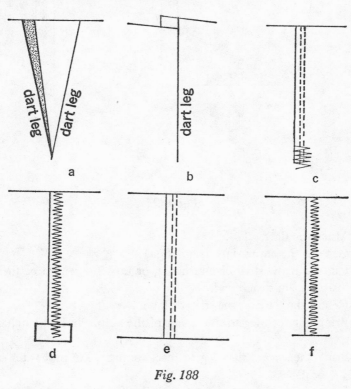

Fig. 188

1. Mark the dart seam lines (legs) carefully.
2. Slash one dart leg to the dart point (Fig. 188a).
3. Overlap the slashed edge on the other dart leg (Fig. 188b).
4. Reinforce the point of the dart with either zigzag stitching (Fig. 188c) or a patch of tape or interfacing (Fig. 188d).
5. Start the stitching at the dart point—the point that requires precision stitching—and stitch to its end. Stitch close to the cut edge. Use either two rows of straight stitching (Fig. 188e) or one row of zigzag stitching (Fig. 188f).
6. Trim away the excess fabric close to the stitching.

JOIN DART LEGS OVER TAPE

This is an excellent method for reinforcing a dart or for stitching a double-pointed dart in the interfacing.

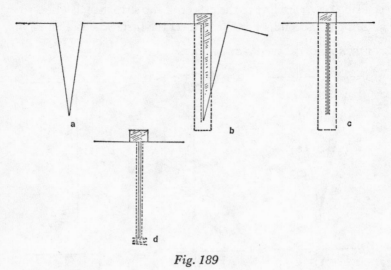

Fig. 189

1. Mark the dart.
2. Cut out the entire dart (Fig. 189a).
3. Cut a narrow strip of interfacing or tape the length of the dart legs plus ¼ inch at each end.
4. Center the dart on the strip of tape.
5. Bring one dart leg to the center of the strip. Pin and stitch (Fig. 189b).
6. Bring the second dart leg to meet the first. Pin and stitch (Fig. 189c).
7. Reinforce each dart point with lock stitching or zigzag stitching (Fig. 189d).

The above method is also a good way to join a shaping seam.

How to Join the Fashion Fabric and the Interfacing or Underlining

The smoothest joining of all results when the fashion fabric and the interfacing or underlining is *each stitched separately* and *each pressed and blocked separately*. Only then are the two layers of material joined. If both fashion and foundation fabrics are joined before stitching, even the best stitching and the most judicious trimming and the most skillful pressing cannot eliminate the unsightly and unnecessary bulk. We are speaking, of course, of the medium- and heavyweight fabrics generally used for tailoring. The method for handling sheer and lightweight materials is different. (See page 259.)

Shaped garments are joined in the same relative position in which they will be worn (fashion fabric topping foundation fabric) and over a tailor's ham to simulate a body curve. This is the order—the tailor's ham representing the body, then the supporting fabric and last, the outer fabric, right side up.

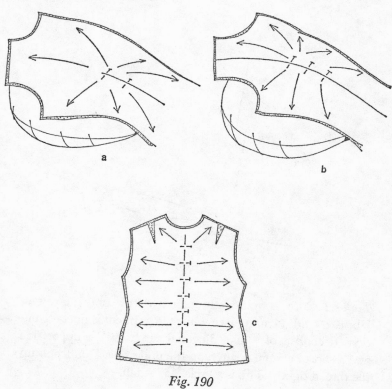

Fig. 190

FRONT

In matching the front outer and supporting fabrics, start at the dart (Fig. 190a) and work toward the outer edges. Pin. When matching shaping seams, start at the crest of each curve and work toward the outer edges (Fig. 190b). Pin to position. You can see how this procedure makes for exact shaping.

BACK

Start the matching at the center back and work toward the outer edges (Fig. 190c).

Because an inside curve is smaller than an outside curve, some of the foundation fabric will extend slightly beyond the edges of the fashion fabric. The excess can be trimmed away after the layers are joined.

Join the fashion fabric and the interfacing or underlining with tailor basting.

Fig. 191

Tailor basting is worked through two (or more) layers of fabric to hold them in place while the garment is in construction. It consists of a long diagonal stitch on the upper side and a short horizontal stitch on the underside. Don't pull up the thread tightly. This is a "relaxed" stitch.

When *sheer or lightweight outer and supporting fabric* are used, the two may be used as one fabric.

1. Cut the outer fabric and the underlining from the same pattern.
2. Transfer the pattern markings to the underlining.
3. Tailor baste or staystitch the fabrics together.
4. Staystitch through the center of each dart.
5. Fold the dart on the staystitching line, smoothing the underlining in place.
6. Pin and stitch the dart through all thicknesses, taking great care as the stitching comes off the dart point. (Start the stitching at the wide end of the dart.)

You can see how difficult this would be in any but sheer or lightweight fabric.

Eliminate Hair Canvas from Construction Seams

While stitching a dart through many thicknesses is hazardous, it is fairly safe to include most supporting materials in the major construction seams. Not hair canvas. It is too springy and too resilient to be pressed flat. There always are exceptions, however. Hair canvas in the armhole seam serves a purpose. It is often included when the sleeve is stitched. Trim the underarm seam allowance of the hair canvas close to the stitching. Use the overarm seam allowance to support the sleeve cap.

If you would like the support of the hair canvas in the sleeve cap but find it easier to set and stitch the sleeve into the armhole without including it in the seam, try the fold-back method.

The *fold-back method* of eliminating hair canvas from the seams:

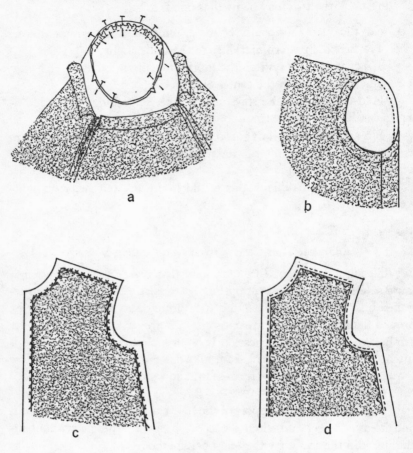

Fig. 192

1. Fold back the hair canvas from the armhole seam. Pin it out of the way (Fig. 192a).

2. Stitch the sleeve into the armhole in the usual way.

3. Bring the hair canvas back to position. Permanently baste it to the seam allowances just beyond the seam line (Fig. 192b).

4. Trim away the underarm seam allowance close to the stitching.

The *cut-away method* of eliminating hair canvas from the seams:

1. Mark the seam line on the hair canvas.

2. Pin or baste the canvas to the outer fabric close to the seam line.

3. Trim away the seam allowance of the hair canvas.

4. Catch stitch the cut edge to the seam line (Fig. 192c). Use a matching single thread, pick up only one yarn of the outer fabric so the hand stitches do not show on the right side. Do not pull up the thread too tightly—just enough to secure the interfacing.

5. To join the sections, stitch *beside* the interfacing, not through it (Fig. 192d).

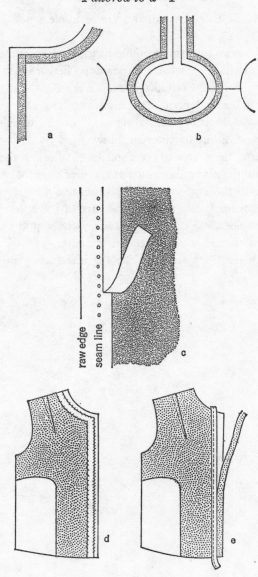

Fig. 193

The *taping method* to be done after the sections of the garment are joined:

This method not only eliminates the bulk of the interfacing from the seam line but stays the length and shape of the outside edges. It is used by professional tailors around the neck, lapels, and closing edges of a jacket or coat.

1. Trim away ¾ inch of the interfacing from the neck, lapel, and front edges.

2. Preshrink the ⅜-inch cotton or twill tape.

3. Cut a length of tape to fit the entire neckline. Cut a length of tape to fit each lapel-and-front edge. Tape is always overlapped at corners (Fig. 193a) rather than darted or mitered. The latter two create bulk.

4. The tape is swirled to fit curved edges—neck, lapel, or style line (Fig. 193b). It is pressed smooth on all straight edges.

5. Apply the tape so the outer edge clears the seam line and rests on the outer fabric. The inner edge of the tape lies on the interfacing. The tape straddles the cut edge of the interfacing (Fig. 193c).

6. Using a single matching thread, hem the outside edge of the tape to the outer fabric with tiny, "easy," invisible hemming stitches, lifting only a single yarn of the fabric at a time. Hem the inner edge of the tape to the interfacing. Catch only the interfacing (Fig. 193d). Do not come through to the garment fabric.

7. When joining garment sections, stitch *beside* the tape, not through it.

In some cases it is possible to stitch the inner edge of the tape to the interfacing by machine (Fig. 193e) before applying the interfacing to the outer fabric. However, one would have to be very sure that all needed adjustments (occasioned by the precise matching of seams and darts of fashion fabric and supporting material) were made before the tape is set. Trim away the hair canvas from the taped edge as in Fig. 193c.

HELP WANTED

To Make Hems Stay Down and Shoulders Stay Up

How to Keep a Good Hem Down

You can't depend on gravity alone to keep a good hem down. A little assistance is in order. Interfacings, underlinings, and weights come to the aid of any hem that has a tendency to ride high.

An Interfaced Hem

For a crisp edge:

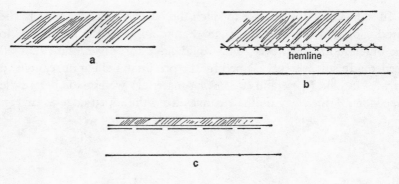

Fig. 194

1. Cut a bias strip of interfacing the width of the hem plus ½ inch and as long as needed plus two seam allowances.

2. Overlap the straight-grain ends of the bias strip, stitch, and trim the seam allowances close to the stitching (Fig. 194a).

3. Place the interfacing against the garment with the lower edge along the foldline of the hem. Lightly catch stitch the lower edge to position (Fig. 194b).

4. Turn up the hem. Fasten the edge of it to the interfacing with permanent basting or catch stitching (Fig. 194c).

5. Fasten the upper edge of the interfacing to the garment in a tailor's hem.

For a soft edge:

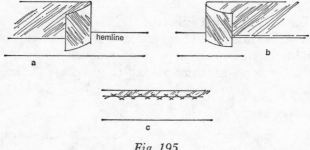

Fig. 195

1. Cut a bias strip of interfacing the width of the hem plus 1 inch and as long as needed plus two seam allowances.

2. Overlap the straight-grain ends of the bias strip, stitch, and trim the seam allowances close to the stitching.

3. Place the interfacing against the garment with the lower edge ½ inch beyond the foldline into the hem (Fig. 195a).

4. Permanently baste the interfacing strip to the hem slightly in from the foldline *toward the hem*. (Fig. 195b). Pick up only one thread of the hem fabric in loose stitches.

5. Turn up the hem. Fasten the edge of it to the interfacing with permanent basting or catch stitching (Fig. 195c).

6. Fasten the upper edge of the interfacing to the garment in a tailor's hem.

Note that in both of the above hems ½ inch of the interfacing extends above the hem in order to grade the thicknesses. It is the method used when a lining is brought down over the hem edge. When there is no lining, the grading is reversed: make the interfacing ½ inch narrower than the hem depth.

An Underlined Hem

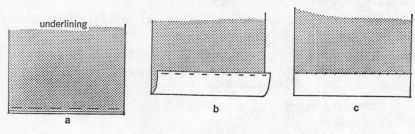

Fig. 196

1. Carry the underlining of the garment down to the very edge of the hem. Baste it to position (Fig. 196a).

2. Turn up the underlined hem and trim it to an even depth (Fig. 196b). Finish the edge in any appropriate manner.

3. Fasten the hem to the underlining (Fig. 196c). Do not let any stitches come through to the right side.

A WEIGHTY MATTER

Sometimes weights are the answer to holding a hem down. A hem may be *weighted uniformly* with a chain. Chains are available in assorted lengths, weights, and metals. Stitch the chain every other link along the top and bottom from facing to facing at the lower edge of the garment (Fig. 197a) or just below the lining (Fig. 197b).

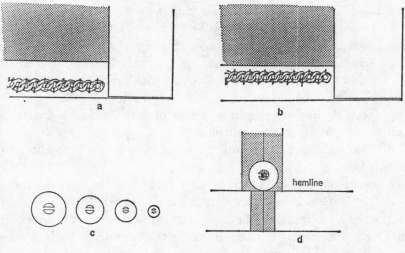

Fig. 197

A hem may be *weighted in spots*. Use dressmaker's weights—lead disks that come in a range of sizes up to 1½ inches in diameter (Fig. 197c). So they will never be seen they are inserted into the hem at seam lines and are stitched to the seam allowances (Fig. 197d). (Dressmaker's weights are used in dressmaking wherever an anchor is needed to hold a detail in place—a cowl neckline, for instance.)

In a circular garment (a skirt, a cape, a coat) a dressmaker's weight stitched to the garment at each deep fold will guarantee that the ripples will always fall into their planned positions.

Padding Firms the Shoulder Line

Remember a time when broad shoulders denoted strength, virility, and protectiveness in a man and when narrow, sloping shoulders was thought to make the little woman look more feminine—and desirably helpless? When the first liberated women rejected this stereotype and took over men's tailoring, they took the shoulder padding that went with it.

Fashions evolve. Today broad padded shoulders are no more fashionable for men than they are for women. However, a light shoulder support does give that trim look long associated with fine tailoring. For a set-in sleeve pad to do just this, it should be squared off at the front shoulder and tapered at the back (Fig. 198a). A shoulder pad for a kimono or raglan sleeve should be shaped to cup the shoulder (Fig. 198b).

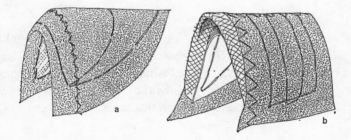

Fig. 198

Such pads are commercially available but a little hard to find. You can make your own of a little stiffening, a little wadding, and, if the garment is unlined, a covering fabric.

Recipes for Home-made Pads

Use the garment pattern. If the pattern is in several sections, pin together all those that make the front-shoulder-and-armhole area and those that make the back-shoulder-and-armhole area.

A SHOULDER PAD FOR A SET-IN SLEEVE

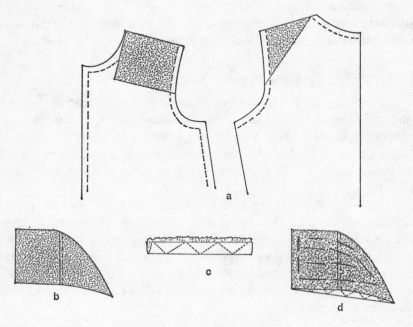

Fig. 199

1. Draw the shape of the shoulder pad on the front and back patterns. Come halfway down the armhole at both front and back. Square off the front; taper the back. (That square front helps to fill out the hollow just below the shoulder.) Make the shoulder length of the pad equal to the shoulder measurement from the neckline to the armhole seam (Fig. 199a).

2. Trace the front and back shoulder pad patterns onto a fresh piece of paper.

3. Cut them out of hair canvas on straight grain.

4. Join the front and back canvases by overlapping the shoulder seams. Stitch. Trim away the seam allowances close to the stitching (Fig. 199b).

5. Cut a strip of bias muslin 9 inches long by 2½ inches wide. Fold it in half lengthwise. Insert a layer (or layers) of wadding (cotton batting, quilting cotton, or flannel). Machine pad stitch (rows of diagonal machine stitching used to hold the padding in place [Fig. 199c]).

6. Stitch the padded muslin strip to the underside of the hair canvas, extending it to about ¾ to ½ inch at the shoulder-armhole edge and tapering it to nothing at each end.

7. Pad with layers of wadding cut to shape. (This is your great chance to get a shoulder pad just to your liking—not too thick, not too thin.) The thickest part of the pad should be at the armhole edge of the shoulder. Taper the thickness toward the neck and toward the ends.

8. Quilt the pad with rows of hand or machine stitching to hold all the stuffings in place (Fig. 199d).

A PAD FOR A DROPPED-SHOULDER, KIMONO, OR RAGLAN SLEEVE

Here is an easy-to-make pattern for this type of pad—and a chance to use your knowledge of geometry.

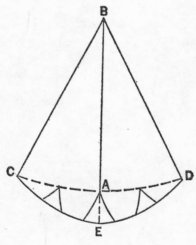

Fig. 200

AB equals the shoulder length.
AC equals half the front armhole.
AD equals half the back armhole.
AE equals the desired depth of the pad over the shoulder. Shape this area with darts.

1. Using this pattern, cut the pad of stiff shaping material.

2. Slash one dart leg of each dart and overlap on the other dart leg. Pin. Fit the pads carefully to your shoulder. Curved darts provide a better cupping.

3. Stitch the darts. Trim away the excess.

4. Pad with any of the wadding materials suggested for the set-in sleeve pad to the desired thickness.

5. Pad-stitch to hold all the thicknesses in place.

You don't have to follow the above recipes for shoulder pads exactly. You may use other ingredients—foam rubber, Pellon, or crinoline for more stiffness. You may combine or vary the ingredients to suit your taste.

How to Set and Stitch the Shoulder Pads in Place

A SET-IN SLEEVE SHOULDER PAD

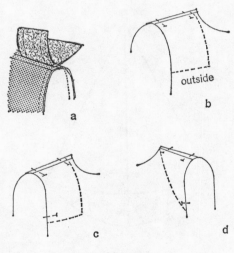

Fig. 201

1. Turn the garment to the inside.

From the inside:

2. Place the pad so that the shoulder line of the pad matches the shoulder seam of the garment and the edge of the pad extends ⅜ inch to ½ inch into the sleeve cap (Fig. 201a). This prevents the cap from collapsing. Remember that the squared part of the pad is the front.

From the outside:

3. "Pinch" the pad, holding it firmly in place. Reverse the garment to its normal wearing position. Slip the shoulder pad under the neck facing.

4. Pin the pad securely at the shoulder and at the neck (Fig. 201b).

5. Slip the hand under the pad. Smooth the material down from the shoulder. Locate the point at which the tip of the shoulder pad meets the front-armhole seam. Pin (Fig. 201c). Do the same for the back (Fig. 201d). Don't force this. Let the tips of the pad go where they want to go even if this means that they go off the armhole seam. Sometimes the shape of the garment or the shape of your shoulders makes this happen. If you force the positioning of the pad tips on the armhole seam you will create a bulge in the shoulder area.

6. Fasten the end of a matching single thread on the underside at the point where the shoulder pad meets the armhole seam at either front or back. Use over-and-over stitches. Bring the needle up to the right side directly into the armhole seam. Fasten the shoulder pad to the garment along the armhole seam with stab stitches.

> To make a *stab stitch* take a tiny stitch on the surface directly into the armhole seam straight through the garment and the shoulder pad. Bring the needle up through all the thicknesses into the armhole seam for the next stitch about ½ inch away. Repeat until you reach the other end of the shoulder pad. Keep the stitches relaxed—not tight. Fasten on the underside with over-and-over stitches.

7. Fasten all loose, unattached points of the shoulder pad to the interfacing with swing tacks (see page 130).

THE DROPPED-SHOULDER, KIMONO, OR RAGLAN-SLEEVED SHOULDER PAD

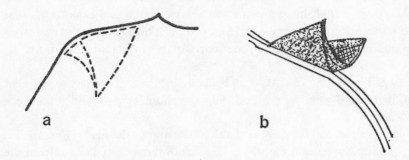

Fig. 202

In these styles, there is no convenient armhole seam to guide the setting. You will have to try on the garment and slip one shoulder pad into position cupping the shoulder (Fig. 202a).

1. Pin the pad in place from the outside. Remove the garment. Measure carefully the distance from the neck to the shoulder-point setting.

2. On the inside, set the second shoulder pad in exactly the same position on the other shoulder (Fig. 202b).

3. Slip the neck end of the shoulder pad under the neck facing.

4. Using a single matching thread fasten the shoulder pad securely to the shoulder seam in the same way as directed for the set-in sleeve.

5. Fasten the tips of the shoulder pads in place with swing tacks *or* catch stitch the entire front and back edges of the pad to the front and back interfacings.

Coax Up the Cap

If not sufficiently supported, some fabrics have a tendency to collapse at the cap of the sleeve.

TRY A CAP UNDERLINING

One way to rescue the cap is with an underlining of lamb's wool padding. (Lamb's wool padding is a different material than lamb's wool interlining. The former is a soft, fuzzy, loosely woven material, the latter is more like a regular fabric.)

Use the sleeve pattern to cut a cap. Place it in position. Fasten with tiny hand stitches to the armhole seam (Fig. 203a).

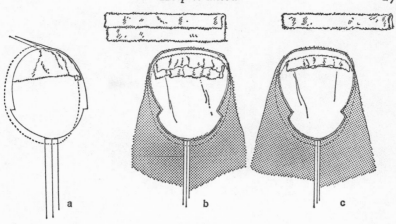

Fig. 203

OR, A CAP LIFT

Another way of providing soft support is with a cap lift.

1. Cut a bias strip of lamb's wool padding. (Self-fabric, flannel, Siri, muslin, or any other similar soft fabric will also do.) Make the strip 4 inches to 6 inches long by 3 inches wide.

For light padding make a 1-inch lengthwise fold. Slipstitch the folded edge to the armhole seam (Fig. 203b).

For more thickness fold the strip into thirds lengthwise.

2. Place the lift into the sleeve cap with one folded edge along the armhole seam—half to the front, half to the back (Fig. 203c).

3. Fasten with slipstitches to the armhole seam.

LININGS

Silver and Otherwise

The Lining, the Last Construction Step in Tailoring

It may not be a silver lining but it certainly is a harbinger of good news. By the time you reach the lining, the end of the project is in sight. The lining is the very last construction step in tailoring.

Make the Lining by Machine

1. Make the same alterations in the lining as you made in the garment.

2. Cut, mark, and stitch the lining with the same care and precision as the fashion fabric.

3. Stitch all darts and all seams with the exception of the shoulder seams. Leave them open (Fig. 204a). Press.

4. Stitch the sleeve seams and press them open. Make two rows of

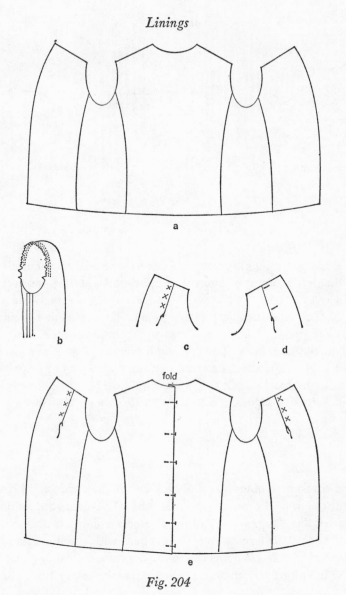

Fig. 204

gathering stitches across the sleeve cap. Draw up the gathering to form the cap shape. Distribute the fullness evenly (Fig. 204b).

5. Lay a soft fold at the front shoulder and pin to position. Fasten through all thickness with cross-stitches (Fig. 204c) or with bar tacks (Fig. 204d).

6. Lay a tentative soft fold at the center back and pin to position (Fig. 204e). Adjustments can be made on the center-back fold as needed.

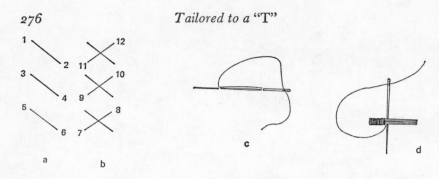

Fig. 205

CROSS-STITCHES

Using a single matching thread. Fasten the thread on the underside. Bring the needle out at 1, insert it at 2, bring it out at 3, insert it at 4, bring it out at 5, insert it at 6. This makes three diagonal stitches all going in the same direction (Fig. 205a). To complete the stitches, make three diagonal stitches going in the opposite direction. Bring the needle out at 7, insert it at 8, bring it out at 9, insert it at 10, bring it out at 11, insert it at 12. Fasten off on the underside (Fig. 205b).

Do as many cross-sitches as are necessary to hold the lining in place for 1 inch to 1½ inches. Keep them small enough and even enough to be pretty.

BAR TACK

Use a single matching thread. Fasten on the underside and bring the needle through to the right side. Take several ¼-inch stitches directly over each other (Fig. 205c). While these do a fine job of anchoring, they are not particularly pretty. Cover them with small over-and-over stitches worked very close together to give a smooth, satiny effect (Fig. 205d). (In embroidery these are called satin stitches for this reason.)

Attach the Lining to the Garment by Hand

Place the jacket or coat over a tailor's ham with the right side against the ham and the inside up. By inserting the lining in a reverse curve an extra bit of ease is added.

Work from the front toward the center back. Do the same operation on each side before going on to the next.

Fig. 206

1. Place the wrong side of the lining against the wrong side of the garment. By this placement the construction seams will be hidden.
2. Match the side seams of garment and lining. When there are no side seams, match the side-front or side-back seams instead.

3. Join the seam allowances close to the stitching line with loose permanent basting. Leave a jacket lining free for about 4 inches from the bottom and a coat lining free for about 6 inches from the bottom (Fig. 206a).

4. With permanent basting, stitch the lining firmly to the armhole seam allowance close to the seam. Start at the underarm and work toward the shoulder. Leave the back armhole lining free for about 2 inches from the shoulder (Fig. 206b).

5. Turn under the seam allowances at the front edges of the lining. Pin in place over the front facings, raw edges matching.

6. Slipstitch the front edges of the lining to the facing leaving the bottom free for about 4 inches from the hemline of a jacket and about 6 inches from the hemline of a coat (Fig. 206b).

7. Baste the front lining to the back-shoulder seam allowance.

8. Clip the neckline curve of the lining.

9. Turn under the lining seam allowance at the shoulders.

10. Lay in the center-back pleat making any needed adjustments. (This is the advantage of working from the front to the center back. That back pleat is an excellent place to hide any miscalculations in measurement.) The fold is directly on center back. Fasten the pleat at the neck, waist, and lower edge with cross-stitches or bar tacks.

11. Turn under the neckline seam allowance.

12. Pin the lining in position over the front lining at the shoulders and over the back facing, raw edges matching (Fig. 206c).

13. Slipstitch the lining to position.

14. To attach the sleeve lining, clip the sleeve lining on the underarm curve.

15. Slip the sleeve lining into (or over) the sleeve, wrong sides together (Fig. 206d).

16. Draw up the gathering across the lining cap to fit the sleeve cap and distribute the ease.

17. Turn under the seam allowance and overlap the sleeve lining on the garment lining. Bring the fold of the sleeve lining to meet the armhole seam line. Match the underarm, shoulder, and sleeve seams (Fig. 206d).

18. Slipstitch the sleeve lining to the garment lining. Tiny hemming stitches instead of slipstitches are advisable for a jacket that is to get hard wear. They may not look as pretty but they're far stronger.

Lining Hems

When this much of the lining has been inserted, let the garment hang out for a while so that the lining settles before finishing the hem. Then pin or baste the lining to the garment several inches above the hemline of jacket, coat, and sleeves (Fig. 207).

Fig. 207

THE ATTACHED HEM

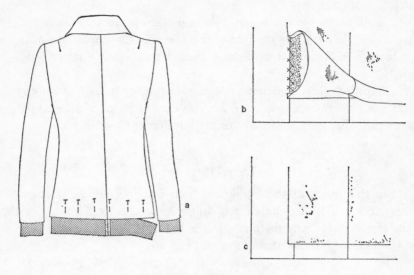

Fig. 208

1. Cut off any lining that shows below the finished hemline (Fig. 208a).

2. Turn under the seam allowance of the lining and pin it over the top of the hem, raw edges matching. Note the small tuck that provides the lengthwise ease (Fig. 208b).

3. Slipstitch the lining to the garment.

4. Smooth the lining down over the hem so the tuck-ease forms a soft fold (Fig. 208c).

5. Close the remaining front edges with slipstitching.

THE FREE-HANGING HEM

(used more often in a coat than in a jacket)

1. Trim the lining 1½ inches below the finished hem (Fig. 209a).

2. Turn up the coat lining to make a 2½-inch hem. This makes the coat lining 1 inch shorter than the coat.

3. The hem of the garment and the hem of the lining are completed separately with any suitable finish.

4. Close the remaining front edge with slipstitching.

5. Attach the lining hem to the garment hem with 1-inch French tacks at all seams (Fig. 209b).

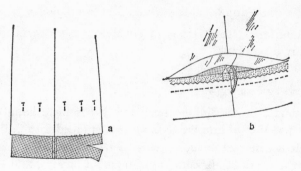

Fig. 209

Lining a Raglan or Kimono-sleeved Style

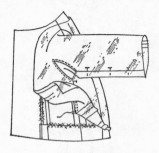

Fig. 210

1. Make such adjustments as were made in the garment.

2. Stitch the *entire* lining together. Clip all curved seams. Press the seam allowances open.

3. Turn the entire garment inside out.

4. Place the wrong side of the lining against the wrong side of the garment so the construction seams are concealed.

5. Match the side and underarm seams. Pin. Baste to position with loose stitches.

6. Pull the sleeve lining over the sleeve. Pin to position.

7. Fold under the seam allowances of all outside edges except the hem.

8. Place the folded edges over the facings, raw edges matching. Slipstitch.

9. Finish the hem in the same manner as directed for set-in sleeve styles.

Warmth Without Bulk: The Interlining

In an interlining, the trick is to get the coat as warm as possible without any excess bulk.

EACH SECTION SEPARATELY

The ultimate in interlining insertion is a complete hand operation where each section of interlining is set and stitched into position individually. It is trimmed in such a way that the edges of the interlining just meet the edges of all seam allowances, all facings, and the top of the hem. All edges are joined by catch stitching (Fig. 211).

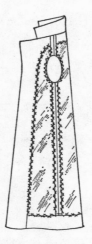

Fig. 211

Perhaps you are thinking this is carrying the flatness fetish a bit too far. Consider this: in addition to the trimness of this type of insertion, it has another advantage. It is often easier to handle one piece of interlining at a time than to insert another great mass of wool into what may already be a voluminous garment.

TWO LAYERS—ONE FABRIC

The opposite extreme is to back the lining and treat the two layers as one fabric. (There is a commercial fabric like this on the market.) However, you can see how the four thicknesses at each dart, seam and pleat, as well as all turn-unders on outside edges would create bulk.

The following compromise method produces excellent results. It cuts down on the work involved in the first method and the bulk produced by the second method.

How to Insert the Interlining

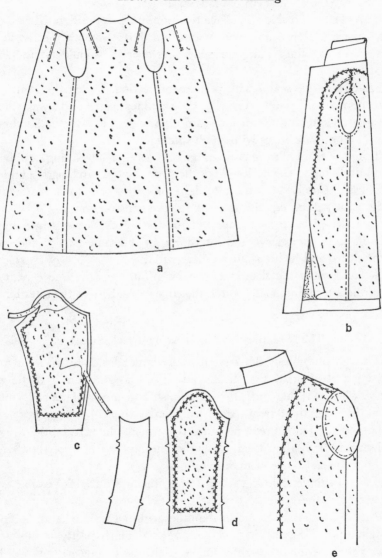

Fig. 212

Cut the interlining from the pattern suggested on page 250. Overlap and stitch all the seams and darts in the same way as for the interfacing. Trim the seam allowances on both sides close to the stitching (Fig. 212a).

Trim the seam allowances of all outside edges. Trim the interlining to meet the top of the hem (Fig. 212a).

Turn the coat inside out. Place the interlining in position. Match the side seams. Match the shaping seams and darts. Smooth the fabric so there is no rippling. The interlining goes over the shoulder pad (Fig. 212b).

Fasten the side seams with permanent basting. Fasten the armholes with permanent basting. Overlap the shoulder seams and fasten them with catch stitching. Trim the seam allowances close to the stitching. Fasten all outside edges with catch stitching.

Trim the seam allowances of a one-piece sleeve interlining. Apply as an underlining to the underside of the sleeve before stitching the underarm seam. Catch stitch the interlining edges to the sleeve seam lines (Fig. 212c). Proceed with the usual sleeve construction.

In a two-piece sleeve, generally only the upper sleeve is interlined. Handle the upper sleeve and interlining in the same way as the one-piece sleeve and its interlining (Fig. 212d).

Set and stitch the sleeve (Fig. 212e). Turn up the sleeve hem to meet the interlining. Catch stitch the edge of the hem to the interlining.

The No-lining Coat or Jacket: Suitable Styles

Though one might think so, it really is not faster to make an unlined jacket or coat. For, if the inside of the garment is to be exposed when it is taken off, then the finish and the workmanship must be nothing less than great. All of which takes time.

Should you really prefer an unlined garment, choose a fabric of such weight and body that it can carry the lines and shaping of the design without the assistance of underpinnings.

Select a simple style so that as few seams and darts as possible will show on the underside.

Choose patch pockets rather than those set in a seam or a slash. That dangling pouch of a set-in pocket is not particularly pretty.

Cut the interfacings slightly smaller than the facings so they will be unseen. Use a softer and lighter-weight interfacing than one would normally use for a lined garment. This avoids too much difference in thickness or stiffness between the interfaced parts and the rest of the garment.

Shoulder pads should be covered with self-fabric or lining fabric of a matching color.

Bind all raw edges: seam allowances, facings, hems. Or, turn under all raw edges and either press or stitch to position.

Avoid raw edges entirely by making a flat-fell or welt seam.

Seams in Unlined Garments

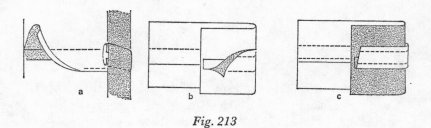

Fig. 213

A FLAT-FELL SEAM

1. Stitch the seam as usual.
2. Press the seam allowances to one side.
3. Trim the under seam allowance.
4. Turn under some of the upper seam allowances.
5. On non-bulky fabrics, machine stitch close to the fold (Fig. 213a). On bulky fabrics, slipstitch the fold in place, or, better yet, make a welt seam.

THE WELT SEAM

Steps 1, 2, and 3 are the same as for the flat-fell seam.

4. Make a row of machine stitching through the upper seam allowance close to the raw edge. The under seam allowance is enclosed but not caught in the seam (Fig. 213b).

A DOUBLE-STITCHED WELT SEAM

1. Make in the same way as the welt seam.
2. Add a second row of machine stitching close to the original seam line (Fig. 213c).

Darts in Unlined Garments

Darts in unlined garments generally remain uncut. They may be stitched to resemble a single or double-stitched welt seam.

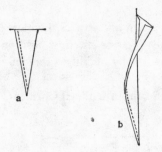

Fig. 214

Press the dart to one side and stitch the folded edge (Fig. 214a).

A wide dart may be treated like a welt seam (Fig. 214b). The foregoing methods of stitching the seams and darts are applicable in the making of a reversible garment from a reversible fabric.

As you can see, no lining is really no short cut.

Anything Goes!

Do as much or as little inner construction as will provide the lines you want for your garment. Just remember, that when it comes to buttressing the shape of fashion, anything goes!

PRESS YOUR IRON INTO SERVICE

One of the hallmarks of fine tailoring is the pressing. One cannot think of great tailoring without also thinking of those crisp edges, the flat seams, and that subtly blocked-to-shape sculptured form. As important as pressing is to dressmaking, in tailoring it is raised to a fine art.

Sewing without pressing is an incomplete act. You may be the greatest sewer in the world but your work will look unfinished and amateurish if not well pressed. Nor can you wait until your sewing is completed for one mighty pressing binge. You must press as you sew!

"Press" vs. "Iron"

Have you noticed that we've used the word "press" rather than "iron"? There's a difference.

To get the wrinkles out of a handkerchief, you push the iron along the surface. That's ironing—a gliding motion. Pressing is an up-and-down motion: lower, press, lift. Ironing must be done on a flat surface. Pressing can be done on a shaped pad as well as a flat surface. Save the ironing for the smooth-surfaced flat work. For shaped garments (which is just about all of them) press on a shaped press pad. There is this, too: fabrics that can be laundered are ironed smooth—cottons, linens, synthetics. Garments that require dry cleaning, either because of their fibers, their texture, or the inner construction, are pressed. Since tailoring generally has all of these latter characteristics, tailored garments are always pressed.

Some General Hints for Pressing and Ironing

Whatever the fabric and whether it's dressmaking or tailoring, your garment will look so much better if you:

press every dart and seam before stitching it to a cross seam.

press each section of a garment before stitching it to another.

press open every enclosed seam before turning the facing back to the underside (collars, cuffs, welts, lapels, closings).

And, it's so much easier:

to topstitch an edge when it has been pressed flat first.

to insert a zipper when the seam allowance is pressed back first.

to achieve a smooth and flat hem if the fullness at the raw edge is ease-pressed before finishing and attaching.

to set a sleeve when the cap has been ease-pressed first.

Set up your pressing equipment along with your sewing equipment. The rhythm of work is always sew and press, sew and press, sew and press.

Place a chair or table close to the ironing board to support any fabric that may otherwise trail on the floor. If you have to clean a garment before you even wear it, it won't feel new.

Don't press darts, seams, folds, pleats, or anything else unless you are absolutely sure they are exactly where you want them. It is often impossible to press out the sharp crease produced by pressing.

Pressing is directional. Press all woven fabrics with the grain. Off-grain pressing pushes material out of shape or stretches it. Press all knit fabrics with the lengthwise rib. Pressing across the ribs stretches the fabric. Press all napped materials with the nap.

You may do your ironing on the right side but for pressing the wrong side is the correct side. If the right side must be pressed protect it with a suitable press cloth. Direct contact with the iron is a sure way to produce a shine.

Keep trimming scissors handy. Clip or notch where needed to make a seam or dart lie flat. Slash and grade to reduce bulk.

When seam allowances are pressed in one direction, press in the direction that produces the least bulk.

In double thicknesses of fabric (facings, hems, etc.) press the underside first, then the upper.

All darts and curved seams should be pressed over an appropriate press pad. Also, all straight pieces destined to fit curved areas should be blocked to shape over a suitable press pad. This applies to collars, lapels, sleeve caps, dartless bodices, and skirts of bias or knit fabrics.

Avoid over-dampening and over-pressing. Settle for the best results you can get. Don't attempt the impossible for the fabric.

Hang up each pressed section as soon as the pressing is complete. If you must store your work in progress, don't fold any more than necessary. Or, fold over tissue paper as if for packing.

Ingredients for Pressing: Heat, Moisture, Pressure, Protection

Both pressing and ironing are accomplished by heat, moisture, and pressure. Some fabrics need protection more than pressure. How much of each depends on the fabric. Every fabric is an individual pressing problem. The safest thing to do is to test-press a scrap of fabric.

HEAT

Use the heat setting on the iron suitable for the fiber:

high heat for the *vegetable fibers*—cotton, linen. (After all, you can boil vegetables.)

moderate heat for the *animal fibers*—silk, wool. (Any gal can tell you that moderate heat is a beauty aid—setting your hair, getting a tan—but high heat can scorch hair and skin.)

low heat for the *man-made fibers*—all synthetics. (Too much heat will melt away the chemicals of which the synthetics are made. Even when the heat is not enough to disintegrate them, it produces a shine.)

In *combinations of fibers,* use the heat setting for the most delicate fiber present. For instance, handle cotton-and-acetate as if it were all acetate, a synthetic fiber.

Holding the iron on one spot for any length of time intensifies the heat. For slow work, reduce the heat of the iron.

MOISTURE

Most fabrics press better with some degree of moisture. Whether you apply it by hand, by eye dropper, by press cloth, whether you sprinkle, spray, sponge, or steam—it depends on the fabric.

Dampened cottons and linens are ironed until they are dry. They wrinkle and muss when limp.

Woolens, however, must never be pressed dry. Allow them to dry naturally. Handle them very carefully while damp since they are easily manipulated out of shape.

No moisture for silks and synthetics: press them dry. It is not that water may injure them but that the dyes will water spot.

PRESSURE

All fabrics require some pressure to smooth them. The very word "press" implies this. Pressure may be anything from a loving pat to the 1600 pounds per square inch applied to the edge of a man's coat in a clothing factory.

For some fabrics, the pressure of the iron is sufficient. Some are pressed then patted with a press mitt. Heavy or firmly woven woolens are beaten and pounded with a pounding block. The latter is the home sewer's answer to the pressure exerted by the factory pressing machines.

PROTECTION

Pounding and patting are fine for some fabrics but disastrous for others. One certainly wouldn't want to flatten out a raised surface that is the main attraction of a fabric. Many materials need protection rather than pressure.

Self-protection

A press cloth of self-fabric is about as good a protection as one can get. There are always scraps of material that fall away in the cutting. Save one that is a little longer and a little wider than your iron to protect the area on which the iron will be pressed.

When the raised surface of the fashion fabric is pressed against the raised surface of the self-fabric strip, the naps interlock, thereby preserving each other. There is this too: naps so pressed tend to adhere. As the two layers of fabric are separated, the naps are lifted.

In the event that you don't have enough self-fabric for a press cloth, use a strip of terry cloth or any other raised-surface material.

Double Protection

When the right side of a fabric is turned to the wrong side for a hem or a facing, that, too, needs protection. (One never knows when one may be needing the under layer for an upper layer.) Use a self-fabric press cloth both under and over the two thicknesses for double protection.

Protected from Itself

A garment needs to be protected from itself—from its seam allowances, pockets, welts, flaps, hems, pleats, lapels, collar, cuffs, buttonholes—indeed, any applied, folded over, or more-than-single thickness. The damage comes in pressing when the outlines of these details are imprinted on the garment unless they are prevented from doing so.

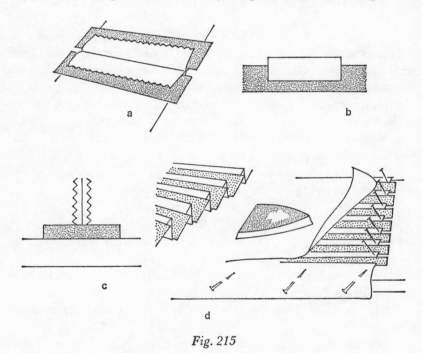

Fig. 215

The simplest and best protection is a strip of brown wrapping paper to cushion the pressure. The strip should be of sufficient length and width so that it can be folded into thirds lengthwise.

Slip the wrapping-paper pad under seam allowances (Fig. 215a), pockets, welts, or flaps (Fig. 215b), hems (Fig. 215c), pleats (Fig. 215d), etc. Let the wrapping-paper pad come between the garment and whatever it is to be protected from.

Press Cloths

In pressing, the iron should never come into direct contact with the fabric. Use a press cloth for protection. Since a few inches are all one ever presses at a time, the press cloths can be fairly small, rectangular strips, a bit longer and a bit wider than the iron so there is no danger of leaving its imprint on the fabric.

Other than self-fabric, the press cloths can be of muslin, lawn, drill, linen, cheesecloth or terry cloth. Wash the cotton cloths thoroughly to make sure that all sizing and all lint have been removed. Because they meet all these requirements, old, worn sheets, pillow cases, table napkins, dish towels, and Turkish towels make fine press cloths.

Pressing Equipment

It is so much easier to do any job well if you have the proper tools with which to work. Not only easier, it's more effective. After all, equipment is devised to get results.

Pressing equipment, like the sewing machine, is a long-term investment. Fortunately none of the following tools costs very much. Some may already be in your household. Others can be made by your father, brother, husband, or favorite beau.

Of the many useful pieces of pressing equipment available or desirable, the following are the minimum you should have.

Iron: as important to sewing as the sewing machine. It may be a dry iron (preferable for tailoring) or a steam iron (which has its uses too).

Ironing board: well padded, of a good working height, and sturdy enough for the "beating" it will take (literally).

Table-top ironing board (Fig. 216a): very useful for pressing small areas.

Sleeve board (Fig. 216b) (often the second side of the table-top ironing board) or a sleeve roll (Fig. 216c): used for pressing the sleeve seams and for blocking the sleeve cap. You can make the sleeve roll to the dimensions given in the illustration. Make it of the same materials as for the tailor's ham (see below).

Pounding block (clapper or spanker) (Fig. 216d): used for pounding into submission those hard-to-get-flat woolens. It is a heavy block of non-resinous hardwood sanded perfectly smooth so that it will not snag any fabric.

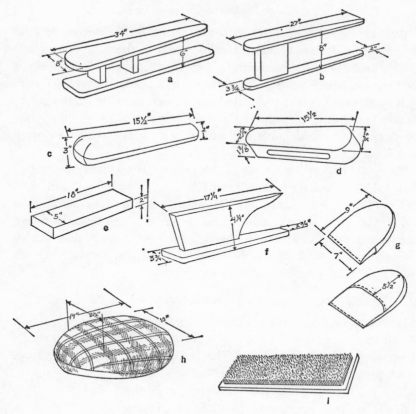

Fig. 216

Press block (Fig. 216e): used in conjunction with the pounding block. Like it, the press block is smooth and of non-resinous hardwood. An old bread board or chopping block will do, provided you retire them from Kitchen Duty and reserve them strictly for your pressing. An extra pounding block to be used as a press block is a good investment. This is particularly effective for sleeve pressing.

Edge and point presser (Fig. 216f): it's easy to get into corners with this piece of equipment. It's also useful for edge pressing.

Press mitt (Fig. 216g): a "handy" piece of equipment for getting into and under hard-to-reach places. It is also good for shaping small areas and for patting flat those materials one dare not pound with the block.

Tailor's ham (Fig. 216h): the most all-around useful shaping pad there is. A must for all sewers. Buy one or make one from the directions that follow.

How to Make the Tailor's Ham

Cut two bias, egg-shaped* pieces of heavy, firmly woven material (silesia, duck, drill, unbleached muslin, wool) to the dimensions given in Fig. 216h. Dart the broader end for more shaping. Machine stitch the two thicknesses leaving the narrower end open. *Pack very tightly* with hardwood sawdust until the ham is quite hard. It cannot do its shaping unless it is. Some sewers use old nylon stockings for the stuffing. The commercial hams are stuffed with cotton waste or wool scraps.

Have you noticed that most of the pressing equipment is made of wood? That's because most woolen fabric requires more steam than that produced by a steam iron. This added moisture becomes a problem on the ordinary well-padded ironing board which tends to reflect moisture rather than absorb it. Wood, on the other hand, does absorb moisture quickly and effectively. This shorter, natural drying time is important in the pressing and shaping of wool.

Optional Equipment for Velvets and Other Nap or Pile Fabrics

It costs more than most of the other pressing equipment but, if you can afford one, a needle board (Fig. 216i) produces professional results in pressing nap or pile fabrics. The board has a flexible base from which protrude closely spaced "needles."

1. Place the nap of the fabric against the needles.
2. Open the seam allowances with finger-pressing.
3. Steam-press using very little pressure. Let the steam do the work.

"I've Got Them on the List"

If you can't afford to rush right out and buy all the equipment immediately, why not make up a suggested gift list and display it prominently? Everyone will be so pleased that you are an enthusiastic sewer and so grateful for the suggestions (it's hard to know what gift to buy!) you'll have all the equipment you need in practically no time at all.

Meet the Press

You could limit your wardrobe to no-iron stuff, if you wish to avoid the whole pressing problem. But who would want to? It's a safe bet that the fabrics you lose your heart to require special handling in

---

* There's a quip about ham and eggs here. Would you like to make it?

pressing. They're hard-surfaced, firmly woven, fleeced, furry, raised, napped, nubbed, slubbed, looped, ribbed, crinkled, blistered, puckered, or embossed. They're either so tough that they require force to subdue them or so touchy you hardly dare lay a finger on them. Don't the difficult ones somehow always turn out to be the most interesting? Better learn how to handle them.

How to Press a Straight, Flat Seam or Crisp Edge in Worsted, Hard-surface, or Firmly Woven Woolens

1. Assemble all the equipment you will need: the ironing board and iron, the press board and pounding block, a press cloth and a small bowl of water, plus two wrapping-paper strips. Place everything within easy reach. This pressing is a *very quick* and *facile* operation.

2. Place the press board on the ironing board. Place the right side of the garment against the press board. The wrong side is up for pressing.

3. Open the seam allowances with finger-pressing. Slip the strips of wrapping paper under them.

> *Finger-pressing:* separate the seam allowances. Run the thumb or forefinger along the seam. Use gentle pressure.

4. Dampen the press cloth. Immerse about one third of it in the bowl of water. Wring it out. Roll up the rest of the press cloth over the wet end until the cloth is uniformly damp. No one part of the garment should be subjected to more moisture than any other.

5. Place the damp press cloth over the opened steam.

6. Use a dry iron set on WOOL. Lower it onto the damp press cloth. Press. Keep the iron on just long enough to create a good head of steam. Lift the iron and set it aside.

7. At this point, you'll wish you had an extra pair of hands. The next two actions are done in such quick succession as to be almost simultaneous. Whisk the press cloth off with one hand while the fabric is still steaming; slap the pounding block on the seam with the other hand. Bring it down with considerable force. (This is a great way to get rid of your aggressions.) Let the pounding block rest there a minute before removing it. Presto! Your magically flattened seam.

One forceful blow should work. If the fabric proves stubborn (some are hard to flatten) or your emotional needs are great, repeat the performance. Some people prefer to beat or spank the seam allowance flat.

8. Move on to the next section and repeat the operation.

This pounding method of pressing may also be effective on heavy or firmly woven cottons or raw silks.

How to Press a Straight, Flat-as-Possible Seam in Fabrics with Nap or Pile

1. Assemble the needed equipment: the ironing board and iron, press mitt, press cloth, small bowl of water, wrapping-paper pads, and a strip of self-fabric.

2. Place the strip of self-fabric on the ironing board with the raised surface up. Place the right side of the garment against it.

3. Open the seam allowances with finger-pressing. Slip the strips of wrapping paper under them.

4. Dampen the press cloth as previously directed and place it over the opened seam.

5. Lower the dry iron (set on WOOL) onto the damp press cloth. Press *lightly* and *briefly*.

6. Whisk off the press cloth with one hand and with the other hand slipped into the press mitt, pat gently.

If, by chance, you have flattened the surface of the fabric, brush it up while damp to restore it.

Don't attempt the impossible with raised-surface fabrics. They can never be pressed as flat as the worsteds. Nor should they be. That would destroy their very special quality.

How to Press Other Fabrics

Deep fleece, or deep, furry naps. Place the right side of the fabric against a strip of self-fabric, terry cloth, or a needle board. Steam from the wrong ide.

Raised, nubbed, slubbed, looped, ribbed structures. Place the right side of the material against another raised surface. Steam-press from the wrong side. Use a light touch; let the steam do the work.

Crinkled, blistered, puckered, embossed, or other novelty surfaces. Finger-press all seams and darts. Press *very* lightly—if at all. Often it is enough to hold the steam iron slightly above the surface and let the steam do the "pressing" rather than the weight of the iron.

Shape Well Before Using

However flat they may look on the cutting board, clothes are meant to fit a more-or-less rounded figure.

With or without darts or shaping seams, clothes will eventually take on some of the shape of the wearer. That's because the body's 98-degree temperature does a bit of blocking on its own. However, one can't rely on Nature alone to do the garment shaping required by most figures. They need the assistance of shaping seams and darts *and contour pressing*. This is particularly true of tailored clothes where not only the outer fabric but each layer of supporting material must be blocked separately before the two can be put together.

All areas of a garment that go over and around some part of the body (which is just about everywhere) are blocked over an appropriately rounded press pad. Come to think of it, it really doesn't make sense to press curves on a flat ironing board. You find yourself pressing out of a garment all the shape you so painstakingly stitched into it.

Assorted Rolls

There is an assortment of rolls and cushions and pads to fit practically every curve of the body. However, the most all-purpose shaping device is the tailor's ham. Somewhere on its rounded surface there is a curve that will match a shaped section of the garment. The other pads are fun to have as extras, but the tailor's ham will see you through most of your blocking needs.

HOW TO PRESS A SHAPING SEAM

1. Place the right side of the garment over an appropriate curve of the tailor's ham. This produces a reverse curve—temporarily. When the pressed garment is returned to its right-side-out position, it will assume its correct contour.

2. Clip the seam allowance where it is necessary to flatten the curve (Fig. 217a). Notch the seam allowance where necessary to remove rippling (Fig. 217b). How far apart the clips and notches are made depends on the degree of the curve. Starting with ½ inch as a standard, make them closer for deep curves, farther apart for shallow curves. Don't overdo it; make just enough snips and slashes to release any restrictions or to eliminate excess fullness.

Some seams require clipping on one seam allowance and notching on the other to make each lie flat. When this is so, notch between the clips so that there will not be too much strain on the stitching (Fig. 217c). Ignore this and your seam will literally be hanging by a thread.

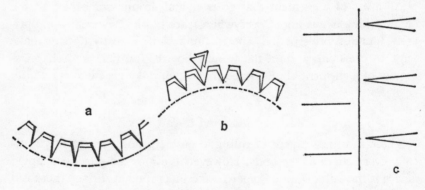

Fig. 217

3. Insert wrapping-paper strips under the seam allowances when necessary.

4. Cover with a dampened press cloth.

5. Press with the lengthwise grain or with the nap (Fig. 218).

6. Remove the wrapping-paper strips. Allow the garment to dry on the tailor's ham. If you remove it while it is still damp, you may lose the shaping.

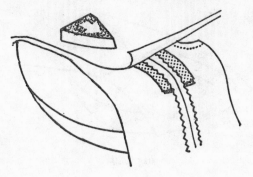

Fig. 218

HOW TO PRESS A DART

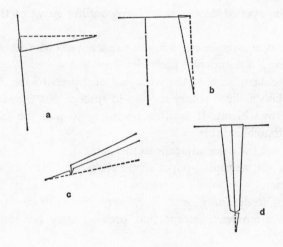

Fig. 219

Very narrow darts, and darts in lightweight fabrics are pressed to one side: horizontal darts are pressed down (Fig. 219a), vertical darts are pressed toward the center (Fig. 219b).

Wide darts and darts in medium-to-heavy fabrics are slashed open to within ¼ inch of the dart point. Snip across the unslashed end of the dart almost to the seam line (Fig. 219c). Press the dart open where slashed, press to one side where unslashed (Fig. 219d). Trim the rest of the dart to ½ to ⅝ inch.

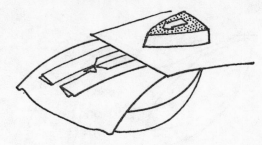

Fig. 220

A double-pointed waistline dart is always clipped at the waistline. Otherwise the dart won't do the shaping for which it was intended. Treat the remainder of the dart above and below the clip as if it were a regulation dart.

1. Place the opened dart over a corresponding curve of the tailor's ham.
2. Slip wrapping-paper strips under the seam allowances.
3. Cover with a dampened press cloth.
4. Press the dart. Start at the wide end and press to the dart point (Fig. 220). Use a slight rotary motion to smooth out the dart point. Try for a perfect blend. It is often necessary to pull the fabric taut while trying to achieve this.
5. Round out the area adjacent to the dart.
6. Remove the wrapping-paper strips. Allow the garment to dry on the tailor's ham.

Interfacing, underlining, and interlining materials are pressed to shape in the same way, except that pressing may be done with a steam iron.

Shaping a "No-shape" Garment

Contour pressing is the means of creating shape in any flat surface —a collar, a lapel, sleeve caps or even a "no-shape" garment, that is, one without darts or shaping seams.

HOW TO BLOCK A "NO-DART, NO-SEAM" GARMENT

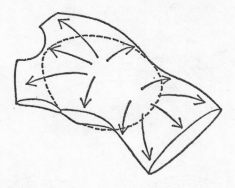

Fig. 221

1. Place the garment on an appropriate curve of the tailor's ham, wrong side up.

2. Press to shape. Start at the center front (or back) and press toward the outer edges (neck, shoulders, armholes, underarm, bust, waist, hips (Fig. 221).

How to Press a Collar into a Neck-shape

Construct the collar as directed on page 339.

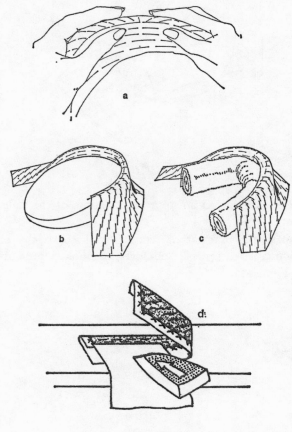

Fig. 222

THE UNDER COLLAR

1. Fold the collar along the roll line (Fig. 222a).

2. Place the folded collar over an appropriate curve of the tailor's ham (Fig. 222b) or a Turkish towel rolled and curled into a neck shape (Fig. 222c).

3. Steam to shape. *Do not* press a crease in the roll line, the collar must really *roll* along this line.

4. Allow the collar to dry in position. A few pins will help to hold the collar in place on the blocking pad.

5. Remove the collar from the press pad when dry.

6. Steam the stand of the collar in an inside curve (Fig. 222d). This will eliminate the ripples that tend to form because of the shorter measurement of the inside curve. Be careful to preserve the curve.

THE COMPLETED COLLAR

1. Mold the completed collar into a neck shape over the press pad. Pin to position if necessary.

2. Steam-press over a protective press cloth. *Do not* press a crease in the roll line.

3. Allow the collar to dry before removing.

HOW TO PRESS THE LAPEL TO SHAPE

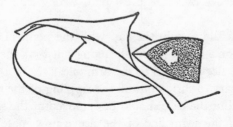

Fig. 223

1. Place the entire front, including lapel, over a suitable curve of the tailor's ham. Steam-press over a protective cloth (Fig. 223). The reverse curve of the lapel is restored to its true contour when the lapel is turned back to its rightful position.

Do not press a crease in the roll line. The lapel must *roll* to position.

How to Shape the Cap of a Set-in Sleeve

The following method is recommended only for such fabrics as can take steam. For a press pad use any of these: the narrow end of the tailor's ham, the broad end of a sleeve board or sleeve roll, the press mitt, or any other similarly shaped pad or board.

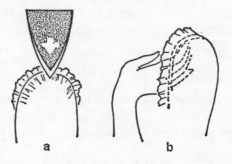

a   b

Fig. 224

1. Stitch the sleeve seam and press it open.
2. Place two rows of gathering stitches—hand or machine—across the cap from front notch to back notch. Draw up the gathering into a cap shape. Distribute the fullness evenly.
3. Slip the sleeve over the press pad, wrong side up. Fit the cap over the pad.
4. Shrink out the ease in the cap with the point of the steam iron (Fig. 224a). Don't worry about shrinking out too much. One can always spread the sleeve cap to fit the armhole.

It is unnecessary to shrink out all the rippling of the seam allowance at the cut edge but the ease should be removed at the seam line. With that disposed of the seam line of the sleeve now matches that of the armhole—all of which makes the setting of the sleeve relatively easy.

5. Block a softly rounded cap ⅜ to ½ inch into the sleeve.
6. When dry, gently push the blocked cap to the right side. You should be able to hold the cap with your hooked fingers (Fig. 224b).

Last-chance Press Before Assembling

Each shell of your garment—the outer fabric, the interfacing, the underlining, the interlining, the lining—should be well pressed and shaped before it is joined to another. Once the layers are applied to each other, one can never get back inside again. A right-side touch-up pressing can never accomplish what thorough pressing and shaping can do as you sew along.

Limp Length to Shapely Set

This chapter should give you some idea as to why the pressers in clothing factories are often more highly paid than the sewers. No doubt about it. Pressing is a special skill. But, by following the rules, you, too, can learn to do a very creditable job. It is worth the effort, for pressing can convert that limp length of cloth into one of shapely set.

ARTFUL DODGES AND CLASSIC
CLOSINGS

You could buckle it, bolt it, tie it, zipper it, loop it, lace it, band it, chain it—artful dodges all.

When it comes to your good tailored clothes—suit, coat, dress, shirt —chances are you will choose that time-honored closing: handsome buttons and beautifully bound buttonholes (Fig. 225).

Fig. 225

Bound Can Be Beautiful

Everyone is just a wee bit apprehensive about making bound buttonholes. After all, a slash in material is so final! Bound can be beautiful, though, if you measure accurately, mark carefully, and stitch as directed.

Start with the Button

The size and placement of the buttons is an essential part of the design of the garment. It is wise to purchase that size recommended on the pattern since the closing extension was planned for it.

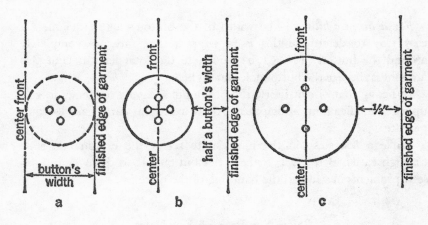

Fig. 226

Wherever the closing—front, back, side, top, bottom—the space between the line on which the garment closes and the seam line at the edge of the garment is exactly the width (diameter) of the button suggested (Fig. 226a). When buttoned, there will be half a button's width between the rim of the button and the finished edge of the garment (Fig. 226b). This placement provides the spacious setting a good button deserves. A cramped setting detracts from the design interest provided by buttons.

You may safely use a smaller button in the same space. However, should you be tempted to use a larger one, make certain that there is at least ½ inch left between the rim of the button and the finished edge (Fig. 226c).

Determine the Size of the Buttonhole

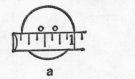

a   b

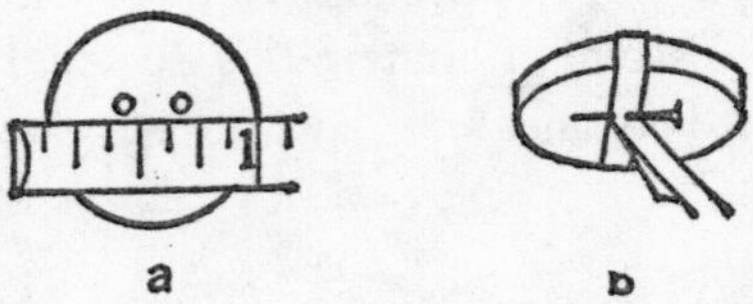

Fig. 227

The size of the buttonhole will be slightly larger than the button so that it can slide through easily. This is the rule:

For a flat button—the width of the button plus ⅛ inch ease (Fig. 227a).

For a bumpy button—the width of the button plus its height. An easy way to determine this is to wrap a tape measure completely around the button (Fig. 227b) and note the total length. Half this amount is the size the buttonhole should be.

In heavy coat or suit fabric the buttonholes have a tendency to end up a bit smaller than anticipated. Allow a tiny bit extra ease to compensate.

Make a test slash in the material to see if the button can slide through easily. Better yet, make a test buttonhole to discover unforeseen problems in size and the handling of the material.

Before You Begin: A Few Notes

Bound buttonholes are made on the right side of the garment and turned to the inside. Therefore the guide markings must be made on the right side.

Bound buttonholes are always made on the garment *before the facing is turned back or attached.* The facing is finished separately much later in the construction of the garment.

When making a series of buttonholes, the work is quicker and more accurate if you do the same operation on each buttonhole before going on to the next step rather than completing one buttonhole at a time.

Guide Markings for Buttonholes

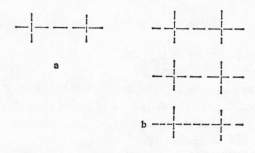

Fig. 228

1. Using a double thread of contrasting color, mark the position of the opening of the buttonhole (slash line). Place cross markings to indicate the beginning and the end of each buttonhole (Fig. 228a).

2. In making a series of buttonholes, make certain that they line up, that they are identical in size and evenly spaced (Fig. 228b).

Reinforce the Slash Line

Any area that is to be slashed should be reinforced before a cut is made in the material. With the exception of hair canvas, the interfacing or underlining can be that reinforcement. Hair canvas is too tough, too resilient, too bulky to be incorporated into the buttonhole. When hair canvas is the interfacing, remove a rectangle of it where the buttonhole is to be constructed and substitute a patch of iron-on material, organza, muslin, or any other lightweight underlining material.

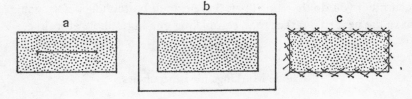

Fig. 229

1. Transfer the buttonhole markings from the right side to the hair canvas on the underside.

2. Draw a rectangle ⅜ inch away from the markings on all sides (Fig. 229a). Don't make the opening any larger than this or you will lose the benefit of the canvas interfacing. It should be just large enough to take the buttonhole comfortably.

3. Cut out the interfacing rectangle.

4. Place the cut-out rectangle on the new backing material as a guide. Trace around it. Draw a new, larger rectangle around the tracing, making it at least ¼ inch larger all around for an overlap (Fig. 229b).

5. Cut out the replacement material.

6. Either insert the new backing in the opening of the interfacing or place it on top of it. You may use the markings of the original rectangle in step 2 as a placement guide.

7. Fasten with catch stitching (Fig. 229c). The iron-on replacement need only be pressed on.

Method I—The One-strip Method for Making a Bound Buttonhole

PREPARE THE BINDING

The following method works well on lightweight to medium fabrics. For heavy or sheer fabrics use Method II.

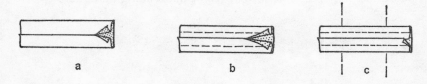

Fig. 230

1. Cut a strip of garment fabric 1 inch wide by the length of the buttonhole plus 1 inch.

2. Fold the strip in half lengthwise, right side outside. Crease or press along the fold. Open out.

3. Fold each lengthwise raw edge to meet the center line (crease) (Fig. 230a). This now makes the strip ½ inch wide.

4. Place a line of hand or machine basting ⅛ inch in from each folded edge (Fig. 230b). Use matching thread.

5. Place the binding on the right side of the garment, centering the strip on the slash line. Baste to position through the center of the strip (Fig. 230c).

ATTACH THE BINDING TO THE GARMENT

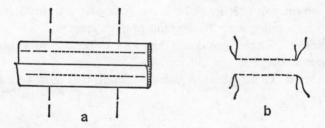

Fig. 231

1. Starting a stitch or two beyond the cross markings, machine stitch the binding to the garment directly over the basting of Fig. 230b (Fig. 231a). *Do not stitch across the ends. Do not lock stitch* at the beginning and end of the stitching.

2. Turn to the wrong side. You will see two parallel lines of machine stitching and the unsecured thread at each corner. Pull all four sets of thread-ends through to the wrong side. Pull them back to the cross markings (Fig. 231b). For perfect corners, each pair of threads must end at the markings and directly opposite another pair. Tie each pair in a square knot (right over left, left over right) and trim the thread close to the knots.

SLASH THE OPENING

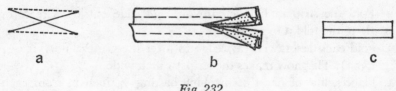

Fig. 232

1. Working from the underside, make a tiny snip in the material at the center of the space between the parallel rows of stitching. Use a very sharp pair of trimming or embroidery scissors.

2. From the small opening slash diagonally to all four corners coming as close to the stitching as you safely can (Fig. 232a). Be careful not to cut the binding on the other side. Note the long triangular flaps that form at each end.

3. Turn to the right side. Slash through the center of the binding strip without cutting the garment (Fig. 232b).

4. Grasp the pair of strips at each end (one pair at a time) and very gently push them through the opening to the wrong side. The binding will assume its rightful position (Fig. 232c). Behold your beautiful bound buttonhole!

Well, almost. There are a few finishing details that must be attended to.

STITCH THE ENDS OF THE BUTTONHOLE

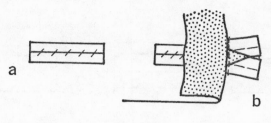

Fig. 233

Adjust the strips so the folds just meet at center without any over-lapping. You may have to do a little coaxing to get them into position.

1. On the right side of the garment, close the lips of the buttonhole with diagonal basting (Fig. 233a). This is very important because the basting holds the binding in place for securing the ends. Omit the basting and you end up with gaping buttonholes.

2. Once again, turn to the underside. Fold back the garment against itself so you can see the long, triangular flap as it lies against the end of the binding.

3. Stitch the triangle to the strip across each end of the buttonhole. Stitch close to the fold but not over it (Fig. 233b). Were you to stitch over the fold you would get a tuck on the right side. Stitch too far away from it and you will find a hole at each end.

4. Trim the excess binding to about ¼ inch from the stitching.

Bound to Be Good

This method of making a bound buttonhole is basic and practically foolproof. The evenness of the lips of the buttonhole is guaranteed in the preparation of the binding. The centered placement of the binding on the slash line automatically puts the stitching lines in the right position. The buttonhole is bound to be good.

In all honesty one must say there are times when this method of con-structing a buttonhole is not entirely satisfactory. In very heavy or very sheer materials it is too difficult to handle the tiny strips. Then, too, a very narrow strip of heavy fabric produces too bumpy a buttonhole. The two-strip method of making a bound buttonhole is preferable for many fabrics.

Tailored to a "T"

Method II—The Two-strip Method for Making a Bound Buttonhole

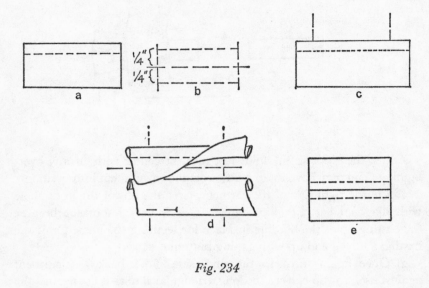

Fig. 234

1. Two separate strips are necessary for each buttonhole. Make them 2 inches wide by the length of the buttonhole plus 1 inch.

2. With the right side outside, fold each strip in half lengthwise.

3. Using matching thread, make a line of guide basting ⅛ inch from the folded edge (Fig. 234a). This will make the ideal buttonhole —¼ inch wide when finished. However, in heavy or bulky fabric, make the binding a little wider. Place the guide basting ³⁄₁₆ inch from the folded edge. This will make the finished buttonhole ⅜ inch wide. It should not be any wider than that.

4. Additional guidelines are necessary to place the larger strips in the same relative position for stitching as in Method I.

Make a line of guide basting above and below the slash line equal to the total width of the finished buttonhole (Fig. 234b). That is, for a ¼-inch wide buttonhole, ¼ inch above and ¼ inch below the slash line; for a ⅜-inch wide buttonhole, ⅜ inch above and ⅜ inch below the slash line.

5. Because of the size of the strips, only one at a time is basted and stitched to the garment. Place strip ⚹1 in such position that the folded edge is against the upper marking. Pin or baste in place.

6. Stitch directly over the basting starting and ending a stitch or two beyond the cross markings (Fig. 234c).

7. Fold back the strip over itself. Pin it securely in this position (Fig. 234d). This reveals the rest of the buttonhole marking.

8. Position and stitch strip ⚹2 in the same way.

9. The rest of the construction of the Method II buttonhole is the same as the Method I buttonhole.

10. Note the wide extensions of each strip of binding on the underside of the buttonhole (Fig. 234e). Grade the thicknesses making the inner thickness narrower than the outer one. Trim the ends.

The use of the zipper foot rather than the regulation presser foot makes it easier to stitch strips of very heavy fabric.

You'll be pleased with the no-bulk, no-ridge buttonhole you have so masterfully created.

Buttonhole Bonus: The Bound Pocket

Here's a bonus for you: a bound buttonhole converted into a bound pocket (Fig. 235a).

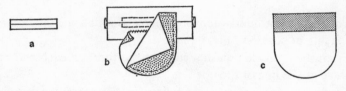

Fig. 235

All you need do is to attach an upper pocket to the lower seam allowance with hemming stitches and attach an under pocket to the upper seam allowance with backstitches (Fig. 235b). (The under pocket is the part against the body; the upper pocket is the part against the outer fabric.)

Make the pocket as wide as the opening plus seam allowance. If you really intend to use it as a pocket, make it deep enough to get your hand into it comfortably.

Make the under pocket of fashion fabric so there will be no break in color or texture at the pocket opening. Another method is to face the under pocket with a strip of fashion fabric only in the opening area (Fig. 235c).

The Finish Through the Facing

By whatever method you choose to make the bound buttonhole on the right side of the garment, a finish is required for the underside through the facing. There are several ways to do this. The first two methods are quick and easy. The third takes more time and care but rewards you with twin buttonholes on outer fabric and facing. It is a particularly good method for a convertible-collar style where both sides of the closing extension must look identical.

FOR ALL METHODS

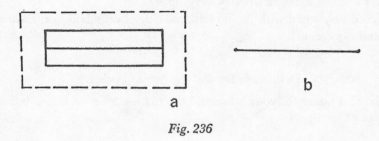

Fig. 236

1. Pin or baste around each buttonhole through all thicknesses to fix the facing in position (Fig. 236a).
2. From the right side, push a straight pin through each end of the buttonhole at the line of the opening.
3. From the facing side, draw a line for the opening with pencil, tailor's chalk, or a line of basting (Fig. 236b). Make certain that the opening is the same distance in from the edge on both right side and facing. Make sure that the length of the buttonhole is the same on both sides. Measure.

Method I—Easiest of All Methods

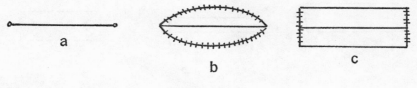

a

b

c

Fig. 237

1. Slash from one end of the marking to the other (Fig. 237a).
2. Turn under the raw edges of the facing to form an ellipse (Fig. 237b). Hem to position.
3. In loosely woven fabrics it is possible to push the opening into the shape of a rectangle with the point of the needle (Fig. 237c). Hem quickly to prevent fraying.

Method II—Takes a Little More Doing

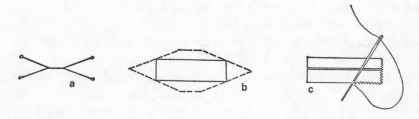

a

b

c

Fig. 238

1. Slash through the center of the marking and clip diagonally to each corner to a depth equal to the width of the binding (Fig. 238a).
2. Turn under each of the four little flaps to form a rectangle (Fig. 238b).
3. Hem tentatively to position with a few quick stitches so the opening is set. Then go back and hem neatly and securely (Fig. 238c). Take several tiny reinforcing stitches at each corner.

Method III—Face the Facing

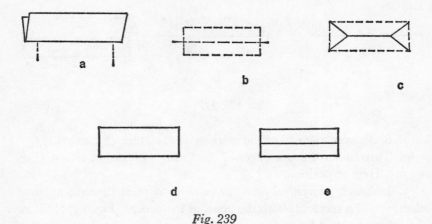

Fig. 239

1. Cut a patch of organdy or organza. (Organza is an ideal material for this purpose since it is practically weightless.) Any color will do since it won't be seen if properly done but a matching color is a safeguard and a nice touch. Make the patch 1½ inches wide by the length of the buttonhole plus 1 inch.

2. Open out the facing. Center the organza over the buttonhole marking on the facing (Fig. 239a). Pin it to position.

3. Stitch the organza to the facing in a rectangle equal to the length and width of the finished buttonhole (Fig. 239b). Count the stitches if this will help you to get it accurate. Or, make a stitching guide by marking the rectangle on the organza.

4. Slash through the center of the rectangle. Clip diagonally to each corner (Fig. 239c).

5. Turn the organza to the wrong side of the facing through the slash. Press or baste to position so no organza shows (Fig. 239d).

6. Place the faced rectangular opening against the underside of the bound buttonhole. Slipstitch to the stitching lines (Fig. 239e).

A PASSEL OF POCKETS

Pockets are more than a place to hide your hands or your treasures.
They can be downright decorative (Fig. 240).

Fig. 240

Like many another detail, they are subject to the whims and fancies of the designer (who may be you). They can be logical or irrational in size, shape, and placement. They may be hidden or boldly displayed. They may be splashed on the surface or set into seam or slash. However little or well they may function as pockets, you'll agree they can add dash to the design.

Surface, Seam or Slash: The Place for Pockets

There are three basic constructions for pockets:

1. There are those applied to the surface like the patch pocket (Fig. 241a). (See directions on page 179).

2. There are those stitched into a seam or a slash (Fig. 241b). (See directions on page 172 for the former and page 312 for the latter.)

3. There are those that have elements of both styles—the welt pocket (Fig. 241c) and the flap pocket (Fig. 241d).

Fig. 241

Flaps and Welts to Hide the Slash

Whereas the binding of a bound pocket is used to finish and protect the slash, flaps and welts can be used to hide it.

In order to do this, the welt or flap is placed on the garment in a position opposite to the way it will look when stitched. When turned to its rightful position, the opening of the pocket is concealed.

For instance, a welt destined to turn up is placed "head down" (Fig. 242a), stitched and turned.

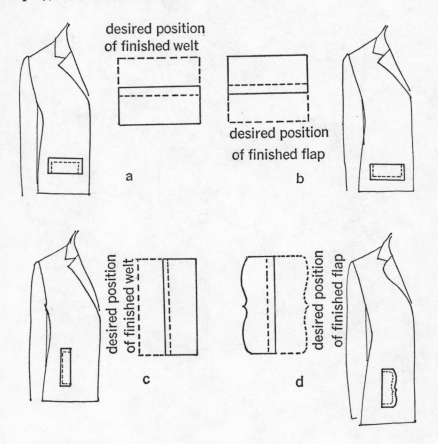

Fig. 242

A flap that will eventually hang down when finished is placed "head up" for stitching (Fig. 242b).

Welts and flaps may appear in other positions (Fig. 242c and 242d) but the rule holds: to hide the opening of the pocket, place the welt or flap in a position for stitching in a direction opposite to the way it will appear when finished.

To Make the Pocket Welt or Flap

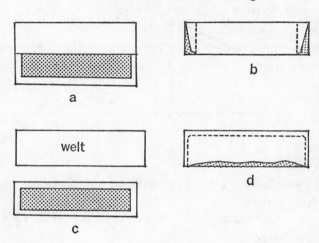

Fig. 243

IN ONE PIECE

1. Cut a strip of fabric the length of the welt by twice its width plus seam allowances.

2. Interface the under half of it (Fig. 243a).

3. Fold the welt in half lengthwise. Set the raw edges of the upper thickness down a little from the raw edges of the under thickness (Fig. 243b). In this way one may utilize some of the seam allowance for the extra length needed to roll the joining seams to the underside. Stitch across the ends (Fig. 243b).

IN TWO PIECES

1. Allow enough fabric on the upper thickness so the joining seam may be rolled to the underside.

2. Interface the facing (Fig. 243c).

3. With raw edges matching, stitch the upper layer to the facing, easing in the fullness. Leave the lower edge open (Fig. 243d).

TO COMPLETE EITHER TYPE OF WELT OR FLAP

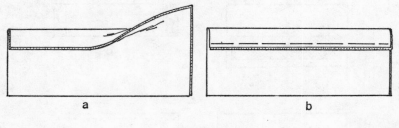

a   b

Fig. 244

4. Press all seam allowances open before turning to the right side. Use the point presser.

5. Grade the seam allowances. Free all corners of bulk. Clip and/or notch as necessary.

6. Turn to the right side and press.

7. In order to make the flaps and welts lie flat when turned to their true positions a little extra length is needed on the upper thickness to negotiate the turn.

With the upper side of the welt on top and the underside against the hand, roll the welt over the fingers making the needed adjustment in length (Fig. 244a). Pin to position. Baste both thicknesses across the lower edge (Fig. 244b).

How to Make the Welt Pocket

ATTACH THE WELT TO THE GARMENT

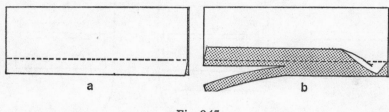

a   b

Fig. 245

1. On the right side of the garment, place the seam line of the lower edge of the welt directly on the slash-line guide basting.

2. Stitch through all thicknesses from one end of the welt to the other (Fig. 245a). *Do not lock stitch.* It's hard to be so accurate that the lock stitches do not go beyond the welt.

3. Pull the thread ends through to the underside and tie each pair with a square knot.

4. Grade the seam allowances of the welt, trimming them close to the seam line (Fig. 245b).

APPLY THE POCKET

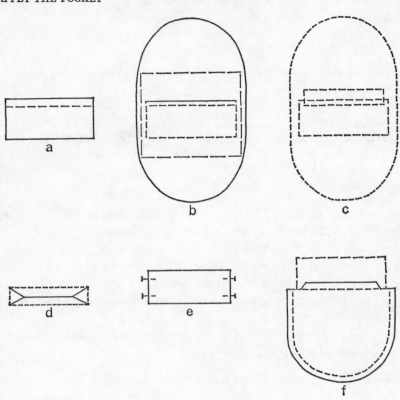

Fig. 246

Fig. 246a shows the welt stitched to the garment along the slash line.

1. Cut the pocket of lining material. Make it equal to the width of the pocket by twice its depth plus seam allowances. Mark the slash line in the center.

2. Place the pocket over the welt, right sides together. Set one stitching line of the pocket directly over the stitching line of the welt. Baste to position (Fig. 246b).

3. Stitch a rectangle for the pocket opening (Fig. 246c). This is easier to do if you turn to the wrong side where the line of stitching that attached the welt to the garment can be used as a guideline. Make the first line of stitching directly over the previous stitching; stitch across one end for ¼ inch; make the third side of the rectangle parallel to the first; stitch across the second end making it parallel to the other end.

Turn the last corner and continue the stitching ½ to 1 inch directly over the first side of the rectangle to secure the stitching.

CAUTION: *Be sure to start and stop the stitching two or three stitches in from each end.* This makes the opening of the pocket a little smaller than the welt. When the welt is turned to its final position, it will completely conceal the opening. Were you to stitch all the way to the ends of the welt, you would wind up with two conspicuous gaping holes at the ends of the pocket.

4. Slash all thicknesses through the center of the rectangle to within ¼ inch of the ends. Clip diagonally to the corners (Fig. 246d).

5. Turn the pocket to the wrong side by slipping it gently through the opening. Pocket and welt will assume their proper positions.

6. Pin the welt in place and slipstitch the ends to the garment (Fig. 246e).

7. On the underside, pin the upper and under pockets together. Note that the upper pocket is slightly longer than the under pocket. This is because of the ¼-inch depth of the opening. Trim it to match the under pocket.

8. Machine stitch the pocket (Fig. 246f).

Flap Pockets

Unlike the welt pocket whose ends are fastened to the garment, a flap hangs free—to flap, of course. A flap can hide the opening of any kind of pocket—patch (Fig. 247a), seam-inserted (Fig. 247b), or bound (Fig. 247c).

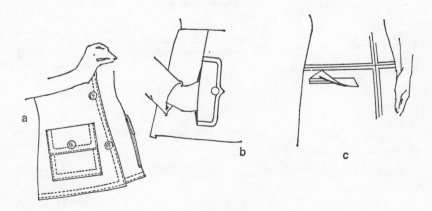

a   b   c

Fig. 247

The Flap Over a Patch Pocket

WELT SEAM UNDER THE FLAP

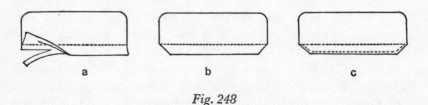

Fig. 248

1. Place the flap in position on the designated placement line. Pin and stitch.

2. Trim the under seam allowance close to the stitching (Fig. 248a).

3. On the upper seam allowance fold under the ends diagonally (Fig. 248b).

4. Turn under part of the upper seam allowance as for a welt seam. Stitch (Fig. 248c).

TOPSTITCHED FLAP

An alternate method skips the stitching under the flap but adds topstitching to hold the flap in place.

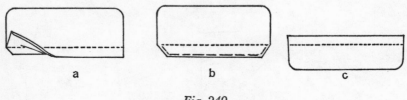

Fig. 249

1. Grade the seam allowances. Clip the ends of the under seam allowance diagonally (Fig. 249a).

2. Fold under the ends of the upper seam allowances diagonally (Fig. 249b). Baste to position.

3. Turn the flap to position. Topstitch an even distance from the fold (Fig. 249c).

A Flap Added to a Bound Pocket

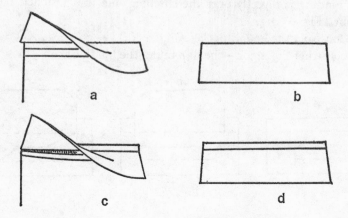

Fig. 250

When a flap is added to a bound pocket it is included in the upper seam. The flap may be inserted over the binding (Fig. 250a) to cover it (Fig. 250b) or under the binding (Fig. 250c) to reveal it (Fig. 250d). Both methods are acceptable. It is merely a matter of design.

To construct Fig. 250a—the flap over the binding:

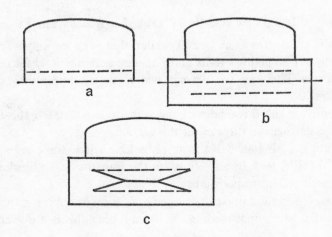

Fig. 251

1. Make the flap and stitch it to the garment ⅛ inch above the pocket opening (Fig. 251a). Trim the seam allowances close to the stitching.

2. Place the binding over the flap so that the stitching line of the upper binding is directly over the stitching line that fastened flap to garment (Fig. 251b).

3. Construct the bound pocket (Fig. 251c).

To construct Fig. 250c—the flap under the binding:

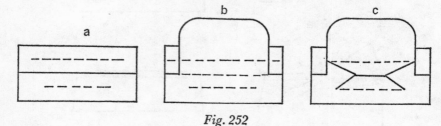

Fig. 252

1. Place and stitch the upper binding the full length of the opening. Stitch the lower binding parallel to the first but tapering in ⅛ to ¼ inch at each end (Fig. 252a). By doing so the flap will cover the opening of the pocket.

2. Make the flap and stitch it in place directly over the stitching line of the upper binding (Fig. 252b).

3. Construct the bound pocket (Fig. 252c).

"It Ain't Necessarily So": Fake Flaps and Welts

Do you think there's a pocket under that welt or flap? It ain't necessarily so! Sometimes welts and flaps are added strictly for decorative purposes. There are two ways in which you can apply these downright fakes.

1. Complete the three sides of the welt or flap. Attach the fourth side to the garment as directed in this section.

2. Complete all four sides first. (Machine stitch three sides, turn to the right side, tuck in and slipstitch the fourth side.) Slipstitch the finished welt or flap to position.

The second method makes a flatter application by avoiding the turnover essential to the first method. In some fabrics this is a decided advantage.

It Is Necessarily So

Pretty or practical, real or fake, pockets can add interest to an otherwise simple design.

TAILOR TALK

Tailored Perfection Takes Time

Your real measure as a tailor is how you handle the classic tailored collar and lapels. Not that the techniques themselves are so difficult, it is just that they take time: time to put in those hundreds of tiny hand stitches—all invisible, all important; time to test and shape and mold. You may go full-speed ahead on less exacting operations but the tailored perfection of collar and lapels takes time. You may be surprised to know that in this age of machines and mass production, the construction of the collar and lapels is still largely done by hand—even in factories.

The Collar-and-Lapel Unit

There are two collars traditionally associated with tailoring. In one (the classic notched collar—Fig. 253a), part of the jacket rolls back to form lapels. A separate collar is set on the neckline and lapels a little distance in from the ends to form a notch (Fig. 253b).

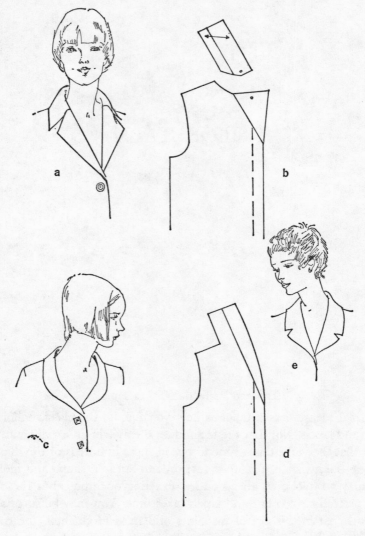

Fig. 253

In the other (the shawl collar—Fig. 253c), the entire collar is part of the jacket front (Fig. 253d).

A simulated notched collar may be created by a cutout on the style line of a shawl collar (Fig. 253e).

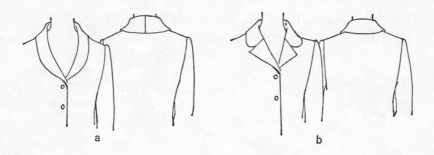

Fig. 254

In the shawl collar, the seam that joins right and left collars is at the center back (Fig. 254a). No seaming is visible from the front.

In the classic notched collar, the seam line that joins collar to lapels is visible from the front (Fig. 254b). The collar may or may not have a center-back seam.

Whether the collar is all in one piece or in two pieces and whether the joining seam is visible or invisible, the collar is thought of as a unit that extends from the center back to the break—the point at which the collar rolls back to form the lapel. Collar and lapels are treated as one unit.

Cut-on and Try-on

Since the shawl collar is part of the front it must be cut when the front is cut. This leaves only one place where an adjustment can be made if needed—the center-back seam.

It is wise to cut-on (add) a seam allowance just in case it is needed for better fit. It can always be trimmed away if not used.

There is more opportunity for perfect fit in the classic notched collar. Since it is a separate collar one can test it in the interfacing material before cutting the collar of one's more expensive or irreplaceable fabric.

To Adjust the Classic Notched-collar Pattern

When the jacket or coat has been carefully fitted at the shoulders, neck, and body seams, and when the garment has been stitched and pressed, proceed as follows.

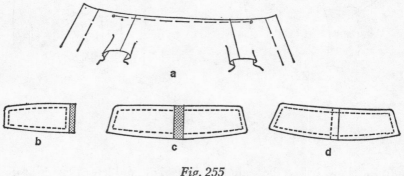

Fig. 255

1. Place a line of guide basting at the neck seam line of the garment. Make longer stitches on the right side and shorter ones on the underside (Fig. 255a).

2. Measure the length of the neck seam line from the center back to the point at which the collar joins the lapel.

3. Measure the neck seam line of the *under collar* pattern from the center back to the point of joining. This is half the length of the entire pattern neckline.

4. Compare the pattern measurement with the garment measurement. The under collar pattern should measure ¼ inch less in length than the garment. (A whole collar measures ½ inch less in length than the garment neckline.) When the two are joined the collar is stretched slightly to fit the garment neckline. This produces a better roll and fit.

5. Make any necessary adjustments to the collar pattern. Up to a seam allowance may be added or subtracted at the center back. If the pattern is cut with a center-back seam, this is easy enough (Fig. 255b). To add length if the collar is cut in one piece: slash the interfacing at the center back, spread the slashed sections, and insert a piece of tissue to the needed amount (Fig. 255c). To reduce the length of the one-piece collar: tuck the center back to the needed amount (Fig. 255d).

When more than a seam-allowance adjustment is needed: slash and spread in several places or tuck in several places. This is done to preserve the style line which would be lost were a big adjustment to be made all in one place.

Trial Run: The Test Interfacing

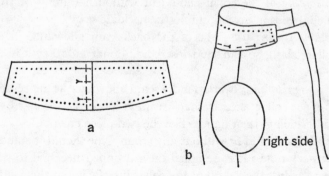

Fig. 256

1. Cut the collar interfacing from the corrected under collar pattern. Mark all seam lines with pencil or dressmaker's carbon.

2. When there is a center-back seam, overlap the seam lines of the interfacing and pin. Place the pins at right angles to the seam for easy fitting (Fig. 256a).

3. *Overlap the collar interfacing on the garment* matching seam lines. Pin. Place the pins horizontally directly on the seam line (Fig. 256b). It is impossible to get a true fitting unless the collar is *overlapped* on the garment.

Match the center backs. On the classic notched collar, match each point on the lapel where the collar joins it. On the shawl collar, clip the seam allowance at the corner where shoulder and collar meet. Match the collar shoulder-marking with the garment shoulder. Stretch the collar neckline between these fixed points to fit the garment neckline. Clip the collar seam allowance where necessary.

4. Try on the garment. If you plan to use shoulder pads, slip them into position. Pin the center front closed from the top button down. Examine the collar for fit. Adjust as necessary.

How the Under Collar Should Fit

The real burden of fine fit falls upon the under collar. The upper collar is just so much decoration.

The collar should fit in length (at the neckline, the roll line, and the style line) and in depth (the stand and the fall). These two dimensions are so interrelated that to change one often means an automatic change in the other.

Fitting the Length of the Collar

The neckline of the collar should fit without straining or rippling. When a change is indicated, unpin the neckline seam.

To relieve strain: use some of the back-seam allowance in a two-piece collar; slash, spread, and insert additional interfacing in a one-piece collar.

To remove rippling: overlap more seam allowance at the center back of a two-piece collar; create a back seam in a one-piece collar by slashing the interfacing, then handle like the two-piece collar.

The roll line should fit without any strain. Nor should it stand away from the neck unless it is designed on a dropped neckline to produce that effect. Adjust the length of the collar interfacing at the roll line by using the center-back seam allowance (when there is one) to add or subtract. When there is no center-back seam, create one by slashing the interfacing.

The style line should lie smoothly around the shoulders without pulling, rippling, or poking out at center back. Add or subtract to the length of the interfacing style line at an existing or created back seam.

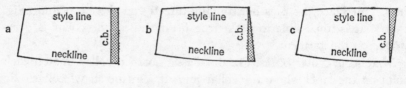

Fig. 257

Adjustments may be balanced, that is, the same amount at the neckline as at the style line (Fig. 257a). Or, they may be made in one place only, that is, change at the neckline but not at the style line (Fig. 257b). Or, retain the neckline measurement but change the style line (Fig. 257c).

Fitting the Depth of the Collar

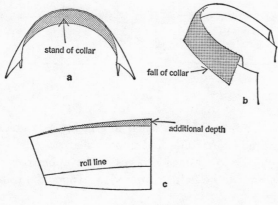

Fig. 258

The stand of the collar is the amount of the rise from the neckline to the roll line (Fig. 258a). It should be neither too high nor too low for *your* neck. When a change is indicated, unpin the neckline seam.

If the stand is too high, lower it by adding length to the collar neckline. If the stand is too low, raise it by shortening the length of the collar neckline. Adjustments are made at the center back.

The fall of the collar is the depth of the collar from the roll line to the style line (Fig. 258b). It should completely cover the neckline seam *plus* at least ½ inch. When the stand of the collar fits well around the neck yet discloses the neckline seam, add depth at the style line (Fig. 258c).

When you are satisfied with the fit of the under collar, mark the roll line with pins from the center back to the break of the collar at the front closing. Work on the side easiest for you to reach. Remove the garment. Unpin the collar. Substitute a chalk or pencil marking for the pins along the roll line. Transfer the roll-line marking to the other half of the collar.

Prepare the Collar

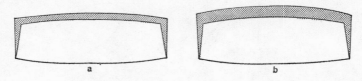

Fig. 259

1. Using the adjusted under collar interfacing as a guide, trace the alterations on the under collar and upper collar patterns.

2. Add roll-ease to all outside edges of the upper collar pattern so the joining seam can be hidden from view. Taper the roll-ease to the neckline (Fig. 259a).

3. When the fashion fabric is heavy, add more collar depth to accommodate the roll of the collar from neckline to style line in the same way that depth was added to the fall (Fig. 259b). Otherwise the collar will flip up when worn.

4. Cut out both upper and under collars in fabric.

5. For a two-piece collar:

    a. Overlap and stitch the center-back seam of the interfacing. Trim the seam allowances close to the stitching line.

    b. Stitch the fabric under collar at the center-back seam. Press the seam allowances open. Trim when necessary.

Collar Contour

In a bodice or skirt it is the darts and shaping seams that produce the garment contour. In a collar, it is hundreds of tiny hand stitches and blocking.

From the moment the collar interfacing is positioned on the under collar, one must stop thinking of the two as flat lengths of material. One must will them, wish them, and sculpture them into a collar contour.

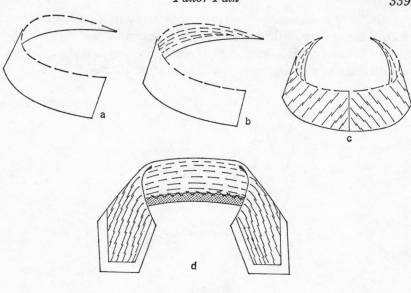

Fig. 260

1. Place the collar interfacing over the wrong side of the under collar. Pin to position.

2. Using matching thread make a row of uneven horizontal basting stitches along the roll line. Make the stitches ¼ inch in length on the interfacing. Catch only a yarn or two of the under collar fabric.

3. When the entire row of stitching along the roll line is completed, tug the thread *slightly* until the collar begins to curve into a neck shape (Fig. 260a).

4. Fill the stand with parallel rows of similar uneven horizontal basting to the neck seam line. Tug the thread slightly at the end of each row. Make the rows ¼ inch apart (Fig. 260b).

5. Hold the collar over the hand in a neck shape while padstitching. Starting at the center back and following the grain of the interfacing, padstitch the fall of the collar from the roll line to the seam line (Fig. 260c). The stitches are ⅜ to ½ inch long; the rows are ⅜ to ½ inch apart.

Padstitches permanently join layers of fabric so they perform as one piece. They are applied to any part of the garment that must maintain a permanent roll as in the collar, cuffs, and lapel. Padstitching is only done on an undersurface where the stitches will never show.

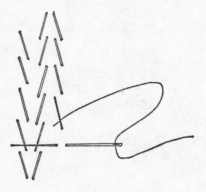

Fig. 261

Padstitching is a series of small, diagonal basting stitches on the surface and tiny horizontal stitches that pick up only a yarn or two of the undersurface (Fig. 261). The smaller the stitches and the closer the rows, the stiffer the padstitched area becomes.

Many sewers like to padstitch the stand heavily (¼-inch stitches, rows ¼ inch apart) and to padstitch the fall lightly (⅜ to ½-inch stitches, rows ⅜ to ½ inch apart). To ensure that the points of the collar and lapel lie flat against the body the padstitches may be made smaller and the rows closer together as they near the points.

Note: The direction of the stitching helps to produce the collar contour. The horizontal stitching of the stand provides the opportunity for determining the neck shape. The padstitching on the fall of the collar utilizes the grain (generally bias) for easing around the shoulders.

6. Trim away all the seam allowances of the interfacing.

7. Trim, clip, and turn up the neck-edge seam allowance of the under collar over the interfacing. Catch stitch in place (Fig. 260d).

8. Crease along the roll line. Block to shape.

To maintain the neck shape of the collar when it is not being worked on, pin it around the tailor's ham, a rolled-up towel, or the neck of a dress form. From this point on it must never be stored flat.

To Complete the Collar

The upper collar is applied to the under collar in one of three ways.

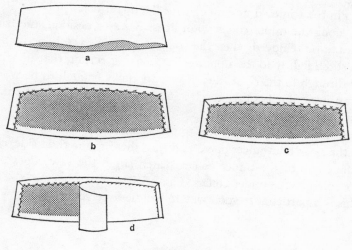

Fig. 262

METHOD I—THE MOST FREQUENTLY USED METHOD

1. Stitch the upper collar to the interfaced under collar around all but the neck edge. That must be left open (Fig. 262a). Use all the tailoring techniques previously learned for easing, stitching, trimming, grading, and pressing.

2. Decide whether the enclosed seam allowances are to be held in place with topstitching or understitching.

When to do the topstitching depends on the style and the method of joining the collar to the garment. Generally, it is done at such time that the entire topstitching of collar, lapels, and closing edge can be done in one continuous line.

When topstitching is inconsistent with the design of the garment, understitch. After the upper and under collars have been joined, pressed, and the seam allowances graded (the upper wider than the under), edge-baste all finished edges to hold the seam in position. Carefully lift the upper collar. Catch stitch the wider upper seam allowance to the tape or interfacing, thereby enclosing (encasing) the narrower under seam allowance. Understitching is done in the same way on the lapels and front facings.

METHOD II—AN EXCELLENT METHOD FOR HEAVY OR PILE FABRICS

1. Trim *all* under collar seam allowances—fabric as well as interfacing.

2. Pin the trimmed under collar to the upper collar, placing its raw edges along the upper collar seam lines. Baste to position, the basting stitches to be removed when the collar is completed. Or, permanently catch stitch lightly to the upper collar, making certain that no stitches come through to the right side. If you are lucky enough to be working with an underlined collar, catch stitch the under collar to the underlining (Fig. 262b).

3. Miter the corners of the upper collar seam allowances. Trim, press the seam allowances open, and turn them to the right side, covering the edges of the under collar. Catch stitch the raw edges of the upper collar to the under collar (Fig. 262c).

This is a particularly good way to handle a velvet collar.

METHOD III—THE FLATTEST COLLAR OF ALL

1. Underline the upper collar.
2. Miter the corners. Turn to the right side.
3. Catch stitch all raw edges to the underlining.
4. Cut an under collar of felt or Melton cloth. Trim away ⅜ inch of all seam allowances, leaving ¼ inch for an overlap.
5. Place the under collar against the seam allowance of the upper collar. Attach with slant hemming stitches (Fig. 262d).

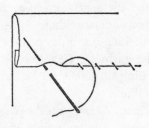

Fig. 263

Slant hemming stitches are fast, strong, but conspicuous. Used only when they won't be seen, they are really tiny, diagonal bastings (Fig. 263).

By whatever method you choose to complete the collar, press all outside edges as flat as possible. Use the pressing technique determined best for the fabric.

Steam and shape the completed collar over an appropriate press pad.

Prepare the Lapel

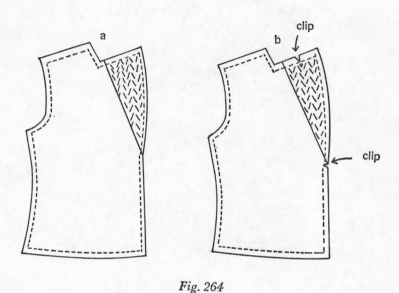

Fig. 264

1. Holding the lapel over the hand in the position in which it will be worn, padstitch from the roll line to the outer edge or to the tape when used (Fig. 264a).

2. Stitch the facing to the front edge of the garment from the hem to the point at which the collar joins the lapel. Clip the seam allowances at this point and at the break of the collar (Fig. 264b). The former clip is necessary for the setting of the collar; the latter, for the change of direction at the turn-back of the lapel.

Use all the tailoring techniques previously described for easing, stitching, trimming, grading, pressing, and handling of encased seams (page 341).

Attach the Collar to the Garment

It's easier, quicker, more accurate, flatter, neater to join the collar to the garment with hand stitching.

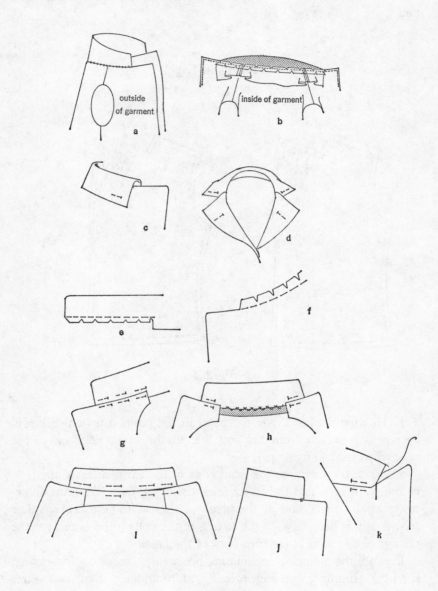

Fig. 265

WORK FROM THE RIGHT SIDE

1. Overlap the finished edge of the under collar on the seam line of the garment neck edge. The garment seam allowance will slip into the opening of the collar.

2. Pin at each point where the collar joins the lapel. Pin the center back. Stretch the collar neckline to fit the garment neckline. Do *not* include the front facing or the upper collar in either the pinning or the stitching.

3. Make sure that both ends of the collar are the same size. Make sure that both lapels are the same size.

4. Attach the *under collar only* (Fig. 265a) with vertical hemming stitches (see page 69). The stitches are tiny, close together, and strong. They are meant to hold the collar intact for the life of the garment.

TURN TO THE INSIDE OF THE GARMENT

5. Trim, clip, and turn down the loose neck-edge seam allowance of the garment over the neckline tape or the interfacing. Press it open with the tip of the iron. Fasten with either permanent basting or with catch stitching (Fig. 265b).

Once more, *back to the right side.*

6. Fold back the collar to the position it will assume when worn, and pin (Fig. 265c). Turn each lapel to position, and pin (Fig. 265d). This will assure enough length on the upper surface for the roll of the collar and lapel.

7. Trim away the seam allowance bulk where collar and lapel join. Trim and clip the seam allowances of the upper collar and the facing (Figs. 265e and 265f).

8. Turn under the seam allowance of the upper collar *into the collar.* Turn under the seam allowance of the lapel *into the lapel.* The folds of collar and lapel meet at the neck seam line. Pin or baste to position (Fig. 265g).

When there is no back neck facing: clip the collar seam allowance at the shoulder (the end of the front facing). Bring it down over the neckline tape or the interfacing from one shoulder to the other, clipping as necessary to make it lie flat. Fasten with either permanent basting or with catch stitching (Fig. 265h). The lining will cover this.

When there is a back-neck facing: attach it to the front facing and press the seam allowances open. Trim, clip, and turn under the entire collar seam allowances into the collar and the entire lapel-and-facing seam allowances into the facing. Pin to position (Fig. 265i).

9. Remove the pins which are holding the collar and lapels in their rolled-back positions.

10. Using matching thread, secure the end with several strong over-and-over stitches on the underside of the collar where it joins the lapel (Fig. 265j). Bring the needle through to the right side at the seam line between the folds of the collar and facing (Fig. 265k).

11. Slipstitch the collar to the facing through the folds. Don't draw up the stitches too tightly. When the stitching is completed, secure the end of the thread with several strong over-and-over stitches on the underside.

12. To make sure that upper collar and facing will always stay in place, anchor them by either of the two following methods:

   (a) Catch some of the under collar seam allowance while slip-stitching collar to facing.
   (b) Gently lift the upper collar and facing, separating them from the under collar and garment. Join the seam allowances of the former to the seam allowances of the latter with permanent basting.

13. Remove all temporary bastings. Press carefully.

AND SEW ON

While this is the standard method for constructing and applying tailored collars, it is an equally good method for making and applying all collars other than standing or ring collars. The technique works well on cuffs too. In fact, it is so easy a method and produces such spectacular results that you will probably never go back to the machine-stitching methods suggested in most pattern directions.

Everything You Always Wanted to Know About Sewing But Were Afraid to Ask

Everything you always wanted to know about sewing but were afraid to ask is an integral part of the tailoring technique. Master that and you will never again be afraid to tackle any sewing problem— dressmaking, tailoring, whatever.

PART IV

GRAB BAG

Assorted Goodies, Sheer to Sturdy

SEW FOR SUNDOWN

By day, you can borrow anything you want from the boys—their blue jeans, their shirts, their vests, their boots. But after sundown, most girls want to look—well, like girls! The look may be billowy or slinky, bold or demure—no matter. What does matter is that one looks appealing in a feminine kind of way.

Often it is not so much the style as the fabric that does the trick: a shirtwaist of satin or brocade, a trench coat of organdy, a shift of velvet. Be the fabrics romantic or razzle-dazzle, they call for special handling.

FOR SHEER PLEASURE

To See and Not to See

What you don't see is often more intriguing than what you do see. To-see yet not-to-see can be the ultimate in allure. Hence, the universal popularity of the see-through fabrics—the chiffons and voiles, the organdies and organzas, the gauzy nets and laces (Fig. 266).

See-through to you, of course, and not to the inner workings of the construction. You wouldn't want that to divert attention from your endearing young charms. Choose styles with unbroken lines, few seams or darts. Small darts are better than large ones. No darts are best of all. No bound buttonholes and no inset pockets. If pockets there must be, strategically placed patch pockets are to be preferred (Fig. 266).

Fig. 266

Fig. 267

For sheer pleasure let the fabric float free, independent of an understructure (Fig. 267a). Make a separate slip or underdress. This not only provides a certain discreet opaqueness, it also presents an opportunity to play with the color of the gown.

For instance:

1. You can intensify a pale pink color by using a deeper, brighter pink under it.

2. You can soften a taupe color by using a pale beige under it.

3. You can green a yellow by placing a blue under it. This produces a lovely shimmer too.

4. You can give dramatic contrast to black lace by placing a white fabric under it.

To create a firmer, opaque fabric of the filmy, see-through variety underline it. Underline the entire dress (Fig. 267b). Or, underline the bodice and skirt only while unlined sleeves veil the arms (Fig. 267c).

Fragile: Handle with Care

Will-o'-the-wisp fabrics require very delicate handling. The crisp sheers are somewhat easier to work with than the soft ones. The latter have a tendency to slip away in cutting and sewing. Fear not! Tissue paper will save the day. It is the great stabilizer of all elusive and unmanageable fabrics.

CUTTING

To prevent slipping, cover the cutting table with a sheet of tissue paper. (If necessary piece the tissue). Sandwich the fabric between the tissue-paper table-cover and the tissue-paper pattern. Place silk pins in the seam allowance so they won't injure the garment. If pins will not mar the fabric, use two rows of sharp pins placed close together, one row on either side of the cutting line. Cut through all layers of paper and cloth.

MARKING

There are several possibilities for marking. Either mark the fabric itself with tailor's tacks or guide basting or mark an underlayer instead.

The underlayer could be the underlining, marked with tailor's chalk or even dressmaker's carbon if that will not show through. The underlayer could also be tissue paper cut from the pattern, marked, applied to the fabric and torn away when the stitching is completed.

In the case of double- or triple-layered sheers, cut each separately. Mark the bottom layer only. Place the identical sections one over the other, all right sides up. Match the grain lines, the centers, and the raw edges. Baste through the center of each garment section. Smooth toward the outer edges and baste (Fig. 268a).

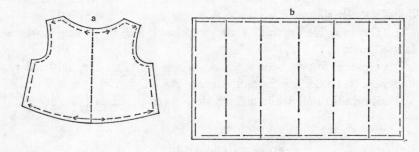

Fig. 268

In large areas, smooth and baste every 6 to 8 inches until the edge is reached (Fig. 268b).

STITCHING

Tension: crisp sheers—average
soft sheers—slightly looser than average
Pressure: light to average
Stitch size: short—15 to 18 per inch
Needle: very fine (size 9), sharp-pointed to prevent snagging
Thread: fine thread of the same fiber as the fabric
Strips of tissue paper placed under the fabric makes stitching easier. Tear the paper away when the stitching is completed.

Seams and Seam Finishes

French seams are classic for this type of construction (Fig. 269a). A double row of stitching trimmed close to the stitching line is also acceptable (Fig. 269b).

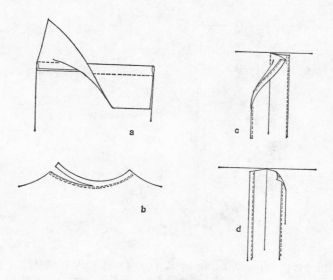

Fig. 269

A seam finish for sheer cottons: turn under the seam allowance and stitch close to the fold (Fig. 269c). Organdies, nets, and scratchy sheers feel more comfortable when all seam allowances are bound (Fig. 269d).

> To make a *French seam:* with *wrong sides* together, stitch the seam on the right side, ¼ inch in from the raw edges. Trim the seam allowances to ⅛ inch. Turn to the wrong side. Crease along the seam line. Stitch a second seam ¼ inch from the edge, enclosing the trimmed seam allowance.

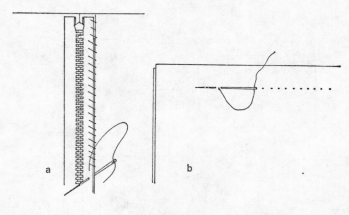

Fig. 270

Use the very thinnest of zippers. If necessary, trim away some of the zipper tape. Overcast the raw edges of the tape to prevent raveling (Fig. 270a).

> To *overcast:* work loose, slanting stitches over the edge, encircling it. The stitches are even in depth and equally spaced.

Zippers are best installed by hand using a prick stitch (Fig. 270b). A prick stitch is a variation of the backstitch. The tiniest of stitches appears on the right side—just over one or two threads. The understitch is the same as the backstitch.

Fastenings Take Cover

COVERED SNAPS, HOOKS, AND EYES

Snaps, hooks, and eyes are best kept under cover. The glint of metal can be a jarring note in an otherwise concealed construction.

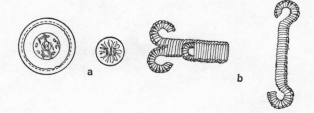

Fig. 271

COVERED SNAPS

1. Cut two circles of matching organza, organdy, thin lining material or self-fabric if it is thin enough. Make them twice the diameter of the snap plus a tiny seam allowance (Fig. 271a).

2. Turn under the seam allowance and gather the outer edges close to the fold.

3. Pierce a tiny hole in the center of one circle and force the ball through it.

4. Draw up the gathering until it fits taut over the snap. Use a cross-stitch or several hemming stitches to secure the closing (Fig. 271a).

5. Cover the socket with the second circle of cloth.

6. Snap the ball and socket together. The exposed ball will create the needed hole in the socket as it is forced into it.

COVERED HOOKS AND EYES

Using a double strand of matching thread, work blanket stitches over the hooks and eyes until they are completely covered (Fig. 271b). The stitches should be very close together.

Buttonholes by Hand

When buttonholes are necessary in sheers they are machine-made or worked by hand. Many of the newer sewing machines have mechanisms for making buttonholes. Consult the sewing machine manual.

For very special projects, hand-worked buttonholes are a couture touch.

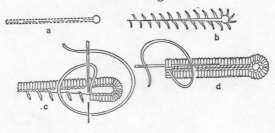

Fig. 272

1. With basting thread, mark the exact placement and length of the buttonhole.

2. Staystitch the length of the buttonhole with machine stitching placed 1/16 inch away from the guideline on both sides and directly over the ends (Fig. 272a).

3. Slash the opening. Overcast the slashed edges (Fig. 272b).

4. Work buttonhole stitches over the overcast edges. Fan the stitches around the end against which the button will rest (Fig. 272c). Make a bar for a finish on the opposite end by covering two or three straight stitches with small overhand stitches (Fig. 272d).

THE BUTTONHOLE STITCH

Use mercerized thread, silk thread, or buttonhole twist. Work from the right to the left. The needle is held vertically and goes through a loop of thread. Form the loop by placing the thread behind the eye of the needle and under its point. Each purl (the knot that is formed by pulling up the intertwisting thread) should be on the edge of the slit. Make the stitches close together and even in depth (Fig. 272c).

The buttonhole stitch is similar to the blanket stitch. The difference is that the blanket stitch has a single purl while the buttonhole has a double purl. The double purl affords better protection.

Hems for Sheers

Allow skirts to hang out for at least 24 hours before setting the hem. Circle skirts take longer. Circles of chiffon will continue to dip outrageously even after careful setting. There is little one can do about it except to correct the dip from time to time.

In sheer fabrics the hem may be turned up and machine stitched, rolled, or doubled. (The first two hems are great edges for scarfs, bows, ruffles, flounces, belts, as well as hems.)

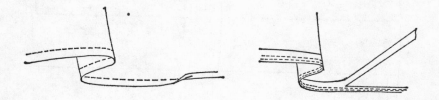

THE EDGE-STITCHED HEM (Fig. 273a above)

Use small stitches (15 to 20 to the inch) and strips of tissue paper under the stitching where necessary to keep the fabric from stretching or puckering. Tear away the paper when the stitching is done.

1. Run a line of machine stitching along the designated hemline.
2. Turn up the hem along the line of stitching.
3. Machine stitch around the edge close to the fold.
4. Make a second row of stitching close to the first.
5. Trim away the excess fabric as close as possible to the stitching.

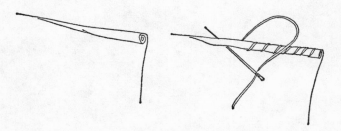

ROLLED HEM (Fig. 273b above)

1. Staystitch close to the edge.
2. Trim close to the stitching.
3. Roll the edge tightly toward you with thumb and forefinger. Moistening the fingers a little helps the roll. Do a small section at a time—½ to 1 inch.
4. For a decorative edging (stitches showing) use the overhand stitch. If you don't wish the stitches to show, use a slipstitch.

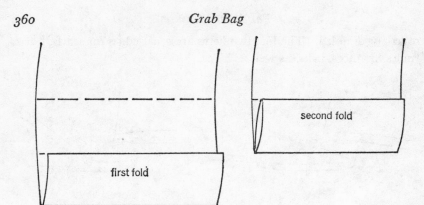

DOUBLED HEM (Fig. 273c above)

1. Mark the hemline. Allow an even amount below the hemline equal to *twice* the depth of the hem.

2. Fold the raw edge halfway into the hem.

3. Fold again to position.

4. Slipstitch the hem to the garment.

LOVELY LACE

The loveliest of lace in the simplest of styles—a formula for a very special dress that requires very special treatment.

Guard the Treasure

Treat your by-the-yard lace as if it were the precious hand-made sort. The same delights, the same problems, the same hazards apply to both.

Somehow it takes more derring-do to cut into lace than into other fabrics. The obvious solution: cut as little as possible. Choose a style with few seams, darts, and dressmaking details.

1. Eliminate seams where you can.

When the pattern has straight, on-grain edges, overlap the seam lines. Pin or Scotch-tape them to position (Fig. 274a). When the pattern has flared edges, remove the flare by drawing new, straight edges parallel to the grain line (Fig. 274b). Join the new straight edges as in Fig. 274a.

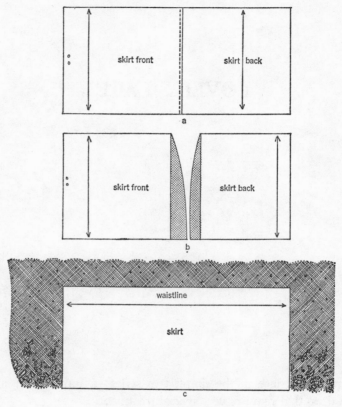

Fig. 274

2. Use a *crosswise layout* so there are fewer seams to match and sew (Fig. 274c). The plus factor in this arrangement is that you can use any shaped self-edge as a trim for the hem, the lower edge of the sleeves, and even (with judicious cutting) for the waistline and the neckline of the bodice.

The Understructure

Lace, like other sheer fabrics, can be made like a cage or shell to be worn over its own underdress or slip. If the style calls for more firmness, it can be underlined. (See Figs. 267b and 267c.)

To retain sheerness and transparency, underline lace with tulle, net or marquisette in a matching color. For an opaque effect, underline the lace with taffeta, crepe, satin, China silk, peau de soie, or any other suitable fabric. For a truly intriguing look combine the "now-you-see-it" of flesh-colored tulle, net or marquisette in strategic places with the "now-you-don't" of an opaque underlining (Fig. 275).

Fig. 275

When an underlining is used, place its right side against the wrong side of the lace so that both right sides face outward and both wrong sides face the body. In this way, no seams or darts will be visible.

Facings and interfacings are unnecessary in lace. In addition to the decorative self-edge previously suggested, edges can be bound with chiffon, satin, ribbon, etc. When an underlining is used, it is brought all the way out to the edges so that no further facing is really necessary.

Hems

The hem edge is often faced with horsehair braid. This is a stiff braid, loosely woven of horsehair. It comes in varying widths from ½ inch to 5 inches. It comes in many colors though the one most frequently used (indeed available) is a translucent, clear almost no-color. Since it is practically invisible, it works well with any color.

TO PREPARE THE BRAID

1. Cut the necessary length plus two seam allowances.

2. Overlap the ends and stitch. Trim the excess material close to the stitching.

3. Because the cut ends of the horsehair braid are so scratchy against the skin, they should be covered. Use strips of appropriate fabric and attach with two rows of machine stitching (Fig. 276a).

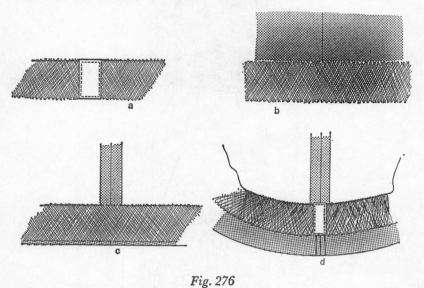

Fig. 276

TO ATTACH THE BRAID TO A STRAIGHT HEM

1. Trim the seam allowance of the garment to ½ inch.

2. Overlap one edge of the braid ¼ inch on the cut edge of the garment. Pin or baste to position.

3. Edge-stitch along the braid using thread that matches the garment fabric (Fig. 276b).

4. Turn the braid to the inside allowing enough roll to hide it (Fig. 276c).

5. Slipstitch or catch stitch the upper edge of the braid to the outer fabric or the underlining.

TO ATTACH THE BRAID TO A FLARED OR CIRCULAR HEM

Use a horsehair braid that has a shirring thread along one edge. Save this edge for the upper edge of the hem.

Steps 1 to 4 are the same as for the straight hem.

5. Draw up the shirring thread to fit the garment (Fig. 276d).

6. Attach the upper edge of the braid to the outer fabric or to the underlining. Use catch stitches or slipstitches.

7. Trim away the excess shirring thread.

A horsehair braid hem is an excellent one for any edge that needs stiffening—whatever the fabric. Bear this in mind for any other of your late-day or evening dresses.

Machine stitching

Tension: slightly loose

Pressure: adjust to fabric

Stitch size: delicate lace—15 to 20 stitches per inch
            lightweight lace—12 to 15 stitches per inch

Needle: delicate lace—size 9: lightweight lace—size 11

Thread: appropriate for the fabric

Tissue paper to the rescue: if the lace puckers, stitch it over strips of tissue paper.

Hand-appliquéd Lace Motifs

An infinitely more beautiful effect is achieved by the hand-appliqué of cutout lace motifs instead of by a regulation seam. The irregular joining, done as invisibly as possible, preserves the over-all design of the lace.

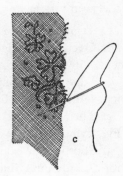

Fig. 277

1. Place the lace motifs where they will look best in the garment.
2. Cut around the design motifs that may land on any seam. Leave an ⅛-inch seam allowance around each motif (Fig. 277a).
3. Turn under the seam allowance and baste.
4. Overlap the motifs on the adjoining section. Attach with whipstitches (Fig. 277b).
5. Trim away any excess lace on the underside close to the hand stitching.

WHIPSTITCH

Use a fine crewel needle, size 10, and find thread to match the fabric. Pass the needle over and under the folded edge enclosing it with the winding thread. The whipstitch is a variation of the overhand stitch. Make the stitches very small and very close together (Fig. 277c).

Pressing

Place the right side of the lace over a thick padding of Turkish towels to preserve the raised surface. Use a steam iron over a dry press cloth.

THE CLINGERS

No dear, a clinging fabric does not make one look like a "clinging vine." Quite the opposite. The look is femme fatale rather than helpless heroine. The clingers call for self-assurance in wearing and a figure worth noting.

Any soft fabric shaped by you rather than by an understructure falls into the clinger's category. The two favorite fabrics in this class are crepe (and crepelike fabrics) and the silky jerseys.

The texture and moldability of crepe are due to its twisted yarns that expand and contract like so many invisible little springs. The elasticity of jersey is due to its meshed construction: loops that straighten when stretched and revert to loops when released.

Both these fabrics are difficult to handle—hard to cut, hard to stitch, hard to press, hard to fit. But the effect? Sinuous, slithery, sexy! So what's a girl to do but learn how to master the necessary techniques?

How to Handle the Creeping, Crawling Crepes

Layout and cutting are best done on a large surface. A cutting board is fine for the fabric can be pinned to it to provide stability. Lacking that, pin the fabric to our trusty tissue paper.

Use lots of pins so the crepe doesn't crawl away in cutting or creep away in stitching. Stitch slowly over tissue paper to prevent stretching.

MACHINE STITCHING

Tension: light
Pressure: light
Stitch size: 12 to 15 stitches per inch
Needle: fine
Thread: appropriate for the fiber
Seams and seam finishes should be as flat and as unobtrusive as possible.

PRESSING

Pressing crepe is a very touchy job. Two bits of advice: test-press a sample seam first and quit when you are ahead. Too much pressing and you'll flatten out the crinkled surface which is the charm of the cloth. Not to mention ending up with a dress several sizes enlarged by the flattening and straightening process. Steam-press the fabric and you'll end up with a doll's dress.

The way to press crepe is with a dry iron over a dry press cloth on the wrong side of the fabric. *Don't overpress.*

CLOSINGS

A hand-stitched zipper is safest. One has more control over the fabric than with machine stitching.

A self-fabric loop-and-button closing is preferable to a buttonhole-and-button closing. If the latter must be used, be sure to reinforce the buttonhole opening with organza or lightweight iron-on material.

FABRIC LOOPS

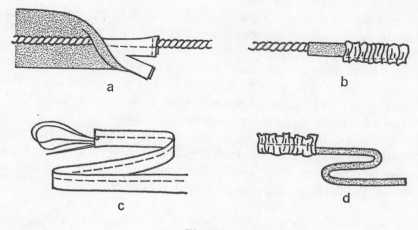

Fig. 278

To make a *firm* loop of self-fabric:

1. Cut a 1-inch strip of bias.

2. Cut a length of ⅛-inch cable cord or firm string twice as long as the bias strip.

3. Midway through the cord, fold the bias strip over it, right side against the cord, wrong side out.

4. Hand or machine stitch across the bias strip at the middle of the cord (Fig. 278a).

5. Using the cording (or zipper) foot, stitch close to the cord but leave a little room for the seam allowance when turned (Fig. 278a). Make the beginning and the end of the tubing a little wider so the turning will be easier.

Note: when stitching bias, loosen the tension and use smaller stitches so there will be more thread to accommodate the bias stretch. Also, stretch the bias a little as you stitch to provide more elasticity.

6. Trim the seam allowances to ⅛ inch.

7. Reverse the bias over the other end of the cord (Fig. 278b). Smooth the bias over the cord. The right side is now out and the seam hidden. Cut away the unnecessary cord.

To make a *soft* loop of self-fabric:

1. Make a 1-inch bias strip.

2. Fold the strip with right sides inside. Stitch to the desired width of the tubing. Make the beginning and end of the tubing a little wider for easy turning.

3. Trim the seam allowance to a width a little wider than the finished tubing. The seam allowance is used to pad it in place of the cording. A thin fabric requires larger seam allowances to fill the tube. Heavy fabrics need smaller seam-allowance padding.

4. To turn the tubing to the right side, fasten a blunt needle and buttonhole twist to one end. Push the needle through the tubing head (needle's eye) first (Fig. 278c). The thread and tubing will follow through to the right side (Fig. 278d).

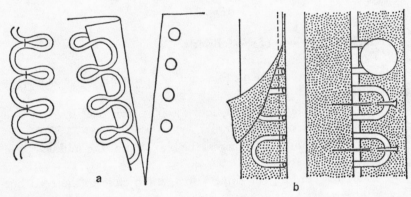

TO MAKE THE LOOPS

Fig. 279

The loops are inserted in the seam that joins facing to garment. They should be large enough to take the buttons with ease (test to see that they do), identical in size, and evenly spaced. The loops may be continuous (Fig. 279a) or cut (Fig. 279b).

In a loop-and-button closing both the loops and the buttons are stitched to the line of the closing. There is no overlap except that made by the loops themselves. There is an underlap.

For frogs, it's an easy jump from tubing to trimming.

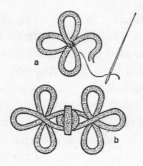

Fig. 280

Twist the tubing into fanciful shapes. Fasten with small stitches on the wrong side at the crossings of the tubing (Fig. 280a). Keep one loop free for buttoning. Stitch a button to the corresponding loop on the opposite frog (Fig. 280b). Center the frog over the closing. Fasten to the garment with slipstitches.

The frogs are only for fun and decoration. Don't depend on them to hold your garment closed. Well-placed covered snaps must do that.

The New Jerseys

This section deals with the thin, silky matte jerseys. With minor variations, the construction methods hold for the heavier single and double knits.

CHOICE OF STYLE

Once more, the best style for this fabric is the simplest. The fewer the seams, the better. The sweater-fit of a no-dart design is pretty, comfortable, and easy to make. Controlled fullness (gathering, shirring, unpressed pleats) takes advantage of the fluid quality of the fabric. In matte jersey, particularly, draping is preferable to darts.

Avoid buttonholes, inset pockets or any dressmaking details that require slashing into the fabric. Use a hand-stitched thin zipper, covered snaps, loops, and buttons instead of buttonholes. (In heavier knits if buttonholes are essential, be sure to reinforce the area with a patch of iron-on material.)

Because of their wonderful built-in ease of movement, the new jerseys can be fitted much closer to the body than woven fabrics.

Some patterns are designed especially for knits and are so marked. Such patterns contain very little ease; they rely on the elasticity of the knit fabric to provide movability.

When a pattern is marked "Suitable for Knits," this refers to the style rather than the cut of the pattern. Since such a pattern was designed primarily for woven fabrics it contains the average amount of ease, most of which needs to be removed for a knitted fabric. Take larger seam allowances on all lengthwise seams.

LAYOUT AND CUTTING

Stabilize the fabric before cutting. Hang it over a well-padded door or shower rod or hanger for at least 24 hours. If the knit is going to stretch in the length, let it do that before you cut and stitch the seams and darts. You certainly don't want them sagging when you've worn the dress a few times.

Jerseys come in flat lengths. The selvage is the vertical grain. Establish the crosswise grain by drawing a chalk line at right angles to the selvage. (Reminder: the folds in a tubular knit are not necessarily the vertical gain. Following one lengthwise rib or wale, cut the tube open. Establish the crosswise grain. Refold the fabric for the layout.)

Knits are directional. Be sure to use the "With Nap" layout.

Use sharp silk pins. Cut with sharp shears.

Staystitch all bias and curved edges immediately on removing the pattern.

UNDERSTRUCTURE

Happily, no understructure is necessary. Since you chose the fabric because of its elasticity and comfort, it seems illogical to eliminate its stretchability with a straight-grain woven lining or underlining, the usual understructure. If line or underline it you must, use a tricot material which, being a knit, has the same properties as the outer fabric. Or, cut the subsurface material on the bias. This, too, has stretch, though not as much as the tricot.

Of course, if you want to ignore the fact that your fabric is a knit and if you would like it to function like a woven fabric, then treat it like a woven fabric. Line it or underline it as you will.

Face necklines and other edges with taffeta, cotton, or silk to prevent stretching in areas where that shouldn't happen. Tape with seam binding any measurement that should be stayed—a waistline seam, an armhole seam, for instance.

MACHINE STITCHING

Tension: light

Pressure: light

Stitch size: 12 to 15 stitches per inch, a tiny zigzag stitch, or a stretch stitch (Some of the newer sewing machines have this feature.)

Needle: sharp-pointed and a size suitable for the weight of fabric

Thread: appropriate for the fiber of the fabric

Stretch the fabric in back and in front of the needle while stitching. Avoid ripping, which is difficult and hazardous. Double stitch any points of stress.

PRESSING

Press seams closed first, then open. Use a steam iron over a dry press cloth. Avoid overpressing.

SEAM AND HEM EDGES

Seam allowance and hem edges can be left just as they are. If you like, they may be finished with hand overcasting. (Machine overcasting causes the edges to ripple—a nice, ruffly effect for something else.) Sometimes, to make sure the knit doesn't run like a stocking, a single line of machine stitching is placed close to the edge. Stretchable lace is another possibility if its roughness does not show through to the right side.

HEMS

Let the skirt hang out at least 24 hours before setting the hem.

The neatest, least visible hem is the tailor's hem. Make loose catch stitches to provide the thread needed for the crosswise stretch of the knit.

THE GLIMMER-AND-GLOW

DEPARTMENT

Satins, Brocades, Metallics, Lames

There's high voltage in their low glow—the satins, the brocades, the metallics, the lamés. Don't touch—unless you have a sure hand in sewing and an accurate eye for fitting.

Satins and Brocades

A trial muslin is a must. True, muslin is not satin or brocade and there will be some changes necessary in the final fitting. But this should be more in the nature of refinement than gross alterations. You really can't afford to make a mistake in the cutting and construction of your expensive fabric. Ripped-out stitching leaves holes and pressing leaves permanent creases. Because of their lustrous floats, these glamour fabrics bruise easily—and never quite get over the hurt.

Since there is very little or no give in the fabrics, allow sufficient ease for close-fitting gowns.

LAYOUT, CUTTING, AND MARKING

Light plays tricks on the directional weave of satin and brocade, which is woven on a satin ground. It makes the fabric have one color and sheen going up and another going down. This means that all pattern pieces must be placed so they head in one direction—neck to hem. Use the "With Nap" layout.

Avoid anything that will leave a permanent mark in a conspicuous place. Instead of pinning the grain line (usually right in the middle of the pattern section) weight it with books, sewing equipment, dressmaker's weights, anything heavy and safe.

Use silk pins. Place them in the seam allowance closer to the cutting line than to the seam line.

Mark carefully with silk thread and a fine needle. *Do not* use dressmaker's carbon paper and the tracing wheel.

MACHINE STITCHING

Tension: suitable for the weight of the fabric
Pressure: suitable for the weight of the fabric
Stitch size: medium, 12 to 14 stitches per inch
Needle: medium—size 14, make certain that the point is sharp
to avoid snagging the floats
Thread: suitable for the fiber of the fabric

Hold the fabric taut while stitching to keep the two thicknesses feeding through the machine at the same rate. Stitch slowly.

PRESSING

Press very lightly. Don't try for ultra-flat seams or sharp edges. Save that for your tailoring. A soft edge is the one called for in all the dress fabrics. Many designers dramatize the softness with layers of lamb's wool padding or soft flannel. (See Fig. 281.)

Satins and brocades are very touchy. Press on the wrong side with a dry iron. Steam and moisture destroy the luster and leave an imprint of the iron. Do protect the fabric with a dry press cloth.

When brocade fabric has an ornamented or raised surface, place the right side against terry cloth or a Turkish towel. Should the fabric be woven with a metallic thread, treat it as if it were an all-metallic fabric.

THE LOOK IS SOFT, THE FEEL IS SOFT

The couturier touch, a luxury touch—a soft edge padded with layers of lamb's wool padding or soft flannel used in addition to or in place of an interfacing.

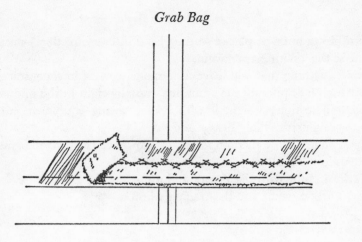

Fig. 281

1. Cut a 3-inch strip of bias padding to fit the edge to be padded. (The strip may be slightly wider or narrower so all thicknesses at the edge are graded.)
2. Fold up 1 inch of the strip.
3. Place the fold of the padding along the fold at the edge.
4. Using matching thread, attach the padding to the garment (or interfacing or underlining) with long, permanent basting. Make it close to the fold toward the hem or facing (Fig. 281).
5. Catch stitch the upper edge of the padding to the garment, interfacing, or underlining as the case may be.
6. Turn back the hem or facing and finish in the usual manner.

HEMS

The very nicest finish is a dressmaker's hem. Enclose the raw edge of the hem with seam binding. Attach with running, basting, or catch stitching.

Metallics and Lamés

Everything said of satins and brocades holds equally well for metallic and lamé fabrics—plus a few extras. Select simple patterns with few seams and darts. Let the beauty of the fabric carry the drama of the design. Avoid details like buttonholes or inset pockets which require slashes in the material. Metallic fabrics have a tendency to ravel. Staystitch all edges immediately after cutting. Work quickly.

LINE TO PREVENT SCRATCHING

Metallic threads are scratchy against the skin. Unless you enjoy being wounded, you had better line the dress completely with a soft but closely woven lining material. If you insist on leaving the dress un-lined, at least use silk fabric for all the facings and be sure to bind all the raw edges. In the end, you'll probably find that it takes more time to do all this than to line the dress.

PRESSING

Metallic threads are permanently creased by pressing. Dampening may cause tarnish. So, press very lightly with a warm, dry iron. Protect the fabric with a dry press cloth.

Add Your Own Fireworks

If you think the fabric doesn't have enough sparkle, add your own fireworks with beads, rhinestones, sequins, paillettes, and jeweled buttons. These blazers are not restricted to the Fourth of July. They're year-round high fashion.

BEADS, RHINESTONES, SEQUINS, PAILLETTES

It takes lots of time, handwork, patience, and lots of beads, rhine-stones, sequins, or paillettes, but the resulting brilliance is worth the work.

Follow the design of the fabric: bead a floral motif, sequin a stripe or plaid, pick up a check with paillettes. (Paillettes are like sequins but larger.) Or, make your own design and transfer it to the fabric by the stencil method (Fig. 282).

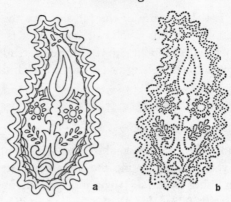

Fig. 282

1. Draw your design on tracing paper (Fig. 282a).

2. Perforate the tracing paper with a sharp-pronged tracing wheel or any similar sharp-pointed instrument (Fig. 282b).

3. Pin the tracing to the right side of the fabric.

4. Dust with chalk, starch, or flour tied in a little bag.

There are two methods of applying the beads, rhinestones, sequins: the tracery method and the backstitch method. Use fine needles (a beading needle for the beads) and matching thread, or, better yet, a transparent nylon thread that blends with all colors. Fasten the beginning and the end of the stitching on the wrong side with tiny backstitches.

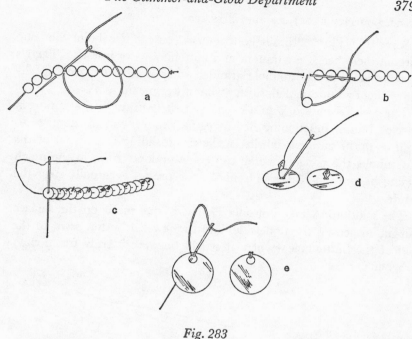

Fig. 283

THE TRACERY METHOD (Fig. 283a)

This method requires two needles and two long threads.

1. String the beads, rhinestones, or sequins on one thread.
2. Place along the outline of the design.
3. With the second needle and thread, tack in place between each bead, rhinestone or sequin or between every third or fourth one.

THE BACKSTITCH METHOD (Fig. 283b)

1. Back the area to be decorated. (The underlining will do.)
2. Sew each sparklet on individually with a backstitch.

The sequins may be sewn on like the overlapping scales of a fish (Fig. 283c) or singly with a bead for a center (Fig. 283d). Paillettes are generally sewn on in solitary splendor (Fig. 283e).

Spare the sparkle and spoil the effect. Don't be stingy. Mass the fireworks and you'll be sure to appear in a blaze of glory.

JEWELED BUTTONS ON FAKE BUTTONHOLES

Some things just naturally go together. You can hardly imagine one without the other. Take buttons and buttonholes, for instance. There's no point at all to a buttonhole stranded without a button. And, a button without a buttonhole just isn't what it was meant to be.

The jeweled button is in a class by itself. Because of its setting, a jeweled button functioning like a regular button can do damage to itself or to the garment fabric. In the much sliding in and out of the buttonhole, the precious stones can come undone. And, in the much sliding in and out of the buttonhole, the prongs eventually snag the fabric.

The solution? A fake buttonhole, that is, one made on the surface but unfinished on the underside, and the jeweled button sewn to the end of the buttonhole (where it would be were it truly functional) (Fig. 284a).

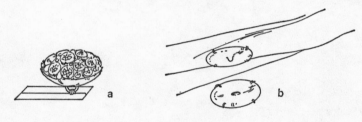

Fig. 284

How does the garment actually close? With covered snaps stitched in place under the fake operation (Fig. 284b).

THE THIRD DIMENSION OF
THE TWO V's
Velvet and Velveteen

The third dimension of the two V's (velvet and velveteen) adds an extra dimension to their beauty. Pile in fabric, however, makes piles of problems. That lush depth must not only be loved, but honored and protected throughout the entire construction.

Choose a design with little seaming so the velvety softness is unscarred by seam lines. No buttonholes—instead use a loop-and-button closing. No pockets that slash into the fabric—only those that can be inserted into an existing seam. No topstitching—the pressure of the presser foot and the stitching mar the fabric.

On the positive side: do keep in mind that velvet drapes gracefully. There is a richness in its texture and an incomparable way in which velvet takes the light. For a very elegant gown, one could not do better.

Follow the Arrow

The color of pile fabrics is richer when the nap runs up toward the face. (Velvets are always cut in this way.) There is this to be said for the nap that runs down: the fabric shows less wear. (Velveteens and corduroys which will get hard use are cut so.) Because the nap has been pressed flat in panne velvet, there is no choice. The fabric must be cut with the nap going down just as other napped fabric does.

To determine the direction of the nap, place your fingertips lightly on the surface of the material. Jiggle them gently—back and forth—riding the surface. If the fabric feels smooth, the nap is running down. If there is resistance against the fingertips, the nap is running up. Mark the direction in which the nap moves along the selvages with chalked arrows (Fig. 285). In this way you will always be certain which way the nap is going. No need for uncertainty and frequent new decisions.

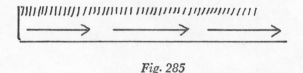

Fig. 285

Layout, Cutting, and Marking

To avoid a patchwork of colors, place the pattern on the fabric in a directional ("With Nap") layout. Should you make the sad discovery that the nap is running in the wrong way, stick with it. It is more important to be consistent though the nap is cut in the wrong direction than to switch direction in mid-cutting and have two different colors.

Normally, fabric is folded with the right side inside for layout and cutting. When you do this with velvets, velveteen, or corduroy, you find that pile-against-pile sticks together like a burr. In this instance, it is easier to fold the fabric with the right sides outside. To avoid a fold altogether, use a complete pattern placed on the right side of the material opened to full width.

Use fine hand needles rather than pins to set the grain. Remove them as soon as the rest of the pattern is pinned. Use silk pins placed in the seam allowance for the rest of the pattern.

For wrong-side marking, use chalk. For right-side marking use silk thread. This does not leave its impression on the fabric in the way that cotton thread may.

When basting is necessary, use a fine needle and silk thread. Use backstitches every so often interspersed with the basting stitches. This will better hold the fabric in place.

MACHINE STITCHING TO PREVENT CREEPING

Machine stitching is a problem because of the locking of the piles and the tendency of the upper layer to "creep." There are several ways to overcome this.

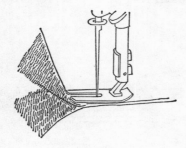

Fig. 286

1. As the fabric is fed into the machine, keep the layers separated until they reach the presser foot (Fig. 286).

2. Place strips of tissue paper *between* the upper and under layers of the fabric. Tear them away when the stitching is completed.

3. Use an "Even-feed" attachment if your sewing machine does not already have this feature built into it.

4. Rather than basting, backstitch both lengths in place before stitching by machine. Though, really, if you are going to do this much handwork, the machine stitching is not necessary. Backstitching as an effective method for joining seams was invented long before the sewing machine. But who wants to be that primitive in this day and age?

MACHINE STITCHING

Tension: light
Pressure: light
Stitch size: 10 to 12 per inch
Needle: medium, size 14
Thread: appropriate for the fiber
Stitch in the direction of the nap.

To reduce bulk, face with lightweight lining fabric and tack the facing invisibly to the backing of the fabric. When joining a pile fabric and a plain fabric, machine stitch with the plain fabric on top.

Press to Preserve the Pile

Let the steam do the pressing rather than the pressure of the iron. Were the iron to be pressed onto the pile, its weight would crush and flatten it.

There are two methods of "pressing" to preserve the pile.

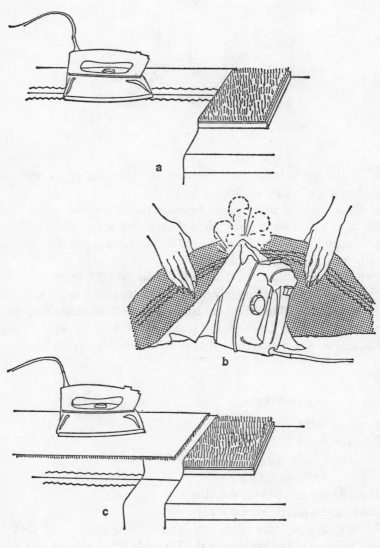

Fig. 287

METHOD I

Place the pile against a needle board or the pile of a strip of self-fabric. The raised surface of terry cloth will also do. Steam-press from the wrong side using *very little pressure* (Fig. 287a). Press over the center of the needle board or the strip of self-fabric. Pressing too close to the edge may leave an imprint of the edge. And, of course, press with the nap.

METHOD II

Stand a hot, dry iron on end and place a damp (rather wet) cloth over it. As it begins to steam, draw the wrong side of the fabric across the steaming iron (Fig. 287b).

Handle pile fabrics carefully while damp as finger marks show easily. (Finger marks can be steamed out and brushed up.)

Be sure to protect the right side of the pile fabric when it is turned back to the wrong side in hems and facings. Use a top needle board in addition to the one on the bottom (Fig. 287c) or use a strip of pile fabric as an upper press cloth.

THE WRAP-UP

A "wrap-up" brings something to an especially successful conclusion. That makes it an eminently appropriate term not only for the final section of a book but also for the final layer of a costume.

Think of all the times when the first impression is of a wrapped-up you. Everyone knows how important an attractive wrapping can be. Why, whole industries are built on this fact.

Think, too, of all the varieties of outfits that need wrapping—bulky clothes and slim ones, short ones and long ones, rough-and-tumble togs and evening finery—cold days, mild days, stormy days—around the clock and through the calendar. With all these needs, you'll surely have room for wraps of some of the just-for-fun fabrics in addition to your more classic types.

FRANKLY FAKE FUR
The "Critter" Fabrics

Have you ever seen a purple leopard or a shocking pink tiger? Only a touch will tell whether it's real seal or a reasonable facsimile thereof. Anything's possible when it comes to fake fur.

The "critter" fabrics are not only high fashion, they're warm, they're comparatively inexpensive, they're wildly imaginative, they're fun. What's even more important, you can wear them with a free conscience knowing that the real animals are alive and well and romping in field and forest with their dear friends and families.

To carry out the illusion of authentic fur, choose a design with style lines and details for your fantasy fur that one would commonly find in a true fur garment. Choose a pattern with few seams. Or, eliminate the unnecessary seams.

Two pattern sections may be joined as one, thereby eliminating the joining seam, *if:*

1. The edges are on straight grain.
2. The seam is not a shaping seam.
3. The fabric is wide enough and long enough to accommodate the enlarged pattern.

Fig. 288

To join sections *overlap the seam lines* and Scotch-tape. Note that this can be done to join a facing to a garment* so the two are cut as one (Fig. 288a). When side seams are joined (Fig. 288b), the front and back can be cut as one piece. A yoke joined to a lower section (Fig. 288c) makes a complete front or back.

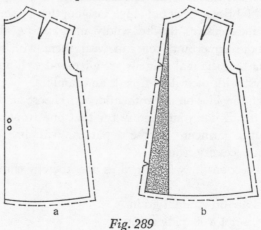

Fig. 289

* In a fur fabric there will be less bulk at the opening edge if you face the garment with fabric that has no nap. Or, eliminate the facing entirely. Instead, bind the edges or bring the lining all the way out to the edge.

A two-piece straight back can be cut in one piece by cutting off the seam allowance and placing the center-back seam line on a fold of fabric (Fig. 289a).

Flare can be removed (Fig. 289b) so the resulting straight edge can be placed on a fold or be joined to an adjacent pattern piece.

You'll agree there is not much point in doing a lot of extra work when the seams won't even be visible when finished.

Layout, Cutting, and Marking

Use a "With Nap" layout. Place the pattern so the nap or pile runs down—neck to hem. (Who would dare ruffle one of the Big Cats by stroking from the tail up?)

Only smooth, flat fur fabrics can be cut on a fold with the fur side outside. Those with pile require that each section be cut separately and in entirety. This means that you must convert each half pattern to a full pattern and make a duplicate for every pattern piece that says, "Cut two."

Place the pattern on the fur side so you can match any shading or distinctive markings. Pay particular attention to the grain. You certainly would not want that very visible nap or pile hanging otherwise than in a plumb line.

Pin the pattern to the fabric using long, sturdy pins.

SMOOTH FUR FABRICS

1. Cut with sharp shears from the right side.
2. Mark darts with tailor's tacks. Mark notches with thread loops on the edge of the fabric.

PILE FABRICS

1. Outline the pattern by placing pins along the cutting edge.
2. Show darts and notches with pins.
3. Turn to the wrong side and trace the pin markings with tailor's chalk.
4. Remove the pins and the pattern.
5. *Cut the fabric from the wrong side* with a razor blade or an Exacto knife. In this way you will cut only the backing and avoid cutting the hair or pile. The uncut hair is used to cover the seam, thereby making the joining invisible.

Machine Stitching

Stitch all seams by machine in the direction of the pile.

Tension and pressure: light

Stitches: 8 to 10 to the inch

Needle: coarse

Thread: heavy duty

Should the fabric creep or pucker in stitching, baste first using occasional backstitches to hold it in place.

When the stitching is completed, work the pile or hair out of the seam on the right side with a blunt needle until the seam is completely concealed.

A special technique to eliminate bulk in the seam is to shave off the fur for 3/8 inch of the 5/8-inch seam allowance. Use a razor or an Exacto blade. Stitch a regulation seam. Work the hair out of the seam on the right side.

Avoid topstitching for obvious reasons.

Tailoring techniques

Use all previously learned tailoring techniques for:

1. Interfacing.
2. Taping.
3. Applying collar.
4. Stitching and setting sleeves (most fake furs have a knit backing which makes it comparatively easy to ease the cap—especially if the fur is shaved from the seam allowance).
5. Handling the hems and the facing.
6. Inserting the lining.

HAND STITCHING

Hand stitching furs and fur-type fabrics is easier with the use of the Glovers needle, Number 7. This is a suture needle; its spearlike point pierces the skin without tearing it.

All stitches catch only the backing of the fabric. They never come through to the right side.

PRESSING (SUCH AS IT IS)

Fur fabric requires very little or no pressing. When pressing is done, use a steam iron. Press the seam allowances over a needle board (best of all), a strip of self-fabric or a Turkish towel. Brush up the nap after pressing.

FASTENINGS

Are you shuddering at the thought of making buttonholes through the depths of the fabric. Relax. They are not necessary. Use furrier's fastenings: large hooks and rings, large covered snaps, braid loops and buttons.

And now, let the fur fly!

TWO-FACED BUT TRUSTY

The Inside-out Wrap

Trust a two-faced fabric to be a friend. The inside-out coat or cape can be a lot of fun and serve you well. You can be practical on one side and glamorous on the other (Fig. 290a); discreet on one side and bold on the other (Fig. 290b).

There are two types of reversibles: those made of fabric whose two layers are joined in the weaving and those that you can join by putting together two separate fabrics. The problems of pattern selection are the same for both types but the construction differs.

Almost any simple pattern can be used for a reversible garment even if it hasn't been designed as such. The best choice is an unfitted style with no intricate seaming or details. Use only one thickness throughout—no facings, no hems. A kimono or raglan sleeve is easier to handle than a set-in sleeve. When a set-in sleeve is used, it is stitched into the armhole first, then, like a kimono sleeve, the underarm of the sleeve and the side seam of the coat can be stitched in one operation.

Patch pockets applied to one or both sides of a garment are best for convertible garments. Other types are not reversible. If you belt a coat, you will eliminate the buttonhole problem. Bound buttonholes are impossible in a double-faced fabric, and difficult in a two-layered job. Even were you to use hand-embroidered or machine-made buttonholes, there would still be the problem of where to put them since right and left fronts are reversed when the garment is worn inside-out. If you are truly determined to use buttonholes, make them on right *and* left fronts. Use a set of link buttons to join them.

Fig. 290

The Two-faced Fabric Garment

Baffle your friends with this tricky treatment. So successfully are darts and seams hidden by the following method, no one will ever guess their whereabouts.

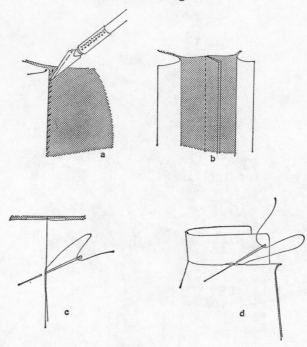

Fig. 291

1. Separate the two layers of fabric at all edges to be stitched. Do this by slicing through the perpendicular threads that join the layers for about 1½ inches (Fig. 291a).

2. Machine stitch the seams of one thickness (Fig. 291b).

3. Press open the seam allowances as best you can with the tip of the iron. (Being small, a traveling iron is great for this purpose.)

4. Trim and turn under the seam allowances of the second side so the folds meet directly over the seam line of the first side (Fig. 291c). Slipstitch.

5. Set the hem. Add seam allowances. Trim the excess fabric.

6. For the hem and all outside untrimmed edges: separate the two layers of fabrics and slice the perpendicular joining threads as for the other seams. Turn under both seam allowances toward each other. Slipstitch along the edge.

7. The collar: slice back 1½ inches of all edges. Turn under and slipstitch all untrimmed outside edges. Turn under both seam allowances on the collar neck edge but leave it open.

8. Slip the garment neck edge into the collar opening (Fig. 291d).

Slipstitch the folds of the collar edges to the neck seam line of the garment.

(Cuffs can be attached in the same way.)

The Sew Must Go On: As-usual Construction

Another method of constructing a two-faced fabric garment is one that completely disregards the double-identity of the fabric and treats it as any other single-layer fabric. The exposed seams and darts are stitched with the flat-fell or welt-seam construction used for an unlined jacket or coat. See page 285.

The Two-fabrics Reversible

In the two-fabrics reversible coat or cape, two identical garments are completed separately, then joined on all outside edges. The kind of "double exposure" one can create with this construction is an exciting challenge to the imagination.

1. Use the same pattern for both outside and underside.
2. Stitch all seams and darts as usual since they will be concealed when the separate garments are joined.
3. Interfacing is optional.
4. Press and shape each of the two single layers.
5. Stitch one collar to each neckline. Stitch one cuff to each sleeve.
6. For an untrimmed edge, place the right sides of both completed garments together. Pin carefully. Stitch all except the hem edges. Press open, trim, and grade the seam allowances. Clip and notch as necessary. Turn to the right side.
7. With the outside seam directly on the edge, baste both layers together. Since both sides are to be used, there is no permanent underside, therefore, it is unnecessary to observe the usual tailoring technique in regard to hiding the joining seams.
8. Inside the two garments, join the sleeves and side seams with long, loose permanent basting stitches in the same way that a lining is attached to a garment.
9. Set the hem. Add seam allowances. Trim the excess. Turn under both seam allowances toward each other and slipstitch along the edge. Baste so the outside seam is directly on the edge.
10. To hold all layers in place, finish with one or two rows of decorative topstitching.

Coming to a Good End

For a decorative trim of outside edges, use ribbon, braid, leather, or bias to bind them.

1. Trim away the seam allowances of the outside edges. (In the two-identical-garments type you had better stitch the two layers together close to the seam line before cutting away the seam allowances.)

2. Fold the binding in half lengthwise and press.

3. Slip the edge of the garment into the fold of the binding. Stretch on all outside curves, ease on the inside curves, miter all corners. Pin and baste carefully through all thicknesses.

4. Cut the binding ¼ inch beyond the planned end of the trimming. Staystitch each end by hand immediately upon cutting so it won't fray or spread. Use small stitches. Turn under the ½-inch seam allowance.

5. Attach the binding.

By hand: slipstitch the edge of the binding to the garment on both the outside and the underside.

By machine: machine stitch close to the edge of the binding through all thicknesses.

Another type of trim might be a crocheted edging in a color that picks up or contrasts with the color of the fabric.

Double the Exposure, Double the Fun

However you make it and whatever the combination of color or texture, you'll find that if you double the exposure, you'll double the fun of any wrap.

IT'S RAINING PRETTY RAINCOATS

You won't be singing, "Rain, rain, go away," if you have a pretty raincoat. Time was when a raincoat was something one always had to buy. The thought of making one was pretty farfetched. Now, with all the bright new waterproofed fabrics and the new methods by which any good cleaning service can waterproof just plain ordinary fabrics, making one's own raingear is a breeze.

Any coat pattern that doesn't have too many seams, darts, or dress-making details will do. Choose an easy, roomy style that will fit over all the layers one is apt to wear on a rainy day. Deep armholes, raglan, or kimono sleeves are best. Consider making a matching hood or hat. And why not a rain suit or a rain cape to add to your collection of rain-chasers?

"The Agony and the Ecstasy" of Sewing Vinyls

Say "Waterproof material" and vinyl comes to mind. Slick and shiny, in colors and prints that make you feel gay. In some ways vinyls are easier to work with than cloth. That's the ecstasy part of the title of this section. Naturally, there are problems too. That's the agony part. But, happily, there are ways of dealing with the problems.

VINYL SURFACES STICK TO EACH OTHER—AND WHAT TO DO ABOUT IT

For storage: keep the fabric rolled rather than folded. For layout: fold with the right side out when cutting double layers.

In stitching: when vinyl surfaces are inside, match the edges and press them together lightly by hand. When the vinyl surfaces are outside, use strips of tissue paper to keep the vinyl from sticking to either the throat plate or the presser foot.

THERE IS VERY LITTLE EASE IN VINYL—AND WHAT TO DO ABOUT IT

The knit-back vinyls are more flexible than the others. Choose a style with simple lines that requires little or no easing. For instance, raglan or kimono sleeves which don't require easing are preferable to set-in sleeves which do.

Because there is no ease in the fabric, there must be plenty of ease in the garment. Make a test muslin so that you are sure of the fit before cutting.

NEEDLES AND PINS LEAVE PERMANENT PUNCTURE MARKS—AND WHAT TO DO ABOUT IT

For layout: use pins sparingly and only in the seam allowance close to the cutting edge. Better yet, use masking tape or Scotch tape to anchor the pattern.

For stitching: don't baste. Use tape (Fig. 292a) or paper clips (Fig. 292b) to hold the thicknesses together for stitching. (They don't need much holding because the vinyl surfaces tend to stick together.)

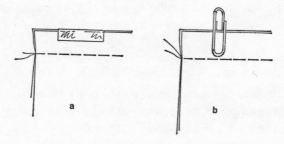

Fig. 292

For marking: Wrong-side marking can be done with pencil or with tailor's chalk. Use a grease-base china marking pencil for right-side marking. It should wipe off without leaving a smudge. Better test first. Caution: avoid tracing wheels. They leave permanent marks on the vinyl.

PLASTICS MELT EVEN AT LOW TEMPERATURES—AND WHAT TO DO ABOUT IT

Keep your cool!

Vinyl is a plastic. Seam allowances in vinyl will curl. They require some flattening but *not with an iron*. Finger-press the seam allowances. Or glue them with Sobo adhesive or rubber cement.

Directions for using rubber cement:

1. Apply a small amount of the rubber cement under each seam allowance.

2. Press the seam allowance flat with your hand or hold the seam allowances flat with the clapper or any other safe weight.

3. When the seam allowances are flattened, lift them gently and remove the rubber cement with a glue ball. This is a little ball of dried rubber cement used like an eraser.

TOPSTITCHING IS A GOOD WAY TO AVOID ANY TYPE OF PRESSING

Use one of the following familiar methods for seams and darts.

1. Topstitched plain seam. (Press both seam allowances to one side and topstitch.)

2. Double-topstitched seam. (Open the seam allowances and topstitch on both sides of the seam line.)

3. Welt seam. (Trim one seam allowance. Press the other over it. Topstitch.)

4. Double-topstitched welt seam. (Topstitch again close to the seam line.)

SEAMS AND DARTS IN CLEAR VINYL

After topstitching, cut away the seam allowances. Trim very close to the stitching.

Machine Construction for a Machine-age Fabric

Construct vinyls largely by machine. Hand stitching is difficult, therefore limited to hems and finishing details.

MACHINE STITCHING

Tension: light to medium

Pressure: light to medium

Stitch Size: medium to long, 8 to 10 stitches per inch.

(Vinyl tends to tear when sewn with small stitches. Like tearing paper on a perforated line.)

Needle: size 14 for medium-weight fabric, size 16 for heavyweight fabric.

(Make certain that needles are new and sharp-pointed.)

Thread: mercerized, cotton-covered polyester, double-duty or heavy-duty threads to match the coated plastics (vinyl); clear nylon thread for the transparent plastics.

Interfacings

Vinyls have enough body to hold their shape. Interfacings are not really necessary. Should you wish to use an interfacing, choose a firm but lightweight one. Use only in the coat fronts and the collar.

Obviously, use none in the transparent plastics.

Fastenings

Buckle, belt, bolt, or button. Use separating zippers or metal snaps. Just so there is enough fastening down the front to keep you protected from wind and wet.

When the raincoat is to have a button-and-buttonhole closing, use machine-made buttonholes on transparent vinyl and bound or machine-made buttonholes on the others.

HOW TO MAKE BOUND BUTTONHOLES IN VINYL

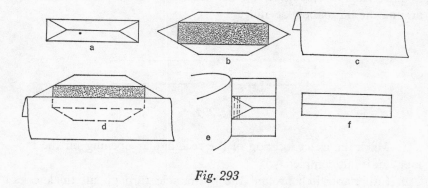

Fig. 293

1. Stay the area to be slashed with a rectangle of lightweight inter-facing.

2. Mark the length and width of the buttonhole with grease pencil.

3. Slash through the center for the opening and diagonally to each corner (Fig. 293a).

4. Turn all four flaps to the underside to form a rectangular opening (Fig. 293b).

5. Prepare the buttonhole binding. Cut two strips of vinyl 1 inch longer than the length of the buttonhole and at least 2 inches wide. Fold the strips lengthwise, making the fold ½ inch in from one edge, right side outside (Fig. 293c). Finger-press or cement lightly to position.

6. On the underside of the garment, center the first strip across the opening forming one lip of the buttonhole (Fig. 293d). The shorter side of the strip is directly against the flap.

7. Stitch the strip close to the foldline of the flap.

8. Place and stitch the second buttonhole strip in the same way. The folds of both buttonhole lips touch at the center of the opening.

9. Fold back each end and stitch the triangular flap to the binding (Fig. 293e). Several rows of stitching will reinforce the ends which bear considerable stress when the garment is worn.

10. From the right side, the finished buttonhole looks just like the fabric bound buttonhole (Fig. 293f). In fact, this is a method often used to make bound buttonholes in fabric.

HOW TO FINISH THE UNDERSIDE OF THE BUTTONHOLE

Since vinyl doesn't ravel, it is not necessary to turn under the facing around the buttonhole opening.

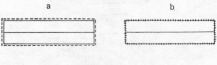

Fig. 294

1. Mark the exact location of the rectangular opening on the facing. Cut it out completely.

2. Either topstitch around the buttonhole through all thicknesses (Fig. 294a), or fasten with small overhand stitches (Fig. 294b).

How to Set and Stitch the Sleeves

Raglan and kimomo sleeves are stitched into the garment as are other garment sections.

When a set-in sleeve is used, it is easier to stitch the sleeve into the armhole *before* either the underarm seams of the sleeve or the side seams of the garment are joined.

STITCH THE SLEEVE CAP INTO THE ARMHOLE

1. Do *not* gather the sleeve cap. Place the sleeve into position in the armhole. "Baste" the sleeve into place with rubber cement, easing as necessary.

2. Because vinyl tends to stretch in stitching, use a start-and-stop method rather than a long line of stitching. It is more accurate.

Start the stitching at the shoulder and continue down the front armhole to the underarm seam. Break the thread. Once again, start the stitching at the shoulder and continue down the back armhole to the underarm. Follow the arrows in Fig. 295a.

3. Pull the starting threads through to the wrong side and tie each pair of threads in a square knot.

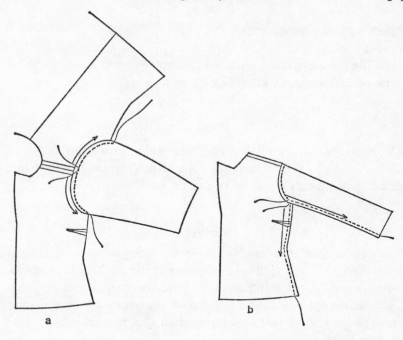

Fig. 295

STITCH THE UNDERARM-SIDE SEAM

1. To close the lengthwise sleeve seam, start the stitching at the underarm and stitch to the sleeve hem (Fig. 295b).

2. To close the garment side seam, start the stitching at the underarm and stitch to the hem.

3. Pull the starting threads through to the wrong side and tie each pair in a square knot.

4. Reinforce the underarm with a second row of stitching close to the first.

Pockets

Patch pockets are topstitched.

Bound pockets are made in vinyl as they are in fabric except that the binding for the opening is made like the vinyl bound buttonhole.

Welt pockets are constructed in vinyl as they are in fabric.

Hems

The easiest way to handle a hem in vinyl is to turn it up and top-stitch it. Another way is to make a tailor's hem. Keep the hand stitches loose and pick up only a yarn or two of the backing of the vinyl.

Linings

Every cloud may have its silver lining but every raincoat need not. The see-through vinyls need none. Opaque fabric may be lined across the shoulders only. (It is important to have some extra protection in the area that is apt to get most wet should you get caught in a downpour.) Having said all that, one must admit that raincoats, like other coats, look prettier when lined.

1. Complete the entire lining, sleeves attached, etc.

2. Place the right side of the lining against the right side of the coat facings. Keeping the lining on top so it can be eased where necessary, stitch the lining to the coat. Use the regulation ⅝-inch seam allowance.

3. Turn both sleeve and lining through to the inside.

4. Trim off any lining that extends below the finished hem of sleeve and garment.

5. Turn under a seam allowance at the lining hem. Place it against the raw edge of the garment hem, raw edges matching. Slipstitch the lining to the garment and the sleeve.

6. Finish attaching the lining at the front edge that was left open.

A Raincoat of Fabric to Be Waterproofed

So many fabrics can be waterproofed these days that almost any fabric is a possibility for a raincoat. Be a little different. Make a raincoat of cool cotton or silk, warm wool or lush velveteen, of unlikely upholstery or drapery fabric. Even the toughs like canvas, duck, and the like make wonderful, swash-buckling raincoats. (Can't you just see the latter with contrasting topstitching, leather binding, hardware for fastening, or even sporting hand-painted designs?)

Just to be sure, choose a color-fast cloth (it would be awful to leave little pools of color behind you on the first wet day). Sponge it before cutting, make the raincoat, then have it waterproofed—lining, trimming, and all.

Suit the style and design to your taste. Suit the tailoring to your fabric. And, when you have finished all that, pray for a rainy day—at least a gray day—that will justify the wearing of your spectacular new raingear.

A FITTING ENDING
How to Fit the Garment

If what you make doesn't fit, forget it! Anybody can do exercises in stitching. The trick is to make what-is-stitched fit. And, fit in a flattering way, at that.

No-shape Garment for All Shapes

There are those no-shape garments that do for all shapes (Fig. 296a)—ponchos, dashikis, mumus, tent dresses, and all those etceteras that at best are marked small, medium, and large. The few points at which these do touch the body can be plotted by arithmetic.

Fitted Garments for Individual Shapes

Arithmetic is not enough for designs that *do* bear some reasonable relation to the figure (Fig. 296b) and for those that actually define it (Fig. 296c).

However simple or complex a design, it must reckon with the body contours of the wearer. *Striking a balance between the lines of the design and the lines of the figure is what the fine art of fitting is all about.*

Fig. 296

ELEMENTARY, MY DEAR

In fitting there are three elements with which we work:

1. The body with all its dimensions, curves, and contours.
2. The fabric with its grain and texture.
3. The lines of the design (both the seam lines that outline the figure and those that are contained within the outline).

So finely meshed are these three elements that if something is wrong with one, it will show up as a flaw in the others. What to do about figure defects is another department entirely. Our concern as sewers is to hide or disguise them. We do have the fabric and all the shaping seams and darts to manipulate for fitting our flawed figures.

Sew-mates

There are many times when a "little help from a friend" is a big help in fitting. There are those places one can't reach. Sometimes we don't see ourselves as objectively as others do. While there is a great deal one can do for one's self, it's a lot more fun to have a sew-mate.

Fit Before You Sew

Pattern directions give a step-by-step sewing sequence. They do not indicate when to do the fitting. (They could hardly do that since there are as many fitting problems as there are sewers.) *You* must decide the appropriate places at which to fit before you sew. It may be necessary to alter the sewing sequence to accommodate the fitting.

Some Words of Advice

Shape up as you will when you wear the finished garment. Wear the right bra and girdle, if any.

Whenever a garment is meant to stand away from the body it is best to prop it up with some of the underpinnings before the fitting. If not, you will be unable to judge the effect which is part of the fitting.

Stand naturally. If your fitting posture is a put-on, your garment won't fit when you lapse into your usual stance.

One cannot fit parts of a garment. You must have the whole front, the whole back.

Don't alter center front or center back. There are too many design features that are balanced on them: darts, shaping seams, buttons and buttonholes, zippers, collars, lapels, styling. Make any needed adjustments toward the sides.

Don't let the fullness fool you. Before the garment can be fitted pleats must be pinned or basted to position. Gathering or shirring must be controlled. Baste it to a predetermined length of seam binding, tape, or a preshaped lining.

Play safe. Use safety pins for crucial points in the fitting. Straight pins have been known to fall out when the garment is taken off after fitting. While this wouldn't be disastrous in a continuous seam line, it could be a calamity with a particular fitting point.

All darts and shaping seams balanced on both sides of the center may be fitted from the wrong side. The fit will not be altered in any way when the garment is reversed to the right side. However, those seams that must be individually fitted (one shoulder higher than another, one side seam bulgier than the other) are fitted from the right side. These are not reversible. Right-side corrections are transferred to the wrong side for stitching. Use chalk or thread for the marking.

The First Fitting: A Pin Fitting

The old saying goes, "As you sew, so shall you rip." To avoid this laborious task, do a pin fitting before doing any permanent stitching. It is the first real test of the accuracy of your pattern changes and cutting.

Are you wondering why a pin fitting is needed when you have made careful pattern alterations to conform with your measurements? You cannot rely on paper changes to produce the needed fit. The unknown factor is the way the fabric will behave. Only in fabric can you get the feel of how a dress hangs and moves.

Pinning is so much easier than coping with long lines of basting. Besides, if the pins are properly placed, the darts and seams will be ready for permanent stitching without the intermediate step of basting. The exception to this procedure: fabrics that bruise easily, or that slither out of place. These should be basted rather than pinned. Use a fine needle and silk thread.

Remember to start the pinning (and stitching) at the wide end of a dart and continue to the dart point.

What to Look for in the Fitting

EASE

Just the right amount of ease is the goal. We don't want you flapping around like a scarecrow or, like June, "bustin' out all over."

You should be able to swish your skirt easily around your hips when standing and be comfortable when seated. You should be able to move your arms with a reasonable degree of freedom even in a fitted set-in sleeve, though it isn't necessary to test your prom dress as if you were swinging a baseball bat. You should be able to breathe even in a snug-fitting bodice and eat even in a tight-fitting waist.

If you constantly have to pull and yank at your clothes because they are riding up or if you must clutch them to hide their bigness or if you are afraid to move for fear of breaking out at the seams, you will feel self-conscious and unattractive. And that means you'll ruin your chances for enjoying whatever it is you are doing.

Unfortunately, only minor changes in ease can be made in the cut-out garment unless you've made fairly large seam allowances. Rescue operations are confined to existing darts and seams. Raise as much as possible. Lower as much as possible. Take in or let out as much as possible. And hope for the best. Remember that even tiny changes in a number of places add up to what you may need to be comfortable.

GRAIN (STRAIGHT OF GOODS)

Grain is the most obvious clue to good fit. This is one reason why we have been so careful of it from the very start of our sewing. Fabric hangs with the grain and this is how it must appear in the garment:

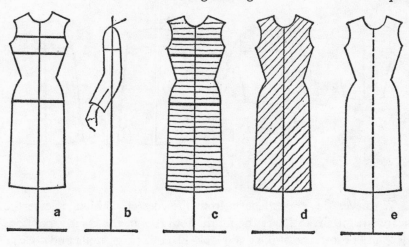

Fig. 297

The center-front and center-back grain hang at right angles to the floor. This places the horizontal grain parallel to the floor. The check points are across the chest, across the bust, across the hips (Fig. 297a).

The vertical grain of the sleeve hangs at right angles to the floor from the shoulder to the elbow. This places the horizontal grain parallel to the floor. Check across the biceps (Fig. 297b). The lower portion of the sleeve—elbow to wrist—will not follow this line since it is shaped by the elbow darts in a one-piece sleeve or by the shaping seams in a two-piece sleeve.

Use any prominent lengthwise or crosswise yarns, stripes, plaids, or checks to locate the grain (Fig. 297c). If the garment is cut on the bias, your only guide is the guide basting (Fig. 297d). It is helpful to mark the vertical grain at the center front or center back with guide basting (Fig. 297e).

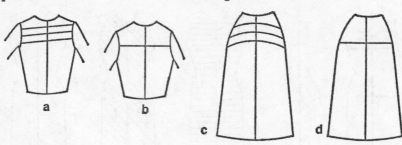

Fig. 298

Whenever the grain departs from the correct position, release the nearest seam, lift or lower the fabric until it is in the correct position. Repin. For instance, if the grain looks like this (Figs. 298a and 298c), make it look like this (Figs. 298b and 298d).

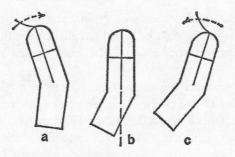

Fig. 299

If the lengthwise grain of the sleeve tilts forward (Fig. 299a) or backward (Fig. 299c), unpin the sleeve and *dial* the cap to its correct position (Fig. 299b).

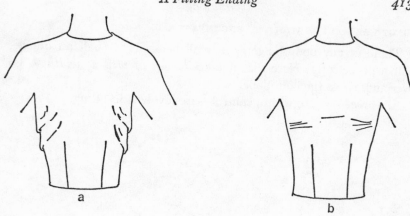

Fig. 300

Sometimes out-of-position grain indicates the need for a larger dart or a smaller dart. In the former, the drooping grain with its unsightly wrinkles and folds cries out to be included in the control (Fig. 300a). In the latter, the off-grain straining struggles to be released from the control (Fig. 300b).

DART CONTROL DOES IT

The right amount of control in just the right place is the secret of successful shaping.

All darts must head toward the high point of the curve being fitted. All shaping seams must pass directly over the high point or within 1 inch on either side of it.

If the darts or shaping seams produce bulges above, below, or beside the high point, unpin the garment and reposition them correctly.

Bulges or poufs at the dart point mean the dart is too large. Less control is needed: make a smaller dart and/or reshape the garment at the nearest seam.

Wrinkles or folds mean that a larger dart is needed—more control. Push the excess material into the nearest seam or dart. Or, where there is no dart or seam, create one.

LENGTH AS WELL AS WIDTH TO ENCOMPASS A CURVE

Think of any body bulge as a small hemisphere (half an orange, half a grapefruit). Note that it takes *length as well as width* to go over and across the half globe.

All three—length, width, control—are involved in fitting.

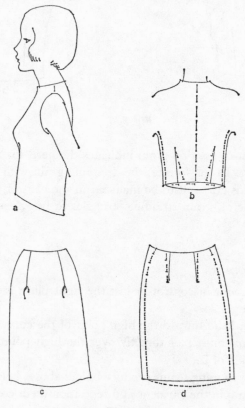

Fig. 301

For instance: *"hiking up"* or *"poking out"* (Fig. 301a) indicates not enough length or shaping. Release the side seams and darts. Straighten the center front or back. Push the excess fullness into the nearest seam or dart. Add length where it is needed (Fig. 301b).

Too long, too bulgy indicates too much length and too much shaping (Fig. 301c). Reduce the amount of control in the nearest seam or dart. Take the excess width off the side seams. Cut off the extra length where necessary (Fig. 301d).

Where It Won't Show

You choose a pattern because you like the design. Don't distort or destroy the style lines in an effort to make the garment fit. Fit only that part that can absorb the change in an unnoticeable manner.

Fig. 302

For instance: the dress in Fig. 302a can be fitted on the lower seam line of the upper bodice and on the upper seam line of the skirt. That interesting shape of the midsection band must be left intact or the chief design interest of the dress will be ruined.

In Fig. 302b, additional fullness for a larger bust may be added to the seam line of the side front section only, while the seam line of the front section remains as the designer intended it. In this way, you are both preserving the style line (which intrigued you) and making it fit your figure as well. No one will be the wiser since you haven't tampered with the distinctive lines of the design.

Corrections for a smaller bust are made on the same seam line. Subtract from the side-section fullness.

MAKE THEM MATCH

Whenever a change is made in a dart (either to make it smaller or larger) the seam from which it originates is altered in length. Compensate for this by adding or subtracting as much as is necessary to make it match the seam it must join.

Each pair of dart legs must be made to match in length.

The Outline Seams

The neck, the shoulders, the side seam, the armhole, the sleeve hem, the waistline, and the garment hem outline the garment. This silhouette is dictated by fashion, function, and figure.

Fig. 303

THE NECKLINE

The neckline is anywhere either the designer or you think it should be (Fig. 303). Wherever it is, it must fit flat against the body with no gaping or rippling.

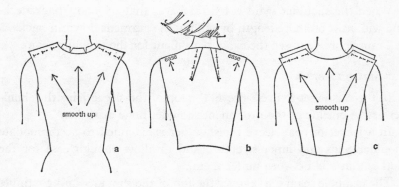

Fig. 304

Where there is gaping or rippling, unpin the shoulder seams. Starting at the center front or back, smooth the material over the body and up into the shoulder seams. Repin (Fig. 304a). Doing this may raise the neckline slightly but that can always be scooped out a bit later. The important thing is to have a neckline that hugs the body.

A back neckline that stands away from the body can be corrected by creating a neckline dart. So there will not be too many darts in one small area, stitch the back neckline dart as a dart but ease the amount of the original shoulder dart into the front shoulder (Fig. 304b). A good steaming over the tailor's ham should take care of this fullness.

Sometimes in correcting a gaping neckline as suggested, the front and back shoulder seams no longer match at the neckline (Fig. 304c). Trim off the neckline wherever necessary to make the neckline seams match. Should this make the neckline too deep, salvage as much as you can of the neck seam allowance.

THE SHOULDER SEAM

Difficult though it is to do, that shoulder seam must be placed in just the right position. Thereby hangs your garment.

The shoulder seam should lie along the crest of the shoulder curve just *slightly* forward of the trapezius muscle from the base of the neck to the prominent shoulder bone (Fig. 303).

If the shoulder line is too far forward the garment will look as if a back extension forms a front yoke. That's all right if a front yoke is part of the design. It's not all right if a front yoke is not part of the design.

When the shoulder seam is too far back, that too-short back neckline will insist on more length by pulling the garment down in back.

Train your eye to see the exact placement for the shoulder seam.

THE ARMHOLE SEAM

In the classic set-in dress sleeve, the top of the sleeve joins the shoulder at the outside of the prominent shoulder bone or socket.

In a jacket or coat sleeve the shoulder is extended to accommodate shoulder pads and inner structure and to allow enough ease for the clothes that will be worn under them.

The armhole seam curves over the top of the shoulder and continues in a slightly curved line to the crease where arm and body meet. Below this point, the seam swings into the underarm curve to a depth 1 to $1\frac{1}{2}$ inches below the armpit (Fig. 303) (somewhat lower in a coat or jacket).

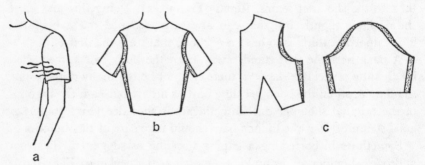

Fig. 305

When there is pulling or wrinkling across the bodice because of tightness (Fig. 305a), add width at both the armhole and the sleeve cap by using some of the seam allowances (Fig. 305b). If there is too much fullness turn under some of the cap or take deeper seam allowances.

An adjustment in the pattern is best of all. Add width or subtract it in the places indicated in Fig. 305c.

Any fitting faults that extend to the armhole become more obvious when the sleeves are set in. Fit the bodice carefully before setting the sleeves.

THE SIDE SEAM

The side seam divides all circumference measurements into front and back. Correctly placed, this seam creates balance between them (Fig. 303).

In profile, the side seam appears as a continuation of the shoulder seam (Fig. 306a).

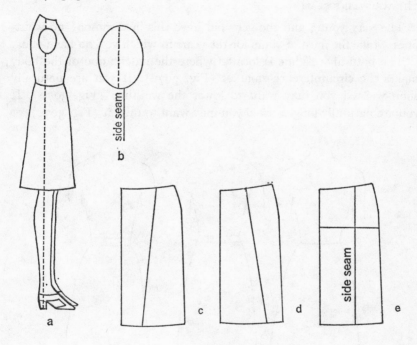

Fig. 306

At the underarm, the side seam starts ½ inch back of the middle of the total armhole (Fig. 306b) and continues in a plumb line to the floor. In doing so, the side seam divides the circumferences so that the front is larger than the back—a variable amount at the bust, about 1 inch at the waist and 1 inch at the hips. Surprised? Did you think the skirt back would be larger? Just the opposite is true.

One good way to test for the correct position of the side seam: allow the arms to hang naturally at the sides. The middle fingers should touch the side seams of the skirt.

If the side seam swings forward at the hem (Fig. 306c) or backward (Fig. 306d) reset the seam in the following way:

1. Release the side seams.
2. Let the fabric hang out naturally.
3. Check the grain and the dart control.
4. Repin the skirt so the side seams hang straight (Fig. 306e).

THE WAISTLINE SEAM

The very young and the very old have this in common: no waistlines. Make the most of yours for the years in which you do have one.

The natural waistline is located where the indentation of the body makes the circumference smallest (Fig. 307a). If you are naturally short-waisted you may want to lower the waistline (Fig. 307b). If you are naturally long-waisted you may want to raise it (Fig. 307c).

Fig. 307

The waistline seam of a garment should be about ½ inch lower than the natural waistline (or the position you've determined for yours). Garments tend to ride up in wearing so the bodice needs a bit of lengthwise ease.

SLEEVE LENGTH

The sleeve length may be anything from short to long. Short is as short as the season, the fashion, and the beauty of your arms permit. The classic long dress-sleeve ends at the wrist bone. (Measure with the arm bent.) Jackets and coat sleeves may be a little longer to cover the garment sleeves worn under them.

THE HEMLINE

Set the hemline as high, low, in-between as fashion and your figure dictate.

All circumference seam lines are curved to follow the natural curves of the body: neckline, bustline, waistline, hipline, and hemline. The only time when one would depart from this rule would be when, for design's sake, it would be more pleasing to follow the straight line of a check, stripe, plaid. When this is done the length, width, and shaping sacrificed for the straight line must be compensated for elsewhere. For example:

Fig. 308

Fig. 308a: the fullness of the skirt compensates for its length.

Fig. 308b: when the yoke seam is a straight line, the necessary shaping comes off the lower bodice.

Fig. 308c: if the side seam is kept straight, shaping and flare can appear on center front or back.

Fit to Flatter

As important as knowing when to follow the rules of fitting is knowing when not to follow them. For instance: if following the rule for the side seam leaves you with a bustle, move the side seam back more. If placing the shoulder seam forward as directed makes you look more round-shouldered than you are, move the shoulder seam back a bit. If fitting your wide shoulders as per the rule makes you look like a football hero in full regalia, by all means set the armhole seam in to narrow the shoulders.

Clothes must not only fit, they must flatter.

SEW LONG

It's comforting to know that there is no one right way to make anything. Of the many sewing methods currently in use one may be more valid than another simply because *it* gives the best result with the least effort for a particular design in a particular fabric.

There! That should free you from the fear that you are not doing it *the* right way. There are many right ways. And that puts some burden on you. Making a choice calls for know-how as well as judgment. Hopefully, this book has provided that background of information on which sewing judgments can be made.

Ideally, if you want to produce something great, you should know everything at the start of a study that you will have learned by the end of it. Unfortunately, that's not the way it works for any skill, sewing included.

Everyone has to start somewhere and the beginning is about as logical a place as any. Now that you're all through the graded projects in this book, you can go back to the beginning again and lightly and perfectly (with all your new-found knowledge) toss off all those "little nothing" items (worth their weight in gold cloth) that will proclaim your expertise. Sew Well and Sew Long.

INDEX

646.2   MAR

Fashion sewing for everyone.

646.2   MAR   CUR   c.1
Fashion sewing for
everyone.

June '74   CUR   88